DAILY ARMOR

Brian Brooks

WestBow Press books may be ordered through booksellers or by contacting:

WestBow Press
A Division of Thomas Nelson & Zondervan
1663 Liberty Drive
Bloomington, IN 47403
www.westbowpress.com
1 (866) 928-1240

ISBN: 978-1-9736-4677-8 (sc)
ISBN: 978-1-9736-4679-2 (hc)
ISBN: 978-1-9736-4678-5 (e)

Library of Congress Control Number: 2018914083

Print information available on the last page.

WestBow Press rev. date: 02/19/2019

DEDICATION

I dedicate this book to my daughter, Jessica, and my son, Scott. You are my inspiration for this daily devotional. I have tried to set the example for you just as my father set the example for me. Forgive me when I have failed to do so. Hopefully, the good has outweighed the bad.

As you embark on your college years, I want to impress upon you the importance of the Written Word. My time with you is nearly over. Although I will never be more than a phone call way, before long, you will be on your own, deciding for yourself what type of man or woman you will be; what type of husband or wife you will be; what type of father or mother you will be. Now is the time for you to realize the importance of the Word and to discipline yourself to have some Jesus time each day. I cannot think of a better way to show this importance other than to send you a "verse of the day", your daily reminder. Read it; treasure it; hide it in your heart. It is God's love letter to you.

And, where would I be without my beloved, my wife, Tina. I would not be the man I am today without her encouragement and support. Thank you, my love, for all your ideas and recommendations on themes and verses. Your confidence in me is reassuring.

INSPIRATION

Back when my children were still in middle school, God laid upon my heart to memorize Ephesians 6:10-17, where Paul discusses the armor of God.

"Finally, be strengthened by the Lord and by His vast strength. Put on the full armor of God so that you can stand against the tactics of the Devil. For our battle is not against flesh and blood, but against the rulers, against the authorities, against the world powers of this darkness, against the spiritual forces of evil in the heavens. This is why you must take up the full armor of God, so that you may be able to resist in the evil day, and having prepared everything, to take your stand. Stand, therefore, with truth like a belt around your waist, righteousness like armor on your chest, and your feet sandaled with readiness for the gospel of peace. In every situation take the shield of faith, and with it you will be able to extinguish the flaming arrows of the evil one. Take the helmet of salvation, and the sword of the Spirit, which is God's word."

I even made a postcard with the 6 pieces of armor written on it and taped the postcard to all the bathroom mirrors in the house so that we could all see it each morning as we got ready for our day. I began a little ritual each morning before I would leave the bathroom and head off to work. I would go through the motions of actually putting on my spiritual armor. Here is how it goes:

(1) Place my hands around my waist and say "the belt of truth"
(2) Brush both hands across my chest and say "the breastplate of righteousness"
(3) Point to my feet and say "the gospel of peace"
(4) Raise my right arm in the shape of an L and say "the shield of faith"
(5) Go through the motions of placing a helmet on my head with both hands and say "the helmet of salvation"
(6) Raise my left hand, and with a clutched fist, say "the sword of the Spirit"

Then I put a smile on my face and burst out of the bathroom ready to take on another day!

I shared this with my children one day and wanted somehow to remind them each day to put on their armor. Even though it may appear corny to do, I wanted to encourage them to actually go through the motions and put on the armor of God. So with each "verse of the day" I close with "Get your armor on!"

I challenge you to do the same. Before you leave your house each day, get prepared for battle. Get your armor on!

TABLE OF CONTENTS

WAYS OF GOD VERSUS WAYS OF THE WORLD

Blessed is the one who does not walk in step with the wicked or stand in the way that sinners take or sit in the company of mockers, (Psalm 1:1 NIV)

Your first day of college. My how your Mother and I have prayed for this day and I cannot believe it is here! The world is at your fingertips! Look at what the psalmist says here. How happy is he! Happy, overjoyed, hilarious is he who does not follow advice of the wicked, or take the path of sinners, or joins a group of mockers. There will be a wealth of seekers who will try to pull you away from the path of the straight and narrow. Be aware of your surroundings and be happy swimming upstream. Honor God and He will honor you!

Get your armor on!

Trust in the Lord with all your heart and lean not on your own understanding; in all your ways submit to him, and he will make your paths straight. (Proverbs 3:5-6 NIV)

I know you are 18 now and you can do what you please. I know you think you know everything there is to know. Hey, I remember those days. Do not forget I was 18 once, too. We can get ourselves in a mess if we rely too heavily on what we think we know and not enough on what the Lord knows. Blessings abound when we trust in His ways and allow Him to guide our paths.

Get your armor on!

WAYS OF GOD VERSUS THE WAYS OF THE WORLD

Do not be anxious about anything, but in every situation, by prayer and petition, with thanksgiving, present your requests to God. And the peace of God, which transcends all understanding, will guard your hearts and your minds in Christ Jesus. Finally, brothers and sisters, whatever is true, whatever is noble, whatever is right, whatever is pure, whatever is lovely, whatever is admirable—if anything is excellent or praiseworthy—think about such things. (Philippians 4:6-8 NIV)

There will be days of anxiety ahead for you: a mid-term exam, that first date with the cute boy/girl in your English class, whether to rush a sorority, which sorority to join, do I live off campus or not, where to live off campus, which organization to join, which church to attend, do I attend this awesome party that "everyone" is going to, and so much more. What Paul is telling the Philippian church is to not worry about ***anything***, but in ***everything***, go to God in prayer. Do not consider this a cop-out. It is the greatest and most important thing you can do. Great or small, it does not matter. God wants to hear from you.

Get your armor on!

but those who hope in the Lord will renew their strength. They will soar on wings like eagles; they will run and not grow weary, they will walk and not be faint. (Isaiah 40:31 NIV)

What a great verse of encouragement! Have you not seen in pictures, on TV, or, in real life, an eagle flying? What grace they show and what power they have as they spread their wings and just glide effortlessly through the air. Close your eyes and envision you doing this for a moment. When you have had a rough day and think, "why did I come here? I want to go home", or "I hate this teacher, I am dropping this class", or "I cannot take this anymore, I need to change my major", draw from the strength of this verse. Trust in the Lord. He will give us the energy we need to make it through another day.

Get your armor on!

WAYS OF GOD VERSUS THE WAYS OF THE WORLD

Blessed is the one who trusts in the Lord, who does not look to the proud, to those who turn aside to false gods (Psalm 40:4 NIV)

Well, you have finished your first week of classes. I trust you are meeting tons of people and establishing some lifelong friendships in the process.

You want to be happy? Joyful? Blessed? I mean **really** happy, joyful, and blessed. Put your trust in the Lord! Do not put trust in yourself, others, or those who are going through the motions with no drive or ambition. That path leads to nowhere. On the other hand, trusting in the Lord will bring blessing upon blessing. It will bring about a joy that cannot be quenched, regardless of the circumstances.

Get your armor on!

LOVE OF THE WORLD

Am I now trying to win the approval of human beings, or of God? Or am I trying to please people? If I were still trying to please people, I would not be a servant of Christ. (Galatians 1:10 NIV)

Have you ever heard of "feel good" preachers? You know, those preachers that do not really preach the gospel, the penalties of sin, and how sin separates us from Christ. This type of message tries to make us feel good about ourselves and does not bring about conviction of sin or call for a change in behavior. As you embark on the world, be careful not to be a people pleaser. Doing those things to try and make people like you. Doing those things that make you fit in with the crowd. Doing things so that you do not stand out in the crowd. Do things that will find favor with God. Strive to please God more than man.

Get your armor on!

Do not love the world or anything in the world. If anyone loves the world, love for the Father is not in them. For everything in the world—the lust of the flesh, the lust of the eyes, and the pride of life—comes not from the Father but from the world. (1 John 2:15-16 NIV)

I know you will meet many people in the days and weeks ahead. Some of them will appear to have more things that you do. Nicer / newer car, nicer clothes, cooler laptop, popularity, better grades. It will be so easy to fall in line with the "world" and desire to have those things. But keep in mind they are merely things. Look at what the Apostle John is telling us. If we love these things, the love of the Father is not in us. Desire a relationship with the Father more than you desire anything else. It is the only thing that will last.

Get your armor on!

LOVE OF THE WORLD

If only for this life we have hope in Christ, we are of all people most to be pitied. (1 Corinthians 15:19 NIV)

Might need to explain this one a bit...if we put all our hope in this life, the life we live on earth and value material possessions we have more than we value our relationship in Christ, we will never be satisfied and our lives will be most miserable.

You have so many people today striving for what I call the three P's: power, possession, and position. Achieving any or all three would seem to provide satisfaction, or so people think. However, all that we achieve or collect on earth is for nothing. We take none of it with us. For if in this life, we find hope or joy or satisfaction, we are truly most pitiful. I am not telling you not to pursue any of the three P's. Just do not devote all of your efforts there. Develop a heavenly perspective. For our true hope, our true joy, our true satisfaction will only be accomplished when we see the Father face-to-face.

Get your armor on!

No one should despise your youth; instead, you should be an example to the believers in speech, in conduct, in love, in faith, in purity. (1 Timothy 4:12 NIV)

Many discount the ability of youth to be a dangerous disciple. Paul was addressing this very issue with Timothy in today's verse. Timothy was a young preacher, but very capable of leading the early church. Many religious leaders may have been ridiculing Timothy or reducing his message because he was not as learned as they were. Paul told Timothy not to listen to their rebuke. Instead, continue to set the Christian example in 5 different ways: in speech, in conduct, in love, in faith, and in purity. Do not ever let the world tell you that you cannot make a difference because you are young. That is a lie straight from the pit of Hell. Get MAD today. **M**ake **A** **D**ifference.

Get your armor on!

LOVE OF THE WORLD

Do not let anyone look down on you because you are young, but set an example for the believers in speech, in conduct, in love, in faith and in purity. (Romans 8:18 NIV)

You know, sometimes, life is just not fair. I mean, why do good things happen to bad people and bad things happen to good people? Some things we just cannot explain. We must trust the Lord has His reasons and purposes. But one thing we can say for sure, that even though we might experience "sufferings of this present time", these sufferings do not come close to the "glory that is going to be revealed in us." When we love this world, we will be disappointed. When our focus is on this present time, we will face frustration, dissatisfaction, and aggravation. When that time comes, and it will come, focus on our future – the glory that will be revealed in us. What we go through today does not even begin to compare with that glory! Can I get a hallelujah!

Get your armor on!

SPIRITUAL FREEDOM

It is for freedom that Christ has set us free. Stand firm, then, and do not let yourselves be burdened again by a yoke of slavery...You, my brothers and sisters, were called to be free. But do not use your freedom to indulge the flesh; rather, serve one another humbly in love. (Galatians 5:1, 13 NIV)

Freedom! The favorite word for newly turned eighteen year olds. There will never be another time in your life where you are more free than these next four years. Oh, to be eighteen again and in college. Yes, you are free to do what you want, when you want, and with whom you want. However, with that freedom comes responsibility and accountability.

In Christ, we are free from the rules and regulations of the Old Testament in terms of earning salvation. We no longer need to do certain things (i.e. perform sacrifices) to obtain forgiveness. Verse 1 is telling us we are free from the harness of these rules and regulations and do not let anyone place conditions on earning salvation and forgiveness. But our freedom in Christ does not give us the liberty to do as we please. If we do what we want, when we want, we are right back into the slavery of sin and the grips of our sinful nature. That is what verse 13 is saying. We are free to live in Christ as Christ would have us live. Just make sure we do not use that freedom to do as we please, when we please, and thus destroy our freedom. The best use of our freedom is to serve others with love and compassion.

The beauty of our salvation is we have freedom to choose. The beast of our salvation is that our freedom has consequences, both good and bad. Choose and choose wisely.

Get your armor on!

SPIRITUAL FREEDOM

"I have the right to do anything," you say—but not everything is beneficial. "I have the right to do anything"—but I will not be mastered by anything. (1 Corinthians 6:12 NIV)

With each passing year, you gain "permission" to do certain things. At 15, you can get your driver's permit. At 16, you can start to drive. At 18, you can vote. At 21, in some states, you can purchase alcohol. However, just because you have permission to do certain things does not mean that you should do those things.

Some Corinthians thought that since Christ had forgiven all sin, they were free to live as they pleased. Paul pointed out that type of reasoning was absolutely not true. Still other Corinthians said certain things are not specifically forbidden in the Bible and therefore ok to do. Paul again pointed out that type of reasoning was false. Yes, we have freedom to choose and while some things may not be strictly forbidden and therefore ok to do, it may not always be beneficial. We must always guard our decisions with this: Will that action draw me closer to Christ? Will that action cause someone else to come closer to Christ? If the answer is no, then guess what, do not do it. If that answer is yes, by all means, do it even more!

Just because you can does not mean you should. So be wise in your decisions.

Get your armor on!

SPIRITUAL FREEDOM

Live as free people, but do not use your freedom as a cover-up for evil; live as God's slaves. (1 Peter 2:16 NIV)

What an oxymoron. As slaves, we are to live as free people. OK, Peter, just how do we do that? In effect, Christians should live as slaves to God, doing His will, not ours. The beauty of this perspective, is, if we do live this way, we are free indeed. Free from the slavery of sin and sin's impact on our lives. However, we must be careful not to use our new found freedom to conceal evil. That is, not to use our free will in Christ to choose as we want and therefore choose to do evil. Or have an evil intent hidden behind the disguise of good.

Freedom we have indeed! But be careful how you use it.

Get your armor on!

Be careful, however, that the exercise of your rights does not become a stumbling block to the weak. (1 Corinthians 8:9 NIV)

God did not make robots. He gave us a free will to choose, even knowing that some would not choose Him. What we have to realize is that our right to choose does not just impact us. It also affects those around us. We must pay close attention to our decisions, especially around new believers in Christ. I would hate to know that a decision I made, albeit within my right to make, caused someone else to fall into temptation and commit a sin. Be careful to choose wisely your freedoms and how you express them. Be careful to always build others up rather than provide an opportunity for them to fail.

Get your armor on!

So whether you eat or drink or whatever you do, do it all for the glory of God. (1 Corinthians 10:31 NIV)

Self-explanatory. No commentary needed!

Get your armor on!

THE WORD

All Scripture is God-breathed and is useful for teaching, rebuking, correcting and training in righteousness, so that the servant of God may be thoroughly equipped for every good work. (2 Timothy 3:16-17 NIV)

God's Word. The Sword of the Spirit.

The Word of God is powerful, transforming. All of it comes from Him. This tiny word, All, is the largest word in this verse. All of it is inspired. You either accept it all, or you do not accept it at all. Yes, man may have written it, but they wrote what the Spirit inspired. Why was it written? So that man would be equipped for every good work! Read it, study it, memorize it, do it. It will change your life forever.

The Bible. It does a body good! Read it and find out for yourself.

Get your armor on!

Keep this Book of the Law always on your lips; meditate on it day and night, so that you may be careful to do everything written in it. Then you will be prosperous and successful. (Joshua 1:8 NIV)

Joshua is talking about the Torah, the first 5 books of the Bible. At that time, the only Bible people had. However, you can infer that Joshua is referencing the complete Bible that we have today. What does he tell us here? That this book should not depart from us, but that we must recite it day and night. In other words, memorize it. Meditate on it. Why? So that we may know what it says to do and do it. And why is that important? Only then will we prosper and succeed in whatever we do. If we keep the true Word of Life on our minds throughout the day and are careful to do as it instructs, we cannot lose. What a guarantee!!!

Get your armor on!

THE WORD

These are the commands, decrees and laws the Lord your God directed me to teach you to observe in the land that you are crossing the Jordan to possess, so that you, your children and their children after them may fear the Lord your God as long as you live by keeping all his decrees and commands that I give you, and so that you may enjoy long life. Hear, Israel, and be careful to obey so that it may go well with you and that you may increase greatly in a land flowing with milk and honey, just as the Lord, the God of your ancestors, promised you. Hear, O Israel: The Lord our God, the Lord is one. Love the Lord your God with all your heart and with all your soul and with all your strength. These commandments that I give you today are to be on your hearts. Impress them on your children. Talk about them when you sit at home and when you walk along the road, when you lie down and when you get up. Tie them as symbols on your hands and bind them on your foreheads. Write them on the doorframes of your houses and on your gates. (Deuteronomy 6:1-9 NIV)

Ok, I know this is a bit long. But I wanted you to have a little bit of the background of the main theme. Moses is talking to the children of Israel and relaying the importance of keeping God's commands and passing them down from generation to generation. The benefits of doing so are listed in the first section: that you may have long life and that you may prosper and multiply greatly.

Now God does not expect us to follow these verses literally in that we are to write them on our hands and or on our foreheads or on the doorposts of our houses. But think about what these verses are saying. In essence, the Word of God should be evident in our lives. They should always be on our minds. They should always guard our conversations. They should always guide our paths. Our hands should do the work of the Word. We should memorize them in order to "repeat them to our children" and friends. When we leave our house, or dorm room, the Word should be evident in our appearance. When we sit around our house, or dorm room, we should not be ashamed to speak the Word. When walking along the sidewalks to class, the Word should always been on our minds. Do not you see how great the Word of God can be! And what a comfort the Word of God brings! Nowhere else can you find peace and truth than in the Word of God! It truly is the greatest treasure on earth.

Get your armor on!

How can a young person stay on the path of purity? By living according to your word. I seek you with all my heart; do not let me stray from your commands. I have hidden your word in my heart that I might not sin against you. (Psalm 119:9-11 NIV)

Now personalize the verses.

How can Jessica/Scott Brooks stay on the path of purity? By living according to Your word. Jessica/Scott seeks You with all her/his heart; do not let her/him stray from Your commands. Jessica/Scott has hidden Your word in her/his heart that she/he may not sin against You.

Takes a whole new meaning, does not it?

So, what is the question here? King David is asking how a young person can keep his way pure. The answer – know God's word. Why? So you will not sin! Now obviously, we are going to sin. That is a given. BUT, the more we keep God's word, the less likely we are to sin. The more we truly treasure His word, the less likely we will want to sin.

Many people only look at verse 9 and 11, but I just love verse 10. "I have sought you with all my heart, do not let me wander from your commands." The old King James says it even more passionately. "With my whole heart have I sought after you; oh let me not wander from your commandments."

That is my prayer for you, Hermana Chica / Hermano Chico.

Get your armor on!

THE WORD

Your word is a lamp for my feet and a light on my path. (Psalm 119:105 NIV)

Short and sweet but oh so powerful! The Bible is much more than a mere book. Look what the write of the psalm is telling us. What does a lamp/light do? It illuminates a clear path in the dark. God's word can do the same for us as we walk through the path of life. Use the Word to guide your every move, thought, action, reaction.

Get your armor on!

PRAYER

Very early in the morning, while it was still dark, Jesus got up, left the house and went off to a solitary place, where he prayed. (Mark 1:35 NIV)

Notice that the Son of Man got up early, went out to a deserted place, and prayed. Now if the Son of Man did this, how much more should we do it! Notice, too, that He went to a deserted place – no cell phone, no laptop, no people, no distractions – just He and His Father.

I know you are not a morning person (just like your mother!!). But, I strongly encourage you to carve out some time during the day and have some alone time with the Father. Maybe even go to the 2nd floor deck at Collins and sit on a chair, alone, just you and God.

There will not be a more rewarding time in your life than time spent with the Heavenly Father!

Get your armor on!

In the same way, the Spirit helps us in our weakness. We do not know what we ought to pray for, but the Spirit himself intercedes for us through wordless groans. (Romans 8:26 NIV)

Have you ever knelt to pray and did not have any idea what to pray for? Or how to start praying? If so, remember this verse. The Holy Spirit will guide our words if we just start speaking. Talk to God like you would a best friend. When we do that, the Holy Spirit will intervene on our behalf and plead with the Father with terms that cannot be expressed in words. Now how great is that!

Get your armor on!

PRAYER

This is the confidence we have in approaching God: that if we ask anything according to his will, he hears us. And if we know that he hears us—whatever we ask—we know that we have what we asked of him. (1 John 5:14-15 NIV)

If you remain in me and my words remain in you, ask whatever you wish, and it will be done for you. (John 15:7 NIV)

These verses were so similar and pertained to the same subject, that I just grouped them together. So how about that – a 2-for-1 special today!

Read theses verses carefully. They do not mean we can ask for whatever we want and receive. 1 John says "according to His will" and John starts out with a very large word, "IF". So when we are walking with the Lord and in His will when we pray, we will only ask for things that will glorify His name. When we do that, we have the confidence that He will not only hear us, but He will answer us!

Take this all in for a moment. The God of the universe, the Creator of all mankind, the God who has no beginning and no end, hears our prayers. But not only does He hear us, He answers us. Now how great is that!

Get your armor on!

PRAYER

For we do not have a high priest who is unable to empathize with our weaknesses, but we have one who has been tempted in every way, just as we are—yet he did not sin. Let us then approach God's throne of grace with confidence, so that we may receive mercy and find grace to help us in our time of need. (Hebrews 4:15-16 NIV)

Have you ever felt like you were the only one in the world going through a particular problem? I know I have. But look at the assurance we have in these verses. Jesus was tested in every way we are. He has gone through every emotion we have. When we feel like we are the only ones with this problem, which is simply not true. Jesus has been there, too. He can sympathize with us. So, because of that, we can approach the throne of grace at any point for any reason. When we do, we will receive mercy and find grace to help us at the proper time. Wow! Is that not amazing! Go to God for anything and everything, no matter how great or how small. He is waiting. Do not make Him wait too long.

Get your armor on!

"Ask and it will be given to you; seek and you will find; knock and the door will be opened to you. For everyone who asks receives; the one who seeks finds; and to the one who knocks, the door will be opened. (Matthew 7:7-8 NIV)

If at first you do not succeed, try, try again. Ever heard that? Same thing with prayer. If you do not hear God's answer right away, try, try again. Look at the confidence we have in these verses. These are the very words of our Savior, Jesus Christ. IF we keep asking, IF we keep searching, IF we keep knocking… Persistent prayer is a must. Do not feel as if you are nagging God. He is telling us right here to keep doing it until we find the answer. Just make sure to keep an open mind to the answer – it may not be the one we want.

So, keep on keeping on! And get your armor on!

UNASHAMED

So do not be ashamed of the testimony about our Lord... Instead, share in suffering for the gospel, relying on the power of God, (2 Timothy 1:8 NIV)

But I am not ashamed, because I know whom I have believed and am persuaded that He is able to guard what has been entrusted to me until that day. (2 Timothy 1:12 NIV)

These words were written by Paul to Timothy. If you recall, Paul mentored Timothy for 14 years. Timothy was a young, energetic pastor. Certainly, he faced many skeptics criticizing him for being young, ignorant, and incapable of leading a new found church. However, Paul knew differently. He could see the passion Timothy had to spread the good news and the ability God gave him to do so. So with these words, Paul encouraged Timothy to not be ashamed of the testimony of our Lord (and indirectly, to not be ashamed of his age).

Now, make it personal. Read it again, only this time, insert your name in place of "I".

Sis/Bub, God has such great plans for you. Do not be ashamed of the testimony!

Get your armor on!

Sustain me as You promised, and I will live; do not let me be ashamed of my hope. (Psalm 119:116 NIV)

And what hope is David talking about here? The hope we have in Christ. All that is in this world will pass away, but we are OK with that because we hope for a better future in heaven with Christ forever!! Do not be ashamed of the hope that is within you!

Get your armor on!

UNASHAMED

Pray also for me, that the message may be given to me when I open my mouth to make known with boldness the mystery of the gospel. For this I am an ambassador in chains. Pray that I might be bold enough in Him to speak as I should. (Ephesians 6:19-20 NIV)

Paul is speaking to the church in Ephesus. Look at his prayer request. When he even opens his mouth, words may be given to him so he can do what? Make known, **with boldness**, the magnificence of the gospel. And secondly, that he would be **bold** enough to speak about God as he should.

Was Paul ashamed of the gospel? Absolutely not! He made known the "greatest story ever told" every waking moment he possibly could. So should we.

Get your armor on!

For [Jessica/Scott is] not ashamed of the gospel, because it is God's power for salvation to everyone who believes, first to the Jew, and also to the Greek. (Romans 1:16 NIV)

Really, look in your Bible. This is how the verse reads!! LOL.

Pretty simple verse that really needs no explanation. The gospel is powerful! Powerful to do anything and everything, even save a poor sinner like your old man. Because of its power, we should not be ashamed of it.

Get your armor on!

UNASHAMED

My eager expectation and hope is that I will not be ashamed about anything, but that now as always, with all boldness, Christ will be highly honored in my body, whether by life or by death. (Philippians 1:20 NIV)

Paul is writing a letter to the church in Philippi. In this first chapter, he is talking about how, even though he was thrown into prison, the message of the gospel is being preached and spreading. In fact, he states in verse 14 that through his imprisonment, some of the other followers of Christ have become even more bold for the gospel. Then Paul states that it is his desire that he, too, will be eager and not ashamed to make known the wonderful news of Christ. We are wise to follow Paul's lead.

Get your armor on!

DO NOT GIVE THE DEVIL A FOOTHOLD

If you do right, won't you be accepted? But if you do not do right, sin is crouching at the door. Its desire is for you, but you must master it. (Genesis 4:7 NIV)

These words were spoken to Cain right after God rejected his sacrifice. The problem was not with Cain's sacrifice, but with Cain's heart. I love the adjectives here. Cannot you just see sin, crouching behind the door, waiting for you to come around, before jumping out in front of you? I think back to the many times you and Scott/Sis tried to scare each other. What did you do? Sneak up somewhere and hide, only to jump out with a scream. That is what sin does. Hides so you do not expect it, then it leaps in front of you with a GOTCHA! But look at what the Lord told Cain. You must master it! God would not have told Cain that if it were not possible. We can master sin. How, you say? By the same method as Christ. When Christ was tempted, what did He do? He used the Word of God (the Sword of the Spirit) as His defense. We must do the same.

Get your armor on!

Be sober! Be on the alert! Your adversary the Devil is prowling around like a roaring lion, looking for anyone he can devour. (1 Peter 5:8 NIV)

Very fitting words not only for a college freshman, but also for a 48-year-old businessman. You see, the enemy is always on the search for you to slip. He is always trying new things to gain a foothold. What he wants is to destroy you, literally, physically, and spiritually. We must always be sober – that does not mean not drunk – but aware of your surroundings.

Get your armor on!

DO NOT GIVE THE DEVIL A FOOTHOLD

Stay awake and pray, so that you won't enter into temptation. The spirit is willing, but the flesh is weak." (Matthew 26:41 NIV)

We are but weak humans who fall into temptation too easily and quickly. Therefore, we must always be sober (be of sound mind, uninhibited by mind altering influences (I do not mean just alcohol either), be alert (aware of our surroundings), be awake (do not ever rest from spiritual warfare – Satan does not), be praying (just like an apple a day keeps the doctor away, a prayer a day keeps Satan away – another dorky saying, but I could not resist!). For when we stop, Satan has us.

Get your armor on!

and do not give the Devil an opportunity. (Ephesians 4:27 NIV)

Paul is talking to the church in Ephesus and is listing several words of encouragement. The entire Chapter 4 is really some good reading if you have time.

Some translations say, "do not give the Devil a foothold." As previous verses this week have suggested, we must always be on the lookout for Satan's evil scheming. He will continue to poke around until he finds your weakest link. Then he will pound away at that link until it breaks. We must recognize our weaknesses and turn that into strength through the power of the Holy Spirit.

Get your armor on!

DO NOT GIVE THE DEVIL A FOOTHOLD

A thief comes only to steal and to kill and to destroy. I have come that they may have life and have it in abundance. (John 10:10 NIV)

Let me re-phrase this verse this way...

Satan comes only to steal and to kill and to destroy Jessica/Scott. I, Jesus, have come that Jessica/Scott may have life and have it in abundance.

Jesus is warning us what happens when we allow Satan to rule over us and allow him to gain a foothold on our lives. On the flip side (and what a flip side it is!), Jesus comes so that we may have life and have it ABUNDANCE! Whoa. Now that is something to hold on to. So hold on to Jesus. He is all you will ever need.

Get your armor on!

CHRISTIAN LIVING - THE DO'S

Therefore, God's chosen ones, holy and loved, put on heartfelt compassion, kindness, humility, gentleness, and patience, accepting one another and forgiving one another if anyone has a complaint against another. Just as the Lord has forgiven you, so also you must [forgive]. Above all, [put on] love—the perfect bond of unity. (Colossians 3:12-14 NIV)

The Christian life is not just a bunch of "do nots"; there are some "do's" as well. In the verses preceding these, Paul lists several things for the Colossians to stop doing (the "do nots). Here, he is telling the church what to do (the do's).

We would do well to do the "do's"!

Get your armor on!

Therefore, be imitators of God, as dearly loved children. And walk in love, as the Messiah also loved us and gave Himself for us, a sacrificial and fragrant offering to God. (Ephesians 5:1-2 NIV)

Here Paul provides us 2 more things to do as Christians. Imitate God and walk in love. In all that you do, imitate God. At the library, at the mall, in studio, in class, walking to and from class, in the dorm room, driving in your car, at Bahama Mamas, at the custard place, at the sporting events, on the phone, on the computer, at the SLIC, at the Huff, in the cafeteria, Everywhere you go, imitate God. Everything you do, imitate God. Ooze love to all those you come in contact with. When people see Jessica/Scott, let them see love. When people hear Jessica/Scott speak, let them hear love.

Get your armor on!

Walk in wisdom toward outsiders, making the most of the time. Your speech should always be gracious, seasoned with salt, so that you may know how you should answer each person. (Colossians 4:5-6 NIV)

Paul is encouraging the church in Colossians to be especially careful how they portray themselves to those outside the church (outsiders). What does salt do to food? It adds flavor. But too much salt puts a bad taste in your mouth. When we come into contact with non-believers, we must ask for God's wisdom on how to approach them. We must add the right amount of "salt" to our conversations so that we know how to answer each person with grace, not condemning them to hell in the first conversation with them. The key to having a Christian conversation with a non-believer is to ensure you have the second conversation with them. So do not overwhelm them and become a turn off, but leave them asking for more. Thus, making the most of your time with them.

Get your armor on!

Pay careful attention, then, to how you walk—not as unwise people but as wise—making the most of the time, because the days are evil. So do not be foolish, but understand what the Lord's will is. (Ephesians 5:15-17 NIV)

Paul is encouraging the church in Ephesus to maintain consistency in their Christian life. We must pay close attention to how we walk (i.e. live, act, react, in our attitude, our outlook on life, our words, what we put into our minds). Remember the acronym GIGO – garbage in, garbage out. OR, God in, God out. Paul says God in, God out. We do that, we are called wise. We do not do that, we are unwise and foolish. We do that, we can understand what the Lord's will is. Paul would not have said it if it were not possible. We can understand the Lord's will. We just need to make the most of our time.

Get your armor on!

But seek first the kingdom of God and His righteousness, and all these things will be provided for you. (Matthew 6:33 NIV)

Jesus was talking about people who worry about things of this world, what clothes to wear, what food to eat, where to live, what kind of career to have, what kind of car to drive. All these things cloud the mind and take our focus off Christ. Jesus mentions right before this verse that the birds have enough food to eat and how the wild flowers are nourished with water and sunshine. If God takes care of these, how much more will He take care of His own? So do not worry about things of this world. IF we seek Him first, ALL of these things will be provided. Do more seeking and a little less worrying.

Get your armor on!

LEARN TO BE CONTENT

Rest in God alone, my soul, for my hope comes from Him. (Psalm 62:5 NIV)

This is a pretty simple verse, but we often fail to adhere to it. We try to fill our lives with things and people around us, things and people that we think will bring happiness and contentment. All too often, though, these material possessions and surface friendships leave us wanting more. All we need is to rest in God's provision for us, knowing that our hope comes from Him and nowhere else.

Get your armor on!

But He said to me, "My grace is sufficient for you, for power is perfected in weakness." Therefore, I will most gladly boast all the more about my weaknesses, so that Christ's power may reside in me. (2 Corinthians 12:9 NIV)

This is probably one of Paul's most significant quotes in all the Bible. Why? Because he is acknowledging that he is not strong enough to do anything on his own. When we try to run our lives and put our trust in our abilities or in someone else or something else, we will surely fail. But, when we acknowledge His strength and His power in us, then we are most powerful. Just remember our strongest position is on our knees before God. If you remember our theme from Youth Camp this summer – FLIP. This is definitely a FLIP – on our knees the world says we are weak, but in Christ, on our knees we are most strong!

Get your armor on!

LEARN TO BE CONTENT

for I have learned to be content whatever the circumstances. I know what it is to be in need, and I know what it is to have plenty. I have learned the secret of being content in any and every situation, whether well fed or hungry, whether living in plenty or in want. (Philippians 4:11b-12 NIV)

Paul has just complimented the church in Philippi on continuing their support for Paul's ministry. Then he tells the church he is not complimenting them so they will give him more. The reason? Because he had ***learned*** to be content with what he had. And goes on to say he had ***learned*** the secret of being content in any and all circumstances. Sis/Bubba, do not get caught up in society's desire to acquire lots of things – what I like to call the three Ps - possessions, power, and position. Be content in what the Lord has given you. Be content in His provision for you. Easier said than done, I know. Paul told us twice in these two verses he had to ***learn*** the secret. Learn and learn well from Paul's example.

Get your armor on!

The Lord is my shepherd; I have all that I need. (Psalm 23:1 NIV)

In Biblical times, a shepherd was vitally important. He kept watch over the flock, providing protection, food, and shelter. The sheep followed the shepherd. He looked after their every need. The sheep did not need to worry about wolves, where their next meal was coming from – nothing! Because the shepherd provided it all. Our Lord and Savior provides the same for His sheep. We lack for nothing because the Shepherd provides it all. Do not let the cares of this world suffocate you and drown you in society's worries. Remember, the Lord is my shepherd; I have all that I need.

Get your armor on!

LEARN TO BE CONTENT

But godliness with contentment is a great gain. For we brought nothing into the world, and we can take nothing out. But if we have food and clothing, we will be content with these... Instruct them to do good, to be rich in good works, to be generous, willing to share, storing up for themselves a good foundation for the age to come, so that they may take hold of life that is real. (1 Timothy 6:6-8,18-19 NIV)

Great words of encouragement from the mentor Paul to his pupil Timothy! Godliness, with contentment, is a great gain. Following the path of the Father and being content with what we have will produce fruit (spiritual fruit) like no tree can. Be content with food and clothing. Again, do not fill your mind with the desire for material possessions. Instead, be rich in good works, be generous with what you have, be willing to share. Doing so will store up for you a strong spiritual foundation so that you can take hold of ***real*** life, not fake life of society.

Get your armor on!

EXTERNAL APPEARANCES

As for those who were held in high esteem—whatever they were makes no difference to me; God does not show favoritism. (Galatians 2:6 NIV)

Paul was writing to the church in Galatia. These new Christians were being confused by those distorting the gospel preached to them. These people tried to bring back obeying the law as part of the gospel message. Later in this book, Paul describes in detail how Jesus Christ freed us from the law. But here, Paul calls them out. They seemed to be important to the church, at least in their own minds! But Paul was not impressed with their reputation. Nor was God, for God does not look on the outside, but the inside, of a person. You see, we can get all dressed up, we can quote scripture, we can pray wonderful prayers, and we can talk the walk. None of that means anything unless our heart is in the right place. Oh, sure, we can impress those around us, make others think we are some kind of wonderful Christian. But God sees right through all the dressing, the "mere appearances". Live for God, not to impress others, but to show the love for our Lord Jesus!

Get your armor on!

God is in charge of human life, watching and examining us inside and out. (Proverbs 20:27 NIV)

When all around may be chaotic, God is in charge. When all around may seem out of control, God is in charge. He is watching us and examining us inside as well as outside. He knows our heart better than we do. He knows our motives better than we do. He knows our desires better than we do. So when we go through the motions "playing church" or showing off our Biblical "head" knowledge (rather than "heart" knowledge), He sees right through it. Do not put up some fake front. It does not do you any good. Let others see the true you, the you on the inside. Because that is the you God sees.

Get your armor on!

EXTERNAL APPEARANCES

What should I bring before the LORD when I come to bow before God on high? Should I come before Him with burnt offerings, with year-old calves? Would the LORD be pleased with thousands of rams, or with ten thousand streams of oil? Should I give my firstborn for my transgression, the child of my body for my own sin? He has told you men what is good and what it is the LORD requires of you: Only to act justly, to love faithfulness, and to walk humbly with your God. (Micah 6:6-8 NIV)

The author here is asking what the Lord requires of His children. Should we bring Him sacrifices? Should we bring Him offerings? Should we bring Him good deeds? Should we bring Him our most prized possessions? While these may be good things to do, we can do these things with deceitful hearts. We can do these things with improper motives – possibly trying to bargain with God. We can do these things without humility. We can do these things just going through the motions without true intent in our hearts. We can do these things for show – so others can see what "great" Christians we are. Much more than these, God has told us what He requires: Act Justly. Love Faithfulness. Walk Humbly. Nothing for show, but all for His glory. Now go and do the same.

Get your armor on!

EXTERNAL APPEARANCES

As the water reflects the face, so the heart reflects the person. (Proverbs 27:19 NIV)

While it is the outside of us that people see, the true you is on the inside. The heart in Biblical times reflected the entire person, all of one's being was described by the heart. Who you are, your thoughts, your character, all was described by the heart. What type of heart do you have? Show others the true you by showing them your heart.

I may have shared this before, and I am sure to share again some other day, but this verse reminds me of a silversmith. He places the silver over the hottest part of the fire to burn away all the impurities. But how does he know when all the impurities are gone and he has pure silver? When he can see his reflection in it! God wants to see His reflection in your heart. That is when He knows He has a pure child. Reflect God in your heart.

Get your armor on!

EXTERNAL APPEARANCES

But the LORD said to Samuel, "Do not look at his appearance or his stature, because I have rejected him. Man does not see what the LORD sees, for man sees what is visible, but the LORD sees the heart."
(1 Samuel 16:7 NIV)

The Lord had instructed Samuel to find Israel's next king. Samuel was led to the house of Jesse in Bethlehem. Jesse had 8 sons and Samuel knew for sure one of them would be anointed king. So 7 of the sons were brought before Samuel and all of them rejected by the Lord. Samuel could not figure out what was wrong. He asked Jesse if he had any more sons. Jesse said yes, but that he was the youngest and out watching the sheep. Remember in Biblical times, a shepherd was one of the lowliest jobs one could have. Surely, the Lord was not calling on a poor little shepherd boy to be the next king!?!? But look at what the Lord told Samuel. Do not look at appearances or position. Do not look at merely the exterior of a person, what is visible. Look inside a person; look at their motives; look at their heart. That is what the Lord looks at; that is what He sees. Do not concern yourself with putting up a good front so others can see you if your heart is in the wrong place. If you do, the Lord will reject you. Make sure your heart is right and then you will not have to worry about the exterior. Others will see you for the true you.

Get your armor on!

FRIENDS

A man with many friends may be harmed, but there is a friend who stays closer than a brother. (Proverbs 18:24 NIV)

This verse may be a bit confusing until you dissect it some and really think about what Solomon is trying to tell us. The first question I had was, "How can many friends be harmful?" But when we think about it, maybe a better word to be used is acquaintances. In today's world of social networking, we will accept almost anyone as our friend on Facebook or add anyone's number to our cell phone for texting purposes. Would you call all of these people friends? Not really. I mean, how can you be friends with 500 people?? You may know of them, but you certainly do not ***know*** them. What Solomon is telling us is that we need to identify that select few, those we will grow to know intimately and personally. Those will be our true friends. Those will stick closer to us than a brother (or sister). I encourage you to really search for your true friends. Be selective. You deserve the right to be choosy. Then stick with them closer than a sibling.

Get your armor on!

A friend loves at all times, and a brother is born for a difficult time. (Proverbs 17:17 NIV)

Why do I need friends? I do not need anyone. I can take care of myself. Have you met anyone like this before? I am sad for those who feel this way. Sometimes we just need a hug. A kind word. A smile from a friend. Other times, we need a friend to help us through difficult times. A shoulder to cry on. A body to lean against. An ear to hear. Friends, true friends, look out for the interest of others above the interest of their own. So why do we need friends? For love and support and encouragement. For help in trying times. Be that type of friend. Give that hug. Give that smile. Be that shoulder. Be that ear.

Get your armor on!

FRIENDS

Iron sharpens iron, and one man sharpens another. (Proverbs 27:17 NIV)

According to Wikipedia, accountability is often used synonymously with such concepts as responsibility, answerability, blameworthiness, and other terms associated with the expectation of account-giving. Accountability is also the acknowledgment and assumption of responsibility for actions and decisions. Accountability can be a dirty word for those not living according to God's plan and desires. Accountability can also be one of the greatest words for those who strive to walk in the Spirit. And it is our friends that hold us accountable either way. We can choose friends who will encourage us to cheat, lie, and steal and thus not hold us accountable. Or we can choose friends who will encourage us to be fair, live in truth, and give of our time, talents, and abilities. We can be that friend that encourages others to cheat, lie, and steal or we can be that friend who will encourage others to be fair, live in truth, and give. Which will it be? No standing on the fence. And remember, a no decision is a decision.

Get your armor on!

So the Scripture was fulfilled that says, Abraham believed God, and it was credited to him for righteousness, and he was called God's friend. (James 2:23 NIV)

Wow! What a testimony. Abraham was called God's friend. If this were stated on my tombstone, I would consider myself to have lived a fulfilling life. We have friends who will turn their backs on us; we will have friends who will disappoint us; we have friends in whom we will lose confidence; we have friends who will just drift off to a distant memory for one reason or another. But that will never be the case with God. He is the friend we can always count on; He is the friend who will stand by our side regardless of the circumstances. Can God call you His friend? Follow Abraham's example and be that friend.

Get your armor on!

FRIENDS

Two are better than one because they have a good reward for their efforts. For if either falls, his companion can lift him up; but pity the one who falls without another to lift him up. Also, if two lie down together, they can keep warm; but how can one person alone keep warm? And if somebody overpowers one person, two can resist him. A cord of three strands is not easily broken. (Ecclesiastes 4:9-12 NIV)

Friends. A person attached to another by feelings of affection or personal regard. A patron or supporter. A person who is not hostile. One who is kind or helpful. We cannot live without them, and sometimes we hate to live with them!! But nothing, besides our relationship with Christ, can make our day brighter, can lift our spirits, or provide encouragement like that of a friend. Sis/Bubba, you are meeting so many new people and building relationships that may last a lifetime. Choose wisely. Be careful to surround yourself with strong Christian friends. Those who make it evident their love for Christ is above anything else. Those who will hold you accountable in your walk with Christ. Those who will encourage you to walk the path of the straight and narrow. For if you do, the three-stranded cord (Christ, your friend, and you) will not easily be broken.

Get your armor on!

GOOD DEEDS

For we are His creation—created in Christ Jesus for good works, which God prepared ahead of time so that we should walk in them. (Ephesians 2:10 NIV)

Good works. Acts of kindness. Good things to do, but these acts do not provide salvation. Paul just told us this in the preceding verses. But that does not mean they are not important, if not vital, things for us to do. In fact, Paul states here that we are created to do those very things. And, he goes even further to state that God has prepared ahead of time those good deeds for us to do. So, while they do not provide salvation, they do provide evidence of salvation. Are you displaying evidence of your salvation through your good works? What type of Jesus do others see in you? God has already prepared good things for you to do. It is up to us to do them. So what are you waiting for?

Get your armor on!

In the same way, let your light shine before men, so that they may see your good works and give glory to your Father in heaven. (Matthew 5:16 NIV)

This is one of my favorite verses. I often close my prayers with this verse. In the verse preceding this one, Jesus refers to His followers as the light of the world. What does light do? It illuminates our paths or guides us towards a destination. In this same way, we are to illuminate the way to Christ and guide others towards our ultimate destination. We are to do this through our good works. The purpose of the good works is not so that man may see us and think, "Wow, what a great person he/she is!" But we do good works in order to give glory to our Father in heaven! Be intentional about the good you do. Give glory to the Father through the good you do.

Get your armor on!

GOOD DEEDS

Therefore, my dear brothers, be steadfast, immovable, always excelling in the Lord's work, knowing that your labor in the Lord is not in vain. (1 Corinthians 15:58 NIV)

Take Paul's encouragement to the Corinthian church to heart. He is urging the church, and us, to be steadfast, unwavering, immovable, firm, and unbendable. He is urging the church, and you, to excel in the Lord's work. Always work enthusiastically for the Lord. Put forth every ounce of your being into doing the Lord's work. Why should we do this? Because we know that our effort, our labor in the Lord, will not return void. It will not be for no purpose. Another translation says that our labor in the Lord "is not futile [it is never wasted or to no purpose]." Still another translation says that we can be confident "that nothing you do for Him is a waste of time or effort." We may never see the fruits of our labor, but know that our efforts for His purpose will bear much fruit.

Get your armor on!

On the contrary, whoever wants to become great among you must be your servant, and whoever wants to be first among you must be your slave; just as the Son of Man did not come to be served, but to serve, and to give His life—a ransom for many." (Matthew 20:26b-28 NIV)

The mother of two disciples, James and John, earlier in this chapter asked that her sons be seated at the right and left of Jesus' kingdom. These were positions of high importance in a king's court. Jesus kind of put her in her place. Instead of desiring to be in a high position of importance where others would serve us, we should desire to become a servant. If we want to become great, we must make ourselves a slave to others. Here we go again with a FLIP. God says the way to become great in His kingdom is to serve others. And He should know; He set the example! Because even the Son of Man came not to **be served**, but **to serve** and give His life for many! Go and do likewise.

Get your armor on!

GOOD DEEDS

What good is it, my brothers, if someone says he has faith, but does not have works? Can his faith save him? If a brother or sister is without clothes and lacks daily food, and one of you says to them, "Go in peace, keep warm, and eat well," but you do not give them what the body needs, what good is it? (James 2:14-16 NIV)

James is a great book about faith in action. Each chapter can be broken down into 1 or 2 major themes about living out your faith. In the second half of Chapter 2, James encourages us to live out our faith through the good things we do. He starts out by asking a rhetorical question: What good is someone's faith if there are no good works to back it up? He even goes as far to say, "Can that type of faith save a person?" Now I am not advocating salvation by works by any means. But the good we do should be an outward expression of what the Lord has done for us on the inside. Look at the example James provides in verses 15 and 16. If someone comes to you in need and you basically tell them, "Hey, I am praying for you. Hope everything turns out ok." But you do not do anything to meet their need, what good is that? If you recall, Jesus often met people's physical needs before He met their spiritual needs. You see, people need to know how much you care before they care how much you know. Live out your faith in what you do for others.

Get your armor on!

CONTROL YOUR TONGUE

Do not let unwholesome [foul, profane, worthless, vulgar] words ever come out of your mouth, but only such speech as is good for building up others, according to the need and the occasion, so that it will be a blessing to those who hear [you speak]. (Ephesians 4:29 AMP)

I like the way the Amplified Bible translates this verse. Foul or profane language. Pretty descriptive. Then added by evil words, worthless and vulgar talk. You know, when we speak ill of those around us and to those around us, our speech is worthless. We might as well not speak at all. It's wasted breath. By contrast, our speech should be good, beneficial, fitting the need and the occasion, be a blessing, and give grace to those who hear it. See the stark contrast of foul and polluting language versus that which gives grace to others. Do not waste your breath. Use your words and your speech to build others up, to encourage them, to benefit them in their spiritual journey.

Get your armor on!

For the mouth speaks from the overflow of the heart. (Matthew 12:34b NIV)

I tell you that on the day of judgment people will have to account for every careless word they speak. For by your words you will be acquitted, and by your words you will be condemned. (Matthew 12:36-37 NIV)

Ouch! Jesus was not pulling any punches with His comments here to the Pharisees. And His comments speak truth today just as they did then. We only speak out of our mouths what is in our hearts. I do not believe in Freudian slips. There are no slips of the tongue. We speak what is on our minds and in our hearts. And we will have to give account for our words one day. When we stand before Christ, we will have to give account for the words we used. Use your words carefully. Do not be careless with them. They show the true you.

Get your armor on!

CONTROL YOUR TONGUE

If you claim to be religious but do not control your tongue, you are fooling yourself, and your religion is worthless. (James 1:26 NIV)

One of the drawbacks of professing to be a Christian is that those around you will automatically begin to pay much closer attention to your actions, reactions, attitudes, behavior and words. Here, James is giving us stern warning to be careful to control our mouths. "If you claim to be religious…" I really do not like this word. Many people are "religious" but so few actually walk with the Lord. So let's paraphrase James and include the word Christian instead of the word religion. So it will read like this…

"If Jessica/Scott claims to be a Christian but does not control her/his tongue, she/he is fooling herself/himself, and Jessica's/Scott's Christian faith is worthless."

Whoa! Now this verse takes on a whole new meaning. If you claim to be a Christian, but talk like any other non-believer, what good are you? And what type of witness are you displaying? You deceive no one but yourself because others can see right through you even if you cannot. And the kicker? Your faith is worthless, of no value at all.

I, for one, do not ever want my faith to be worthless. Do you? If you agree, then watch what you say!

Get your armor on!

but no man can tame the tongue. It is a restless evil, full of deadly poison. With it we bless our Lord and Father, and with it we curse men who are made in God's likeness. Out of the same mouth come blessing and cursing. My brothers, these things should not be this way. (James 3:8-10 NIV)

Here is the double standard with our mouths. Out of one side we speak kindly to others, uplifting them, encouraging to others. Out of the other side, we speak negatively, perhaps spreading rumor or gossip, telling them only what we think they want to hear. Sometimes, we might let out a curse word. James says this should not be the case. Out of the same mouth we speak both blessings and cursing? James asks two rhetorical questions right after these verses. How can a fresh water spring bring about salt water? How can a fig tree bear olives? The answer? They cannot. So why do we? Make sure what comes out of your mouth is sweet to the taste, uplifting to others, and most pleasing to our Lord and Savior. Do not pull the double standard.

Get your armor on!

And coarse and foolish talking or crude joking are not suitable, but rather giving thanks. (Ephesians 5:4 NIV)

Here is more instruction from the Apostle Paul regarding our speech. Let's break down just what type of speech he is talking about, starting with coarse talking. Coarse means vulgar, uncouth, rude, and foul-mouthed. Foolish means stupid, silly, idiotic, unwise, and thoughtless. Crude means rough, unfinished, and unsophisticated. All of this type of talking is not suitable for Christians. On the contrary, speech that is giving thanks is charitable, generous, bountiful, appreciated, and recognized. Do not you see the difference in the meaning of these words? They give a connotation that breeds love, joy, and peace. Besides, they just sound nicer! Follow Paul's instruction.

Get your armor on!

CONTROL YOUR THOUGHTS

But each person is tempted when he is drawn away and enticed by his own evil desires. Then after desire has conceived, it gives birth to sin, and when sin is fully grown, it gives birth to death. (James 1:14-15 NIV)

Look at the progression of sin. It first starts with a desire, a craving, a want, a thought. Satan first puts a thought in our minds – the need to do something or want something. Then, when that thought grows, it gives birth to the act. The act, if allowed to continue unabated, will ultimately kill you, either by physical death or by spiritual death. Therefore, we must control our thoughts. And how do we do that? By controlling what we put into our minds. And how do we do that? By paying attention to the music we listen to, the movies we watch, the TV shows we watch, the people we hang with, what we read. The list goes on... Put some THOUGHT into your day today!

Get your armor on!

One evening David got up from his bed and strolled around on the roof of the palace. From the roof he saw a woman bathing—a very beautiful woman. (2 Samuel 11:2 NIV)

Here is the beginning of the end of David. What started as a casual glance at a woman ended with adultery and murder. Right after this passage we see that David sent messengers out to find out who this woman was. Once he found out who she was, Bathsheba, the **wife** of Uriah the Hittite, he still sent for her. He saw; he thought; he asked; he called; he did. See the progression. Be wise! Learn from David's mistake. Control your thoughts by controlling what you see. Control what you put into your mind, for what you put in will come out – eventually.

Get your armor on!

CONTROL YOUR THOUGHTS

But I tell you, everyone who looks at a woman to lust for her has already committed adultery with her in his heart. (Matthew 5:28 NIV)

Matthew Chapter 5 contains the beginnings of the Sermon on the Mount. Jesus taught the throngs of people about life and explained how He came to fulfill the Old Testament laws, not replace them. Not only are we not to commit certain acts like murder (from verse 21) and adultery (in this verse), but we are not to think it either. The Scribes and Pharisees were so caught up on presenting an outward appearance. Jesus said commitment to Him goes so much deeper. Merely thinking about committing a particular sin is just as bad as the act itself. That is why controlling our thoughts is so vital. That is why controlling what we put into our minds is essential for a stronger, closer walk with our Lord. **THINK** about that!

Get your armor on!

Therefore, I say this and testify in the Lord: You should no longer walk as the Gentiles walk, in the futility of their thoughts. [18] They are darkened in their understanding, excluded from the life of God, because of the ignorance that is in them and because of the hardness of their hearts. (Ephesians 4:17-18 NIV)

Paul's words to the Ephesians should ring loud and clear to us today. Gentiles, similar to today's non-Christians, were futile in their thoughts. In other words, their thoughts were useless, pointless, fruitless, and ineffective. Why? Because they were darkened in their understanding and excluded from the life of God. They had hardened their hearts to the things of God and had become ignorant. That's what happens when we turn away from God and do our own thing. We become ignorant and our thoughts are useless. What a sad state to be in. Make an effort to walk in the ways of the Lord so that your thoughts may be useful, helpful, functional, valuable, and effective.

Get your armor on!

CONTROL YOUR THOUGHTS

taking every thought captive to the obedience of Christ. (2 Corinthians 10:5b NIV)

This verse really sums up our theme on controlling our thoughts. Bring every thought captive to the obedience of Christ. What we think should be under the influence of being obedient to our Lord. No doubt this is hard to do. Sure, we are going to fail daily. But do not let that stop you from trying. It takes work to bring every thought captive to obey Christ. You have evidence of the rewards of hard work – just look at your first semester grades! You did not achieve those grades without a lot of blood, sweat, and tears. In this same way, strive to bring your thoughts captive to Christ.

Get your armor on!

PURITY

For this is God's will, your sanctification: that you abstain from sexual immorality, so that each of you knows how to possess his own vessel in sanctification and honor, not with lustful desires, like the Gentiles who do not know God. (1 Thessalonians 4:3-5 NIV)

Purity – cleanliness, wholesomeness, spotless. That is God's will for you and me. That we be set apart (sanctified) for His purposes. In order to be sanctified, we must refrain from any type of immoral activity. The simple fact that you keep yourself pure sets you apart from the rest. As is normally the case with Paul, when he gives a command or suggestion, he always follows up with the why. In this case, the why is so that we know how to possess our own bodies with honor. That we can hold our heads high and walk with confidence that while others around us are compromising, we stand strong in the power of the Lord. Stand strong!

Get your armor on!

you yourselves, as living stones, are being built into a spiritual house for a holy priesthood to offer spiritual sacrifices acceptable to God through Jesus Christ. (1 Peter 2:5 NIV)

Peter gives us insight to whom and what we really are in Christ. And this verse ties perfectly with tomorrow's verse. As a Christian, we are living stones. Stones used to build a spiritual house. A spiritual house being built for a holy priesthood. In other words, we are the church. Our bodies are the spiritual house hosting the holy priesthood of Christ Himself. Ever thought of that before? If we think of our bodies as the church, we will be more careful how we present ourselves and what we put into ourselves and what we do with ourselves. Think of it this way. Before you do anything, would you do the same thing inside the sanctuary of a church? Keep your living stone holy!

Get your armor on!

PURITY

Beloved, I implore you as aliens and strangers and exiles [in this world] to abstain from the sensual urges (those dishonorable desires) that wage war against the soul. (1 Peter 2:11 AMP)

This translation is from the Amplified Bible. I think it provides a little bit better wording to better understand the intent of the verse. The Apostle Peter was writing this letter to Christians. He refers to them as aliens, strangers, and exiles because, in reality, that is what we are. We were not created to live in this world forever. So, in a way, we are aliens, strangers, and exiles of this world awaiting the new Earth that God is preparing for us. Peter urges us to abstain from sensual desires. What does abstain mean? Desist, withdraw, refrain, withhold, do without, give up. While Peter stresses here our sensual desires, we can infer that he includes any type of earthly desire that pulls us away from Christ. The desire for popularity, money, possessions, authority, individualism, food, attention, any craving that replaces that craving for God. Remember our battles are not against flesh and blood, but against the rulers, against the authorities, against the powers in this dark world and the spiritual forces of evil in the heavenly realms. When these battles come up, run Forest run! Run for your life, literally!

Get your armor on!

PURITY

Let there be no sexual immorality, impurity, or greed among you. Such sins have no place among God's people. (Ephesians 5:3 NLT)

You can be sure that no immoral, impure, or greedy person will inherit the Kingdom of Christ and of God. (Ephesians 5:5a NLT)

This New Living translation is pretty descriptive of Paul's words to the church in Ephesus. I do like, however, how the NIV has verse 3. The NIV lists the same three sins and adds that these not "be once named among you." In other words, do not even give others a hint that you are associated with these sins. That way, if rumors are spread about you, they will be obviously false. Besides, Paul says these sins have no place among God's people. Then Paul adds one more stinging comment – people who associate themselves with these sins will not inherit the kingdom of God.

Sis/Bubba, live a pure life! This goes not only now when you are single, but after you are married as well. Do not even give others the opportunity to spread rumors about you. As the Lord Christ Himself says, Be holy for I am holy!

Get your armor on!

PURITY

Do you not know that your body is a sanctuary of the Holy Spirit who is in you, whom you have from God? You are not your own, for you were bought at a price; therefore glorify God in your body. (1 Corinthians 6:19-20 NIV)

The culmination of Purity! So often we join God's family and think, "OK, now that I have that eternal life thing settled, I can live how I want to." But we fail to comprehend God's intent for each one of His children. Paul clearly states here that the church is not some building with fancy windows and manicured landscaping. You and I are the church! Our bodies are living sanctuaries possessing the Holy Spirit within us. Once we turn our lives over to Christ, we are no longer in possession of our bodies; He is! He bought us with the highest price one could offer – His Son's blood. As a result, we should honor God in our body. Honor God with your body – what you put into it, what you put on it, what you do with it.

Get your armor on!

FORGIVENESS

If we confess our sins, He is faithful and righteous to forgive us our sins and to cleanse us from all unrighteousness. (1 John 1:9 NIV)

Probably the greatest gift, through His Son, that God has given us is His forgiveness. It is unimaginable to me that the Great Creator God can forgive me of my many transgressions. Not just once, but over and over again. But read this verse carefully. It is true that God's forgiveness is granted to us all. However, we must confess our sins before we can receive forgiveness. See how this verse begins, "If..." So before you can claim forgiveness, confess your sins before Him. Then you will know you have been forgiven because of God's faithfulness. He never backs down from a promise. But let's not stop there. Not only does He forgive us, but He cleanses us from all unrighteousness. Kinda like cleaning behind the ears and in all the creases. God gives us a good scrubbing when we confess and ask for forgiveness. To this I say, "Scrub away!!"

Get your armor on!

For You, Lord, are kind and ready to forgive, abundant in faithful love to all who call on You. (Psalm 86:5 NIV)

Our God is so gracious! Look at what the psalmist tells us. Our God is READY to forgive. He is waiting for us to confess and ask for His forgiveness. When we do, He is there ready to forgive us. He is ready to give abundant, faithful love to His children when we come to Him. Wow! How awesome is that! Do not let Satan gain a foothold and tell you that God will not forgive you for doing something (or not doing something). That is a flat out and out lie. Do not believe it. We have no qualifiers in this verse. No if's. No but's. Simply, God is ready, willing, and able to forgive us and give us abundant love when we call out to Him. Start calling!

Get your armor on!

FORGIVENESS

LORD, if You considered sins, Lord, who could stand? But with You there is forgiveness, so that You may be revered. (Psalm 130:3-4 NIV)

This verse takes away any ability of our own to reach perfection. For if we considered our sins, who could stand? No one! But, praise the Lord for the "but". But with You Lord, there is forgiveness. Can I get an AMEN! Because He has provided forgiveness, we ought to revere Him, honor Him, admire Him, respect Him, look up to Him, hold Him in the highest regard, be in awe of Him, and worship Him. Get on your knees and thank God for His forgiveness! What a mighty God we serve.

Get your armor on!

Then I acknowledged my sin to You and did not conceal my iniquity. I said, "I will confess my transgressions to the LORD," and You took away the guilt of my sin. (Psalm 32:5 NIV)

Have you ever committed a sin and the nagging guilt just would not go away? I mean, everywhere you turned, the remembrance of that sin kept coming back. Then you realize, "OK God. I get the hint", and you confess right away. However, that guilt never seems to go away. Satan tries to get to us by causing the guilt to stick around and interfere with our walk with Christ, just like a scab that we keep picking over and over again. It cannot heal unless we stop picking. Read this verse again. The Lord will take away the guilt of my sin. We must recognize when we confess to the Lord, I mean really confess to the Lord, our sins are removed. Not only the sin, but also the guilt of that sin. Confess you sins to Him; repent and turn from future temptations; remember the sin no more.

Get your armor on!

FORGIVENESS

As far as the east is from the west, so far has He removed our transgressions from us. (Psalm 103:12 NIV)

If you go back to the last couple of day's verses, we have been building up to this one. I really just flat out love this verse. You know why? Because this verse tells us just how much God loves us and how much He has forgiven us. As far as the east is from the west! Casting Crowns has a song called "East to West" and in it the verse goes like this... "Jesus, can you show me just how far the east is from the west...from one scared hand to the other." Now why did not the psalmist say as far as the north is from the south? I know this is a bit rhetorical, but think about it. You can go north only so far before you start going south. You can go south only so far before you start going north. But can you ever go west by going east? No. If you start out going west, you will never start going east. That is how far God has removed our sins from us. Is He not just an amazing God!!

Get your armor on!

LISTEN

My dearly loved brothers, understand this: everyone must be quick to hear (James 1:19 NIV)

There is more to this verse but I cut off at this point to make a point. I am sure you have heard this many times before, either from me or someone else. But God gave us one mouth and two ears for a reason. We are to listen twice as much, if not more, than we speak. This especially goes when we are having a conversation with God. Many times in our prayer time, we are the only ones talking. We do not pause enough to let God talk. He does not audibly speak to us, but often does so through His word. That is why it is important to pray after we spend time in His word. Pray about what you just read. Perhaps He gave you a thought while reading. Maybe He convicted you of some unconfessed sin. Or He laid a friend on your heart to reach out to. Read, then listen. Pray, then listen. Most of all, listen.

Get your armor on!

Without guidance, people fall, but with many counselors there is deliverance. (Proverbs 11:14 NIV)

This is some pretty good advice. We all need guidance. All areas of life, all kinds of decisions, I have sought advice. It is not a sign of weakness to ask for help. As it pertains to your Christian walk, there is no greater counselor than The Counselor! In fact, that is one of Jesus' names – Counselor (Isaiah 9:6). Pray for discernment to know when it is Jesus speaking. You pray for it, He will give it to you. Without His advice, you will surely fall. With it, you will find success.

Get your armor on!

LISTEN

Hear this, you foolish and senseless people. They have eyes, but they do not see. They have ears, but they do not hear. (Jeremiah 5:21 NIV)

What a terrible thing to have said about someone. People who refuse to see; people who refuse to listen are foolish and senseless. And that is exactly what can be said about us if we do not listen to what our Lord is telling us. There are a number of reasons we do not want to listen: we do not like what we are being told; we do not want to be told what to do; we are comfortable in our sin; we have our own plans. Do not be foolish. Do not be senseless. Listen with the ears you have. See with the eyes you have.

Get your armor on!

We must therefore pay even more attention to what we have heard, so that we will not drift away. (Hebrews 2:1 NIV)

The writer of Hebrews provides a stern warning to those who neglect what they have heard and been taught. If we just let the advice we receive enter one ear and spill out the other, what good is it? If we hear the word spoken to us, if we receive sound advice, but do not act on it, what good is it? Even now, more than ever, we must pay even more attention to what we have heard so that we will not drift away. It only takes a spark to light a fire. Satan only needs a small crack in our armor to gain a foothold. Pay attention. Listen and learn. Remember the advice of our Lord so that you will not drift away.

Get your armor on!

LISTEN

Then He said, "Go out and stand on the mountain in the LORD's presence." At that moment, the LORD passed by. A great and mighty wind was tearing at the mountains and was shattering cliffs before the LORD, but the LORD was not in the wind. After the wind there was an earthquake, but the LORD was not in the earthquake. After the earthquake there was a fire, but the LORD was not in the fire. And after the fire there was a voice, a soft whisper. (1 Kings 19:11-12 NIV)

These words were spoken to Elijah. He had been faithful to God for such a long time, but saw no fruits of his labor. In fact, he was running for his life at the moment these words were spoken to him. The Lord was going to show Himself to Elijah in an effort to comfort him and remind him that the Lord would always be with him. We see a great and mighty wind. We see an earthquake. We see a fire. But the Lord was not in any of these. Lastly, we hear a voice, a soft whisper. Some translations say a still, small voice. Often times we want God to show Himself to us in great and mighty ways. That way we know He is there. But God does not always work according to our plans. Many times, if not all the time, it is in those quiet moments that God speaks to us. Our job is to be still and listen. Listen for the small voice, the soft whisper, of God.

Get your armor on!

GOD'S PROMISES

Call to Me and I will answer you and tell you great and wondrous things you do not know. (Jeremiah 33:3 NIV)

I thought as you begin a new semester in college, that I would focus the first few weeks on different attributes of God. Different qualities that make our God...well, God. There are so many places to start, but I wanted to begin with His promises to us, His children. Read this verse again. Can you fathom the God of creation, the God of the universe promises to answer us when we call out to Him. And not only answer us, but to tell us great and wondrous things we cannot even imagine! Do not ever be ashamed to call out to the Father. You will not get an "out of the office" message or even a busy signal. He is waiting to hear from you. Do not keep Him waiting too long.

Get your armor on!

He did not waver in unbelief at God's promise, but was strengthened in his faith and gave glory to God, because he was fully convinced that what He had promised He was also able to perform. (Romans 4:20-21 NIV)

Paul is providing the church in Rome an example of falling on the promises of God. The "He" in these verses refers to Abraham. If you remember, when Abraham and Sarah were promised a son, both were in their 90s. So, while it may have appeared preposterous to think that they could bear children at that age, because God promised it, Abraham believed it. More than just believing, Abraham was fully convinced that what God promised, He was able to do. We would be wise to learn from Abraham.

Maybe one day, someone will write: Jessica/Scott did not waver in unbelief, but was strengthened in her/his faith and gave glory to God. Jessica/Scott was fully convinced that what God has promised, He is able to perform!

Get your armor on!

GOD'S PROMISES

Now to Him who is able to protect you from stumbling and to make you stand in the presence of His glory, blameless and with great joy, to the only God our Savior, through Jesus Christ our Lord, be glory, majesty, power, and authority before all time, now, and forever. Amen. (Jude 1:24-25 NIV)

You know these two verses have been made into a praise song which I learned my freshman year in college. I have not heard that song in many years, but I can sing it now just as I did so long ago. God is able to protect us and keep us from stumbling. He allows us to stand in the presence of His glory blameless. Can you imagine? We are covered in our sin, dark and soiled. But we stand in His presence blameless and with GREAT joy! Wow, what a promise! Makes me anxious for the day we will be able to do that very thing.

Get your armor on!

No one will be able to stand against you as long as you live. I will be with you, just as I was with Moses. I will not leave you or forsake you. (Joshua 1:5 NIV)

These words were spoken by our God to Joshua. He was taking over the reins of Moses to lead the children of Israel to the Promised Land. While these words were spoken to a specific individual, at a specific time, for a specific purpose, we can still take comfort in them. Certainly, Joshua must have felt overwhelmed at the task in front of him. And, I can bet you Joshua felt, at times, ill-equipped for what lay ahead. But look at the promise of our Lord and Savior. He tells Joshua that no one will stand against him as long as he lived. Then He adds that He would be with him, just as He was with Moses. And He tops it off with the fact that He would never leave or forsake Joshua. We can take comfort in the fact that when God calls us to do something, He has already equipped us to do it. So we have nothing to fear. We just need to do it. Take comfort in God's promise to never leave you or forsake you.

Get your armor on!

GOD'S PROMISES

We know that all things work together for the good of those who love God: those who are called according to His purpose. (Romans 8:28 NIV)

For I know the plans I have for you"—declares the LORD— "plans to prosper you and not to harm you, plans to give you a hope and a future. (Jeremiah 29:11 NIV)

I like both of these verses so much and I could not separate the two. And from the way things are going for you this week, I thought both were especially applicable.

Romans 8:28 is your mother's favorite verse. Let's look at it closely. All things work together. The little word "All" is a very big word indeed. God leaves nothing out with this word. There is no "but", there is no exception, and there is no "if". **All** things work together. For what? For the good of those who love God. He works everything out for our good. Even if we cannot see the good in it now, He has promised us that His ways are for our good. And we are called according to His purpose, for His purpose. We just need to simply trust Him (which sometimes is not very easy).

Jeremiah 29:11 has received much publicity in recent years. And it gives us a great and comforting promise. Notice how God tells us the He knows the plans the He has for us. The plans are His, not ours, and the two sometimes do not equal each other. Look at the promise in this verse. His plans are for our welfare, our wellbeing, our happiness, our benefit. His plans are not for our disaster, but to give us a future and a hope. Now would you not want those types of plans? They are the best one could offer. Again, it does not make it any easier to accept especially when His plans differ from ours, but we must accept them and be thankful for them because they are for our own good, to give us a future and a hope!!!

Get your armor on!

GOD'S POWER

You are from God, little children, and you have conquered them, because the One who is in you is greater than the one who is in the world. (1 John 4:4 NIV)

I want to share with you the awesome power of our God. At times you will feel like the entire world is caving in around you. Everywhere you turn, everything you do will seem to fall to pieces. Nothing will go your way. But do not be discouraged. Be of good cheer. "Huh? You've got to be kidding! Why should I not be discouraged? Why should I be joyful?" This is the natural human response to these situations. But John's word for us gives us reason for encouragement and joy. The One who is in you is greater than the one who is in the world. Notice the capitalization of the word "one". The **O**ne who is in us is the Almighty God! The **o**ne who is in the world cannot even compare! What power! And we have that same power working in us. We just tend not to use it as often as we should. Be encouraged! Be of good cheer! Our God is greater!!

Get your armor on!

And with great power the apostles were giving testimony to the resurrection of the Lord Jesus, and great grace was on all of them. (Acts 4:33 NIV)

Huh? The apostles were giving testimony to the resurrection of the Lord with great power? These same apostles who were nowhere to be found the night of Christ's death? These same apostles who were behind locked doors in the upper room after the crucifixion fearing for their very lives? These same apostles including Peter, who even denied knowing Christ? Yes, it was these very apostles who are now in the streets, in the cities, by the county sides giving authoritative testimony of the resurrected Lord. What can explain this turnaround but the awesome power of God!! We can infer that this same power that transformed the apostles can do the same for us. Allow God to transform you with His awesome power!

Get your armor on!

GOD'S POWER

I have told you these things so that in Me you may have peace. You will have suffering in this world. Be courageous! I have conquered the world. (John 16:33 NIV)

Jesus is sharing with His disciples about His impending death. In the verses preceding this one, Jesus explains that there will be time when He will be alone and His disciples scattered to their houses. Then He hits them with this verse. You, meaning the disciples, but more pointedly, me and you, will have suffering in this world. It is inevitable. We cannot escape it. However, read the first part again. Jesus is telling us these things so that, in Him, we might have peace. How is that possible? I mean, to have peace in the face of sufferings? Now read the last part – He has overcome the world! Can I get an AMEN! You see, despite any sufferings or difficulties we encounter, we can face them with courage because God has conquered the world. That same power that enabled Jesus to conquer the world's difficulties has been given to us through the Holy Spirit. We just need to tap into that power!

Get your armor on!

But you will receive power when the Holy Spirit has come upon you (Acts 1:8a NIV)

This verse does not say you may receive power; it does not say by chance you will receive power; it says you WILL receive power! Do you realize you have the power of the Almighty God within you? Scripture is very clear than when we become a child of God, the Spirit of God comes within us and dwells within us forever more. So you do not have to question whether the Spirit is with you or not. It is! And because it is, we have POWER! Power to move mountains. Power to stop rivers. Power to leap tall buildings in a single bounce. Oh, sorry, got carried away there. But you see where I am going. Live like you have the power of the Living God within you and you can do anything!

Get your armor on!

GOD'S POWER

Now to Him who is able to do above and beyond all that we ask or think—according to the power that works in you— (Ephesians 3:20 NIV)

Look at this verse in different translations.

Here is the Message translation.
God can do anything, you know—far more than you could ever imagine or guess or request in your wildest dreams! He does it not by pushing us around but by working within us, his Spirit deeply and gently within us. (MSG)

Here is the Amplified Bible translation
Now to Him Who, by (in consequence of) the [action of His] power that is at work within us, is able to [carry out His purpose and] do superabundantly, far over and above all that we [dare] ask or think [infinitely beyond our highest prayers, desires, thoughts, hopes, or dreams]— (AMP)

Here is the New Living translation
Now all glory to God, who is able, through his mighty power at work within us, to accomplish infinitely more than we might ask or think. (NLT)

I do not believe that we truly grasp the power of this verse. I especially like the Message translation. God can do anything! Far more than our wildest dreams! For His power goes beyond our human comprehension, beyond our highest prayers, desires, thoughts, hopes, dreams... Put God to the test. Let Him prove Himself to you! Think (pray) outside the box!

Get your armor on!

GOD'S FAITHFULNESS

Know that Yahweh your God is God, the faithful God who keeps His gracious covenant loyalty for a thousand generations with those who love Him and keep His commands. (Deuteronomy 7:9 NIV)

A key aspect of God's character is His resounding faithfulness. Throughout our lives, we will face those who will disappoint us, not keep their promises, not remain faithful. But one thing we can count on is God's faithfulness to us. Our God is not one who will keep His promises until something better comes along, or for only a short period of time and then move on to someone or something else. Read the verse – He will be faithful for a thousand generations to those who love Him and keep His commandments. Do you get that? A thousand generations. We need not take this literally, but figuratively, for a thousand generations is equivalent to eternity. So while we cannot depend upon others to remain faithful, we can always count on Him to come through. Have faith in His faithfulness. All that He has promised us will come to pass. You can count on it!

Get your armor on!

God is not a man, so he does not lie. He is not human, so he does not change his mind. Has he ever spoken and failed to act? Has he ever promised and not carried it through? (Number 23:19 NIV)

Don't you just hate it when you are told one thing by a professor only the next class period to be told something else! Like what book they will be using for the semester. Really ticks you off doesn't it! I am sure your mother and I have done the same to you and Scott/ Jessica over the years. Well, we do not have to worry about God doing that to us. He is the same yesterday, today, and forever. His message never changes. And He is forever consistent. In fact, God cannot change nor can He lie. It is not within His nature. What He says He will unequivacally do. What He has promised will come to pass. Count on it! Depend on it! Believe it! He is faithful!

Get your armor on!

GOD'S FAITHFULNESS

Give thanks to the LORD, for He is good; His faithful love endures forever. (Psalm 107:1 NIV)

When you read this verse, you might be thinking of the praise hymn based on this verse. Go ahead, sing a few lines!!

While the song and verse may be focusing on His love for us, look again at what type of love He has...faithful love. I just realized we have been focusing on His faithfulness this week, but we have not looked at its meaning. So what does faithful mean? True, real, authentic, accurate, or exact. All these words describe the character of God. Faithful sums it up pretty well. God is true to His word. He is real. He is authentic. His words are accurate. He is exact in everything He does. No artificial coloring; no artificial ingredients; no hidden agenda. He is the real deal! He is faithful.

Get your armor on!

He said: LORD God of Israel, there is no God like You in heaven above or on earth below, keeping the gracious covenant with Your servants who walk before You with their whole heart. (1 Kings 8:23 NIV)

The "He" in this verse is Solomon. Solomon begins a prayer to God with this verse. The next 30 verses contain his complete prayer. The most awesome character trait of our Lord God is that He is completely unique from any other god. There is no god above or below that even compares to Him. Further distinguishing Him from all others is His faithfulness to keep His promises to those who walk before Him with their whole heart, with every ounce of their being. If we are faithful to Him, He is faithful to us. Even when we are not faithful to Him, He remains faithful to us. Try to find anyone else or anything else like that!

Get your armor on!

GOD'S FAITHFULNESS

[Because of] the LORD's faithful love we do not perish, for His mercies never end. They are new every morning; great is Your faithfulness! ***(Lamentations 3:22-23 NIV)***

You know there is a song based on this verse. You may or may not have heard it before. This was mine and your mom's generation!! It goes like this, "Great is Your faithfulness. Great is Your faithfulness. Morning by morning new mercies I see. All that I have Thy hands have provided. Great is Thy faithfulness. Great is Thy faithfulness."

I really cannot add anything more to that. God's faithful love never goes away, never runs empty. His mercies never end. We can see God anew and afresh every day. Truly, great is His faithfulness!

Get your armor on!

GOD'S LOVE

For as high as the heavens are above the earth, so great is His faithful love toward those who fear Him. (Psalm 103:11 NIV)

Lately, we have been focusing on various aspects of God's character. I want to continue that with a look at His love for us. We are talking about God's agape type love; unconditional, unwavering, unending, and any other "un-" word you can think of. Here, the psalmist is attempting to give us a glimpse of just how great His love for us is. As high as the heavens are above the earth! Take a look at the stars tonight. Consider just how far away some of those stars are. Millions and millions of miles away. And those miles do not even compare to His faithful love for those of us who fear (reverently respect) Him! Wow, now that is some kind of love.

Get your armor on!

Look at how great a love the Father has given us, that we should be called God's children. (1 John 3:1a NIV)

I do not know of any greater bond of love than that between a parent and their child. Something happens to a person when their child is born. Your outlook changes. Your focus changes. Your concern changes. All away from you and towards the child (or at least that is what should happen). You do anything and everything for your child. I know of no greater example of that than your mother. There is absolutely nothing she will not do to take care of her babies! As great as our love for you and Scott/Jessica are, our love does not even come close to God's love for you. And to be called God's children. Well, that is icing on the cake. God's love for you is greater than words can describe.

Get your armor on!

GOD'S LOVE

God showed how much he loved us by sending his one and only Son into the world so that we might have eternal life through him. This is real love—not that we loved God, but that he loved us and sent his Son as a sacrifice to take away our sins. (1 John 4:9-10 NIV)

This is the New Living Translation version of these verses. Meditate on this verse for a bit. God demonstrated His awesome love for us through sending His Son, His One and Only Son. We are not talking about some stereotypical type of love, some kind of fake love, or superficial, surface type love. We are talking about REAL love. Love that we are incapable of showing without Him. Love that we do not deserve. In some cases, the type of love that cannot be explained, just accepted. The praise song "Amazing Love" just popped into my head.

Amazing love,
How can it be
That You, my King, should die for me?
Amazing love,
I know it's true.
It's my joy to honor You,
In all I do, I honor You.

Get your armor on!

GOD'S LOVE

For God loved the world in this way: He gave His One and Only Son, so that everyone who believes in Him will not perish but have eternal life. (John 3:16 NIV)

How can we talk about God's love and not reference this verse. This is probably the most famous verse in the entire Bible. This is the very first verse I ever memorized. I am sure it was yours as well. You know how I enjoy personalizing verses, so read it this way:

For God loved Jessica/Scott in this way: He gave His One and Only Son, so that Jessica/Scott would believe in Him and not perish but have eternal life.
What kind of love would cause someone to make such a sacrifice? Can you imagine if Mom or I had to give you or Scott/Jessica up to save the world? Then only to see so many reject that gift!? No way. I could not do it. That just shows you the depth and height of God's love. Which is a perfect prelude to tomorrow's climax verse on God's love. Stay tuned!

Get your armor on!

For I am persuaded that neither death nor life, nor angels nor rulers, northings present, nor things to come, nor powers, nor height, nor depth, nor any other created thing will have the power to separate us from the love of God that is in Christ Jesus our Lord! (Romans 8:38-39 NIV)

The pinnacle of God's love. Paul was fully persuaded, totally convinced that there was no way the love of God could be taken away. He lists nine different things that one might say could have the power to do so. And if that is not enough, he then adds the catch-all "nor any other created thing". Notice he said "created thing". God was not created. He created! So how can anything He created be more powerful than He? Simply, it cannot. God's love is so great, so powerful, and so complete, it cannot be removed. Wow! If that does not give you comfort, nothing will.

Get your armor on!

GOD'S HOLINESS

[Your] eyes are too pure to look on evil, and You cannot tolerate wrongdoing. (Habakkuk 1:13a NIV)

Ever consider God's holiness? I mean really meditate on how holy God truly is? The best illustration I can think of is pure fallen snow. I know living in Texas we do not ever see much snow, but certainly you have seen pictures. The ground completely blanketed by the snow. The snow glistens as the sun's rays bounce off the ground. Untouched by any footprints. Void of any disturbances. Pure. Holy. That is how I picture God's holiness. Untouched by evil. Void of any wrongdoing. Evil is not in His make-up. Sin is counter to His nature. He is pure and holy.

Get your armor on!

"Do not come closer," He said. "Take your sandals off your feet, for the place where you are standing is holy ground." (Exodus 3:5 NIV)

God spoke these words to Moses as he approached the burning bush. I included this verse as a reminder of how we should approach God. All too often we approach God in such a nonchalant way. Casual. Laid-back. Blasé. Mostly I see this in our church attendance, but we must not forget even in our prayer time or quiet times with Him. We do not give God the proper attention that when we come to Him, we are coming to Holy God Almighty. The Creator. The Omniscient, All-Knowing Lord of Lords and King of Kings. I have recently started praying kneeling face down on the floor in awe and reverence to Him. My attempt at acknowledging Him for who He is. Try things like that. Find creative ways to acknowledge God for who He is – the Holy One.

Get your armor on!

GOD'S HOLINESS

He was transformed in front of them, and His face shone like the sun. Even His clothes became as white as the light. (Matthew 17:2 NIV)

Ever tried to look directly at the sun? Mom always told us not to look at the sun or it would ruin your eyes! In these verses, we get a glimpse of God's holiness. This is Matthew's account of the Mount of Transfiguration, where Jesus was miraculously transformed into His glory right before the eyes of Peter, James, and John. His face shone like the sun. His clothes became as white as the light. The Gospel of Mark also records this event in Chapter 9. In Mark's account, Jesus is described as *"His clothes became dazzling and extremely white as no launderer on earth could whiten them."* I pray that after today, each time you see the sun, you will see the Son. Meditate today on God's Holiness.

Get your armor on!

In the year that King Uzziah died, I saw the Lord seated on a high and lofty throne, and His robe filled the temple. Seraphim were standing above Him; each one had six wings: with two he covered his face, with two he covered his feet, and with two he flew. And one called to another: Holy, holy, holy is the LORD of Hosts; His glory fills the whole earth. (Isaiah 6:1-3 NIV)

Yesterday, we read Matthew's account of the transfiguration. Here is Isaiah's account. Note the superior position of the Lord. He is seated on a high and lofty throne. His robe fills the temple. Seraphim, or angelic creatures, stood nearby, awaiting the opportunity to serve the King of Kings. As they flew, look at what they said – "Holy, Holy, Holy is the Lord of Hosts. His glory fills the whole earth." Focus on the phrase "His glory fills the whole earth." Everywhere you turn, you see God's glory. You cannot go a day without seeing how brilliant His creation is. Truly we serve a majestic King. A magnificent Lord. A Holy God.

Get your armor on!

GOD'S HOLINESS

For I am the LORD your God, so you must consecrate yourselves and be holy because I am holy. (Leviticus 11:44a NIV)

Our only natural response to His holiness is to attempt to be holy as well. Not that we would ever reach His level of holiness, but that should be our goal. I want to focus just a bit on the word "consecrate". Another one of those churchy words that you hear often, but really have no clue what it means. Consecrate actually means to make holy, to set apart. As children of the Almighty God, we should set our lives apart from the rest of the world. I have often said this while teaching, "No one should ever have to ask if you are a Christian. They should be able to see it through how you live." I am the LORD your God! Be holy because I am holy.

Get your armor on!

GOD THE CREATOR

You alone are the LORD. You created the heavens, the highest heavens with all their host, the earth and all that is on it, the seas and all that is in them. You give life to all of them, and the heavenly host worships You. (Nehemiah 9:6 NIV)

We continue our look at God's attributes by considering Him as Creator God. Notice how the writer sets the tone right away in this verse. "You **alone** are the LORD." God did not require any assistance and He did not act in cooperation with anyone else. His creation was His alone. And the writer did not leave anything to chance or allow anyone else, or anything else, to take credit for its creation. God made the heavens, the earth, and the seas, and all that is on it or in them. There is nothing that God did not make. Honor God by honoring His creation.

Get your armor on!

Our Lord and God, You are worthy to receive glory and honor and power, because You have created all things, and because of Your will they exist and were created. (Revelation 4:11 NIV)

So why did God create the world in the first place? It's like what do you get someone for Christmas when they already have everything they need / want. One of the reasons for His creation is stated right here – in order to reveal His glory and honor and power. And secondly, He created the world simply because He wanted to. It is because of God's will that everything exists and that everything was created. If God did not want it, He would not have created it. Give glory, honor, and praise to our Creator God. Thank Him for all of creation.

Get your armor on!

GOD THE CREATOR

By faith we understand that the entire universe was formed at God's command, that what we now see did not come from anything that can be seen. (Hebrews 11:3 NLT)

I like this New Living Translation version of this verse. The entire universe – everything you can see for as far as you can see it – was formed on God's command. What kind of God is able to speak things into existence! It is hard for us mortals to understand and comprehend. Let's focus just a bit on the word "formed". At God's command, the entire universe was fashioned, put in order, and equipped for their intended purpose. The earth was set on its axis. The rotation of the planets and stars around the sun was put in motion. Gravity was set with its properties. All this was done at the sound of God's word! Wow! What a mighty God we serve!!

Get your armor on!

From the creation of the world His invisible attributes, that is, His eternal power and divine nature, have been clearly seen, being understood through what He has made. As a result, people are without excuse. (Romans 1:20 NIV)

I have often wondered about those people in certain regions of the world that have never heard the gospel preached. How can those people be condemned to hell if they have never had the opportunity to hear the gospel? Paul tells us very clearly that the eternal power and divine nature of God can be clearly seen and understood through His creation. So much so that man is without excuse. No one can say, "But I never heard..." "I did not know." Be amazed at His creation. Be amazed at how orderly things are. Be amazed and glorify the Creator.

Get your armor on!

GOD THE CREATOR

Where were you when I established the earth? Tell [Me], if you have understanding. Who fixed its dimensions? Certainly you know! Who stretched a measuring line across it? What supports its foundations? Or who laid its cornerstone while the morning stars sang together and all the sons of God shouted for joy? Who enclosed the sea behind doors when it burst from the womb, when I made the clouds its garment and thick darkness its blanket, when I determined its boundaries and put [its] bars and doors in place, Have you ever in your life commanded the morning or assigned the dawn its place, Have you traveled to the sources of the sea or walked in the depths of the oceans? Have you comprehended the extent of the earth? Tell [Me], if you know all this. Have you entered the [place] where the snow is stored? Or have you seen the storehouses of hail, Who cuts a channel for the flooding rain or clears the way for lightning, to bring rain on an uninhabited land, [on] a desert with no human life, to satisfy the parched wasteland and cause the grass to sprout? Can you command the clouds so that a flood of water covers you? Can you send out lightning bolts, and they go? Do they report to you: "Here we are"? (Job 38:4-10,12,16,18,22,25-27,34-35 NIV)

Here is God's response to Job when Job calls out to Him. In a way, God tells Job, "Just who do you think you are talking to?" God then explains, in a series of rhetorical questions, that He is the Almighty Creator, setting everything into motion and giving everything life. Who fixed the dimensions of the earth? Who supports its foundation? Who set the seas in their place? Who made the clouds? Have you ever commanded the sun to rise? Have you ever comprehended the extent of the earth – the depths of the seas, the vastness of the oceans? Who brings the rain to satisfy the earth and cause the grass to grow? And get this – who tells the lightning bolts where to strike? When we consider all that is in the world, and how intricately everything fits together, how can anyone question its origin? Thank our Creator God for His handiwork!

Get your armor on!

GOD'S COMPASSION

Then the LORD passed in front of him and proclaimed: Yahweh—Yahweh is a compassionate and gracious God, slow to anger and rich in faithful love and truth, maintaining faithful love to a thousand [generations], forgiving wrongdoing, rebellion, and sin. (Exodus 34:6 NIV)

Moses probably had the most intimate contact with God than anyone else who ever lived, besides the Lord Jesus Himself. Here, God passes in front of Moses and proclaims a unique characteristic of His being – His unending compassion. Think about all we do against God that disappoints Him. The things we do and do not do. Yet, His compassions never fail. He is slow to anger (boy, how I wish I could say that!). He is rich in faithful love and truth (I think of a treasure chest bursting with gold, silver, and jewelry). He has compassion to forgive our wrongdoing, rebellion, and sin even if we willingly and knowingly act. He is waiting to forgive us and restore fellowship with Him. Praise Him for His compassion. May it never end.

Get your armor on!

But You, Lord, are a compassionate and gracious God, slow to anger and abundant in faithful love and truth. (Psalm 86:15 NIV)

Compassion, we hear the word a lot, especially in church. But do we really know what it means? According to my Random House dictionary, Compassion means "a feeling of deep sympathy for one's misfortune or suffering." Grace, mercy, kindness, understanding, leniency are some synonyms. Because Jesus was fully man while, at the same time, fully God, He knows what we are going through each day. He understands our struggles to walk upright in a wicked world. And because He knows, He is full of compassion. Because He knows, He is slow to anger (there that phrase is again!!!). Because He knows, He is abundant in faithful love and truth. Praise God because He knows.

Get your armor on!

GOD'S COMPASSION

See, we count as blessed those who have endured. You have heard of Job's endurance and have seen the outcome from the Lord: the Lord is very compassionate and merciful. (James 5:11 NIV)

We all know of Job's trials and tests. Satan was trying to get Job to deny and curse God. God, on the other hand, new His servant Job better. Even with everything we consider important removed from him, Job still knelt before God and praised His name. Because of his faithfulness, the Lord had compassion and returned to Job even more than he had before. Look keenly at the end of this verse - "the Lord is **very** compassionate..." He is the same with us today. Endure, keep on enduring, just like Job, and see the compassion of our Lord.

Get your armor on!

"However, if you listen to Me, says the LORD, and do not bring loads through the gates of this city on the Sabbath day and consecrate the Sabbath day and do no work on it, kings and princes will enter through the gates of this city. They will sit on the throne of David, riding in chariots and on horses with their officials, the men of Judah, and the residents of Jerusalem. This city will be inhabited forever. (Jeremiah 17:24-25 NIV)

In preceding verses, Jeremiah conveys God's judgment on the people of Israel for abusing the Sabbath day and failing to keep it holy as God commands. However, in a beautiful display of compassion, God tells Jeremiah to say "However,..." If you search scripture, when God pronounces judgment on a people, He has a "however". Always willing to forgive, always willing to give an exception, always willing to provide a way to escape, our God is full of compassion. Yet we have to act on our "however" to receive His compassion. God did not promise these things if the people continued in their sin. They had to act on their "however" in order to receive. I pray you experience God's "however" today.

Get your armor on!

GOD'S COMPASSION

So he got up and went to his father. But while the son was still a long way off, his father saw him and was filled with compassion. He ran, threw his arms around his neck, and kissed him. (Luke 15:20 NIV)

This is an excerpt from a well-known Bible story – the Prodigal Son. If we read this story from God's point of view, the father in the story is God. The son in the story is you and me. This verse gives us keen insight into the make-up of the Father. The son decides he has had enough of living his way, "enjoying" the fruits of this world. He comes to the realization of Solomon that all was a "chasing of the wind" and returns to the Father. Then look, "...while the son will still a long way off, his Father saw him..." The Father was at home, waiting, looking, and longing for His son's return. Being filled with compassion, He ran to His son, threw His arms around his neck, and kissed him. The Father saw His son coming back home and the Father ran to meet him. He did not wait for the son to reach the house. The Father ran after the returning son and greeted him with great joy. That is exactly how our Father responds to us when we "come back to Him". He does not glare at us with an "I told you so" look. Rather, being filled with compassion, our Father runs to greet us, wraps His big arms around us, and squeezes us tight. May you feel His squeeze!

Get your armor on!

GOD'S SUPREMACY

LORD, who is like You among the gods? Who is like You, glorious in holiness, revered with praises, performing wonders? (Exodus 15:11 NIV)

How often do we try to limit God and put Him in a box so that we can comprehend just who and what He is? Our humanness cannot fully grasp the greatness, the supremacy of our God. Read the verse again. Who is like you among the gods (note the lower case "g")? Who is like You? In other words, who is like our God in terms of His holiness, His receipt of praises, and His ability to perform wonders? In a word – no one! Ok, that is two words, but you get the point. Our God is Supreme!!!! He is the highest, the utmost, the best, the ultimate, the absolute God of all.

Get your armor on!

But will God indeed live on earth? Even heaven, the highest heaven, cannot contain You, much less this temple I have built. (1 Kings 8:27 NIV)

These words were spoken by Solomon at the dedication of the temple. Solomon asked a rhetorical question: If God was to live on earth, where would He live? Now why is that a rhetorical question? Solomon provides us the answer to his own question – nothing on earth, or even in heaven for that matter, can contain God, for God is so much greater than anything man could ever build. The vastness of God, the supremacy of God, is that He is greater than anything seen or unseen, from time past to time eternal. Nothing can contain the Mighty God, much less a temple we may build. Do not put God in a box. He will not fit!!!

Get your armor on!

GOD'S SUPREMACY

LORD, there is no one like You. You are great; Your name is great in power. (Jeremiah 10:6 NIV)

But the LORD is the true God; He is the living God and eternal King. (Jeremiah 10:10a NIV)

Jeremiah is calling out to the only God who can really do anything for him. Israel and Judah were so bent on serving other gods. We often do the same. We look everywhere for security, comfort, and protection. Yet those gods cannot do anything for us. There is no God like our God. He is the one true God we can call. He is great in power. He is the Living God, the eternal King. He is unique; He is supreme.

Get your armor on!

When he stops, the earth shakes. When he looks, the nations tremble. He shatters the everlasting mountains and levels the eternal hills. He is the Eternal One! (Habakkuk 3:6 NIV)

Do you remember the "look of death" you sometimes get from you mother? We all have seen that glare. The stare the cuts a hole right through you. Chills go down your spine. Fear overcomes you. You shake in your shoes. Uh oh. Take a look at what the writer is describing here. Who is He that causes an entire nation to tremble by His piercing look? Who is He that causes the entire earth to shake? Who is He that shatters the mountains and levels the hills? Who is He? God Almighty, the Eternal One! Surely there is no other like Him. He is supreme!

Get your armor on!

GOD'S SUPREMACY

Can anyone hide from me in a secret place? Am I not everywhere in all the heavens and earth?" says the Lord. (Jeremiah 23:24 NIV)

I recall many times wondering how in the world my parents find out about something I had done. It was like they had ESP or some sixth sense or something. Now, as a parent, I recall a few times where you have wondered the same thing about your mom and me. How did we know? I honestly cannot tell you. I do believe God gives parents some sort of ESP to watch over their children. In these verses, God is telling us just how supreme His is by asking a couple of rhetorical questions. Can anyone hide from God? Is God not everywhere in all the heavens and earth? The answers are no and yes, respectively. You cannot hide from God no matter what you do or how secret you keep it. And there is no where you can travel that God has not already been. Rather than try to rationalize it or even try remotely comprehending it, or try to explain it, just accept it as it is. Things will be much simpler if we just accept God for who He is. The SUPREME!

Get your armor on!

GOD'S PERSPECTIVE

Summoning the crowd along with His disciples, He said to them, "If anyone wants to be My follower, he must deny himself, take up his cross, and follow Me. For whoever wants to save his life will lose it, but whoever loses his life because of Me and the gospel will save it. For what does it benefit a man to gain the whole world yet lose his life? What can a man give in exchange for his life? (Mark 8:34-37 NIV)

You may have been encouraged at some point by from a pastor or youth minister or Sunday School teacher to develop an eternal perspective, or a God perspective, on life. You know, to look at life through God's eyes rather than through our own eyes. Jesus was attempting to get his disciples and other followers to develop that type of perspective in these verses. If we want to "save" our lives by enjoying the pleasures this world has to offer, we will eventually "lose" our lives. We will lose that joy of fellowship with the Father and the blessings that relationship brings. However, if we "lose" our lives for Christ, we will actually "save" ourselves from the destruction of the world. Jesus' rhetorical questions really bring this point home. What does it benefit a person to gain the whole world-all the riches, success, popularity, stature in the community, awards, and accolades-yet never trust in Jesus and be condemned to hell for eternity? What part of temporal earth can be exchanged for or equated to eternity? The answer to both questions is "Nothing". The quicker we develop that Eternal Perspective, God's Perspective, the better off in life we will be.

Get your armor on!

GOD'S PERSPECTIVE

Be careful not to practice your righteousness in front of people, to be seen by them. Otherwise, you will have no reward from your Father in heaven. (Matthew 6:1 NIV)

These are the words of Jesus. When I remind myself that the gospels are full of the words of Jesus, I tend to read the verses a bit differently. They seem to carry much more weight.

Today, way too many people "play" church, or "play" being a Christian. Like it is some sort of game or a way to stockpile points. In the end, if you played the game right or accumulated enough points, you win. That is a worldly perspective. Jesus tells us to be careful not to show off in front of others. Be careful not to do things for the sake of being seen by others. Be careful not to desire the praise of man. Is it wrong for others to see you perform good works? Is it wrong for others to compliment you on the good deeds you do? Absolutely not. However, it is always a question of the heart. Why are you doing good things? If the sole purpose is to be seen by others, you will have no reward in heaven. The true test of a person's character is what they do when no one is watching. That is the start of a Godly perspective.

Get your armor on!

GOD'S PERSPECTIVE

Do not be conformed to this age, but be transformed by the renewing of your mind, so that you may discern what is the good, pleasing, and perfect will of God. (Romans 12:2 NIV)

Here is how to develop a Godly perspective. Do not be conformed to this world. Do not let the trappings of this life get you buried. Do not let what is wrong convince you that it is right. Main stream media and especially Hollywood will try to tell you pre-marital sex is ok. Living with your partner is like taking a car on a test drive; you have to try it out to see if you like it. Some people were "made" homosexual. All this is a bunch of lies straight from the pit of hell. Rather than conform, transform! Renew your mind with God's word so that you may discern what is the good, pleasing, and perfect will of God. Develop a Godly perspective on life. Dare to be different.

Get your armor on!

For me, living is Christ and dying is gain. (Philippians 1:21 NIV)

Paul got it. He had developed a Godly perspective. When I first heard this verse, I really did not understand what Paul was saying. To gain a better understanding, you really have to put this verse in context. Read verses 14 through the end of Chapter 1. What Paul is saying is that for him, if he continues to live, he will live for Christ. If he dies, then all the better because he will then live with Christ. So no matter if he lives or dies, Christ will be glorified. That is precisely the type of perspective we need! If we are to continue living, glorify Christ at all times. And certainly, once we die, we will truly live! Be determined! Develop that Godly perspective.

Get your armor on!

GOD'S PERSPECTIVE

Blessed is a man who endures trials, because when he passes the test he will receive the crown of life that He has promised to those who love Him. (James 1:12 NIV)

Why do bad things happen to good people? Good question; one for which I really do not have a good answer. But I can turn you towards Jesus and ask the same question. Why did such a bad thing happen to such a great person? So that He could receive the crown of life promised to Him and so that He could provide the same to you and me. When you are struggling with life in general, whether it be with a particular class assignment, relationships, time management, or temptation, remember the words of James. Notice James did not tell us "blessed is the man who avoids trials." He told us "blessed is the man who endures trials." We know that if we can endure and pass the test, we will receive the crown of life promised to us. That true crown will only come in eternity, albeit we can still enjoy the fruits of that crown here on earth. However, part of developing a Godly perspective is to keep our eyes on the prize for eternity. As we do that, the cares of this world will not really matter that much. Keep your eyes on the prize!

Get your armor on!

GOD'S DELIVERANCE

But I will have compassion on the house of Judah, and I will deliver them by the LORD their God. I will not deliver them by bow, sword, or war, or by horses and cavalry. (Hosea 1:7 NIV)

God's deliverance does not come in conventional means. During much of the Old Testament times, Israel was under captivity. The reason being they were disobedient to the commands of our Lord. During each captivity, God had plans to deliver them to freedom. However, this deliverance was not in the form Israel expected – bow, sword, war, horses, or cavalry. Even though we are not told how in these verses, you can infer it was through the mysterious workings of the Spirit. So when you feel besieged by professors, sorority sisters, friends, homework, exams, etc., know that God will deliver you. But be open minded to how He will show His deliverance!

Get your armor on!

I cry aloud to God, aloud to God, and He will hear me. In my day of trouble I sought the Lord. My hands were lifted up all night long; I refused to be comforted. (Psalm 77:1-2 NIV)

God will hear us if we call out to Him. I want to focus on the last phrase of this verse, "I refused to be comforted." What is the psalmist trying to tell us here? When we call to God and know that He hears us would that, should that, not bring us comfort? I am sure the psalmist felt that comfort. But knowing the comfort was there did not stop him from continuing the call upon the Lord all night long. I equate this feeling to being warm and snuggly in your bed on a cold winter morning. It is so nice and roasty toasty under the covers that you do not want to leave. In fact, you refuse to leave because of the comfort you feel. It is the same way with seeking the Lord. You refuse to leave His side because of the comfort you feel. In times of trouble, He will deliver you. May you be so close to Him that you refuse to leave.

Get your armor on!

GOD'S DELIVERANCE

'Not by strength or by might, but by My Spirit, says the LORD of Hosts. (Zechariah 4:6 NIV)

There is a song by Leslie Phillips based on this verse. I am sure if you cannot recall it, you would remember it if you heard it. It goes something like this:

Sometimes fears can hide your vision
The loss of purpose chains you down
You think I've forgotten all you're dreaming of
But how could I forget the one I love
And it's...
Not by might, not by power
But by my spirit says the lord
Not by might, not by power
But by my spirit says the lord

As I mentioned the other day, God moves in wondrous ways, but not always the ways we expect. Not by strength. Not by might. But by His Spirit! Let His Spirit guide you.

Get your armor on!

I am able to do all things through Him who strengthens me. (Philippians 4:13 NIV)

How about this one! It is your favorite verse. And it really illustrates our greatest deliverance. Notice the little word "all". How can such a small word be so very big? You can do anything...with God's help. For with God's help, you are not using your strength, but His. So next time you feel your world caving in on you and you have no escape, remember this verse. You can do it! Just put your little mind to it... and use the Master's help.

Get your armor on!

GOD'S DELIVERANCE

"Look, I am the LORD, the God of all flesh. Is anything too difficult for Me? (Jeremiah 32:27 NIV)

We face troubles of all sorts throughout life. Relationships, time, money, decisions, wants, and desires pull us in all directions. It can be overwhelming at times. How do we manage? Where do we escape? Unfortunately, many chose other means besides the LORD, the God of all flesh! In the verses preceding this one, Jeremiah is whining to God about all the difficulties he is facing. No wonder he is called the "weeping prophet". God slaps him upside the head. Hey, Jeremiah, it's God here. You know the God of all flesh. Is anything too difficult for Me? Let this be a reminder to you as well. When all things seem to cave in around you, you have an escape. You have a way out. You have deliverance through the God of all flesh. Escape to God.

Get your armor on!

GOD OUR REFUGE

The name of the LORD is a strong tower; the righteous run to it and are protected. (Proverbs 18:10 NIV)

Consider what a tower is used for. Set high on a hill, it can spot the enemy from distances away so the city can be prepared for the attack. The name of the LORD is like a strong tower. Not just any tower, but a strong one. When we run to Him, we will be protected. Notice the verse states run. That does not mean we will casually drop by or if we are in the area, we will go in to be protected. NO! We must run with all our might. Intentionally run to Him. When we do that, we will be protected from any of the flaming arrows the enemy may send. When we are near God, under His wing, the enemy cannot reach us, cannot harm us, and cannot control us.

Get your armor on!

The LORD is my rock, my fortress, and my deliverer, my God, my mountain where I seek refuge, my shield and the horn of my salvation, my stronghold. I called to the LORD, who is worthy of praise, and I was saved from my enemies. (Psalm 18:2-3 NIV)

See all the attributes of our Lord and Savior? Rock, fortress, deliverer, mountain, refuge, shield, horn, stronghold, MY GOD. Wow. What an awesome God we serve. He is all those things and more. And when we call on Him, He will save us from our enemies. Not that we might be saved, or maybe we will be saved, or there is a chance we will be saved. It is guaranteed. We WILL be saved from our enemies.

Have you called on Him? Have you run to Him? Is He where you seek refuge? Is He your stronghold? As you know, all else is like "chasing the wind."

Get your armor on!

GOD OUR REFUGE

God is our refuge and strength, a helper who is always found in times of trouble. Therefore we will not be afraid, though the earth trembles and the mountains topple into the depths of the seas, though its waters roar and foam and the mountains quake with its turmoil. (Psalm 46:1-3 NIV)

IF we use God as our refuge and strength, then no matter what chaos is occurring around us (earth trembling, mountains topple, waters roar [insert your own chaos here]) we will not be afraid. No need to worry, no need to fret. If God is truly our refuge and strength, we have nothing to fear. He is in control. He is a helper who is always found. We do not have to go looking for Him, for He is always near. We do not need to make an appointment, for He is always available. We just need to let Him control.

Get your armor on!

LORD, I seek refuge in You; let me never be disgraced. Save me by Your righteousness. Listen closely to me; rescue me quickly. Be a rock of refuge for me, a mountain fortress to save me. For You are my rock and my fortress; You lead and guide me because of Your name. You will free me from the net that is secretly set for me, for You are my refuge. Into Your hand I entrust my spirit; You redeem me, LORD, God of truth. (Psalm 31:1-5 NIV)

David is clearly claiming our Lord God as his refuge and mountain fortress. When we call out to Him, as David did, He will rescue us from whatever is pulling us away from Him. And the great thing is He does this not because of us, but because of His great name. We must decide to entrust Him with our spirit and allow Him to be Lord over us.

Get your armor on!

GOD OUR REFUGE

It is God who arms me with strength and keeps my way secure. He makes my feet like the feet of a deer; he causes me to stand on the heights. He trains my hands for battle; my arms can bend a bow of bronze. You make your saving help my shield; your help has made me great. You provide a broad path for my feet, so that my ankles do not give way. "I pursued my enemies and crushed them; I did not turn back till they were destroyed. I crushed them completely, and they could not rise; they fell beneath my feet. You armed me with strength for battle; you humbled my adversaries before me. You made my enemies turn their backs in flight, and I destroyed my foes. They cried for help, but there was no one to save them— to the Lord, but he did not answer I beat them as fine as the dust of the earth; I pounded and trampled them like mud in the streets. (2 Samuel 22:33-43 NIV)

OK, so I know this is long, but I wanted you to see what we can do to our enemies if we run to our refuge. And remember it is He who gives us strength to "pursue [our] enemies and crush them", He helps us to "crush them completely", He gives us strength to "humble my adversaries", who makes our "enemies turn their backs in flight" us, we "destroyed my foes" us, we "beat them as fine as the dust", we "pounded them and trampled them like mud." Look at the adjectives David uses as he describes what we can do to our enemies when God is on our side.

Look also at the beginning of the verses. He makes our "way secure", He makes our "feet like the feet of a deer" (we can run swiftly and dodge the enemies arrows), He sets me "on the heights" (so we can see where the enemy is coming from), He trains our "hands for battle" (not physical battle, but spiritual battle), He has given us a "shield" of help, He "provides a broad path for my feet" (we do not have to fear where we place our feet as we will always land on safe ground).

Get your armor on!

GOD OUR ADVOCATE

You go before me and follow me. You place your hand of blessing on my head. (Psalm 139:5 NIV)

I can never escape from your Spirit! I can never get away from your presence! If I go up to heaven, you are there; if I go down to the grave, you are there. If I ride the wings of the morning, if I dwell by the farthest oceans, even there your hand will guide me, and your strength will support me. (Psalm 139:7-10 NIV)

Often times we do not realize what type of God we really have. We like to put God in our little box so we can define Him and keep Him as we want Him to be. However, our finite minds cannot comprehend the God we serve. We cannot put God in a box. He will not fit! I believe the psalmist was figuring this out when he penned these verses. "You go before me and follow me...I can never escape from your Spirit...I can never get away from your presence!" God, our Advocate, is always there for us no matter where we are in our lives. We cannot escape Him. He is with us, forever guiding with His hands and supporting with His strength. What a God we serve! What an Advocate!

Get your armor on!

My little children, I am writing you these things so that you may not sin. But if anyone does sin, we have an advocate with the Father—Jesus Christ the righteous One. (1 John 2:1 NIV)

Remember what an advocate is – one who pleads for or on behalf of another. You know that God is completely and totally holy. He cannot tolerate or associate with sin. So when we sin, we are separate from Him and our relationship is broken. The Apostle John is telling us that when we do sin, guess who is there pleading for and on behalf of us? Jesus Christ, the Righteous One. Jesus Himself is our Advocate. He has our back! Wow! Cannot think of a better advocate!

Get your armor on!

GOD OUR ADVOCATE

But when the Father sends the Advocate as my representative—that is, the Holy Spirit—he will teach you everything and will remind you of everything I have told you. (John 14:26 NIV)

When I mentioned yesterday that God is our Advocate, I really did not go into detail as to what an advocate is. According to my dictionary, an advocate is one who pleads for or in behalf of another; a supporter; a promoter; a campaigner, a sponsor. God as our Advocate is all these things and more. And what is even better is that our Advocate has been intentionally sent to us by the Father to teach us and constantly remind us what our purpose is. This was not by chance or some coincidence. God purposely sent us our Advocate. All we need to do is lean on Him. Remember the lyrics of the song "Lean on Me" –
Lean on me when you're not strong
And I'll be your friend
I'll help you carry on

This is exactly what the Advocate does for us. Lean on HIM!!!!

Get your armor on!

The LORD is for me; I will not be afraid. What can man do to me? (Psalm 118:6 NIV)

This is the ultimate "I got your back" verse. Look at the beginning phrase – "the LORD is for me". God is on your side. He is your biggest cheerleader. Each day, He is rooting for us to win, to be a success. Knowing that, what is there to be afraid of? What can man (this world) do to you? Get up each day with the attitude that you are going to take charge of the day. Think, this is the only Thursday, March 25, 2010 / April 5, 2012 that I will ever have. Then, go out and make the best of what the day brings. After all, what can this day bring that you and God cannot handle together?

Get your armor on!

GOD OUR ADVOCATE

What then are we to say about these things? If God is for us, who is against us? (Romans 8:31 NIV)

Wow! Do you grasp the enormity of this verse? If God is for us, who is against us? Or said another way, "If God is for us, what difference does it make who is against us?" Let me make this point clear, because some people will misinterpret this verse. Paul is not telling us that if God is with us, life will be smooth sailing. You only have to look at the life of Job, Jeremiah, and Christ Himself to know that following God is not always the path of least resistance. But following God is always the right thing to do. For with Him, we cannot lose. We cannot be defeated. Who is against you? With God, it does not matter.

Get your armor on!

GOD'S IMPARTIALITY

For the LORD your God is the God of gods and Lord of lords, the great, mighty, and awesome God, showing no partiality and taking no bribe. (Deuteronomy 10:17 NIV)

You know we serve a great and mighty God. He has no peers and no equal. One keen attribute of God that is often overlooked is that He does not play favorites. And you cannot talk God into doing something selfish for your own good. God does not care who your parents are; what your family has done; how much money you have contributed to worthy causes. He only cares about your heart and whether or not you know His Son. You may come from a long lineage of great and wonderful Christians. Your family may have established one of the greatest foundations in the world, giving to all types of needy causes. You may have given all kinds of money, time, and talents to visiting nursing homes, orphanages, even being a Baylor Buddy. But in the end, God only cares about the answer to one question: Do you know My Son? And that is a decision we all must make on our own. Not based on anything or anyone else.

Get your armor on!

There is no favoritism with God. (Romans 2:11 NIV)

This is pretty short and simple. I like that from God at times. No debate. No argument. Black and white. God does not play favorites. Each will be judged for his/her own actions and decisions, both good and bad.

Keep up the good work Sis / Bubba. You make a father (and the Father) proud.

Get your armor on!

GOD'S IMPARTIALITY

Then Peter began to speak: "In truth, I understand that God does not show favoritism, but in every nation the person who fears Him and does righteousness is acceptable to Him. (Acts 10:34-35 NIV)

This verse emphasizes what we have been talking about this week. Peter came to the realization that God does not show favoritism. He, Peter, thought that the gospel was only for the Jews. However, after meeting with Paul, he realized that Paul was called to minister to the Gentiles (non-Jews) while Peter was called to minister to the Jews. Regardless of how we feel about a person, what they look like, how they talk, how they dress, what their background is, the color of their skin, how much money they have, whether they step on the last nerve of ours, we should share the gospel with them. Why? Because God does not care about the things we care about. He only cares that as many people get to know Him as possible. We may let our feelings interfere, but He does not. Take a lesson from God – do not play favorites.

Get your armor on!

My brothers, hold your faith in our glorious Lord Jesus Christ without showing favoritism. (James 2:1 NIV)

But if you show favoritism, you commit sin and are convicted by the law as transgressors. (James 2:9 NIV)

You know I just love the book of James. It is faith in action. Apparently, James felt it necessary to counsel his readers about playing favorites. Remember, the Jews felt like they were the favored group and wanted to keep the gospel to themselves. James then explained why it is such a big deal to show favoritism. If we do, we commit sin. You know I never really thought about how playing favorites is sinful until I read this chapter. So, put your faith into action.

Get your armor on!

GOD'S IMPARTIALITY

But the wisdom from above is first pure, then peace-loving, gentle, compliant, full of mercy and good fruits, without favoritism and hypocrisy. (James 3:17 NIV)

How do we go through this life without showing favoritism? We must use the wisdom we receive from above. That type of wisdom has these 6 listed qualities without favoritism. Worldly wisdom cannot match this. Wisdom on our own will surely fail. Use the wisdom God has given you.

Get your armor on!

GOD THE SPIRIT

And I will ask the Father, and He will give you another Counselor to be with you forever. (John 14:16 NIV)

Part of the attributes of God includes the Holy Trinity. This is a hard concept for some to accept, but is clearly one of the unique qualities of our Lord. The complete Holy Trinity is seen in this verse. Jesus is speaking. He will ask the Father to give us a Counselor who will be with us forever. That Counselor is the Holy Spirit. The small voice in your conscience that says you better do this or you better not do that. As Counselor, He provides us with advice, guidance, and direction. He gives us warnings. He provides us with encouragement and is our Advocate. We have the Spirit from the time we first accept Christ until the time we see Christ face-to-face! How wonderful to know we truly have a Counselor with us!

Get your armor on!

Teach me to do Your will, for You are my God. May Your gracious Spirit lead me on level ground. (Psalm 143:10 NIV)

The Spirit of God does many things for us. One of those is listed here – to lead us on level ground. Let's think about the implications of being on level ground. Have you ever watched a building being built from the ground up? It seems like it takes forever for the building to actually be built. The construction team works for months and months on the foundation, removing dirt, bringing in dirt, leveling the dirt, drilling holes, and pouring concrete. Why do they take so long? Without a strong, level foundation, the building will never stand. We are no different. The Spirit is like our spiritual foundation. He keeps us level.

Get your armor on!

GOD THE SPIRIT

For you did not receive a spirit of slavery to fall back into fear, but you received the Spirit of adoption, by whom we cry out, "Abba, Father!" The Spirit Himself testifies together with our spirit that we are God's children, (Romans 8:15-16 NIV)

Another function of the Spirit is testifying or confirming we are God's children. When we join the family of God, we receive the Spirit of adoption, meaning we receive confirmation that we are now in God's family. Born into sin, definitely not a part of God's family, we are now adopted into God's family, with full rights as His children. Think about that for a moment. We are as orphans, with no family, no home, no rights to anything. God swoops down and gives us a life we do not deserve. We become a part of His family, with all rights as His children. All confirmed by His Spirit. And through His Spirit, we can call out to God "Abba, Father!" which really means "Daddy!" Any man can be a father. But it takes a special someone to be a Daddy! Call out to Daddy through His Spirit today!

Get your armor on!

For God has not given us a spirit of fearfulness, but one of power, love, and sound judgment. (2 Timothy 1:7 NIV)

Here is yet another function of the Spirit. There are so many more. I urge you to search scripture for more ways the Spirit is used to make us more Christ-like. Some translations use "timidity" in place of "fearfulness" and, to be honest, it is probably the more descriptive word. To be timid means nervous, shy, fearful, hesitant, and apprehensive. The Spirit we have received is nothing like that. Our Spirit is one of power, love, and sound judgment. Power: Authority, Control, Supremacy, Muscle. See the difference? Love: Affection, To Care For, Adore, Worship. Getting the picture yet? Sound Judgment: Secure, Confident, Competent, Sensible, Honest, and Upright. Do not be intimidated with the world around you. Be confident in the Spirit!

Get your armor on!

GOD THE SPIRIT

In Him you also, when you heard the word of truth, the gospel of your salvation—in Him when you believed—were sealed with the promised Holy Spirit. He is the down payment of our inheritance, for the redemption of the possession, to the praise of His glory. (Ephesians 1:13-14 NIV)

This verse gives us some great insight into more functions of the Spirit. At the moment of salvation, the Spirit is poured out upon us. That pouring of the Spirit provides a seal around us. It provides a coating that locks us into salvation like a zip-lock baggie. It is sealed on the inside with no leaks. And there is more! He also provides the down payment of our inheritance. You know, like a deposit. By making a down payment on something, you are telling the vendor, "I want this and am coming back for it. So do not give it to anyone else." Through the Spirit's work, we are set aside for a time when Christ will return for us. Truly, praise His glory for the work of the Spirit.

Get your armor on!

GOD THE SON

For a child will be born for us, a son will be given to us, and the government will be on His shoulders. He will be named Wonderful Counselor, Mighty God, Eternal Father, Prince of Peace. (Isaiah 9:6 NIV)

That child, the Son, is none other than Jesus Christ Himself! Notice the verse says He was "given to us" and "the government will be on His shoulders." That is, He will administer, rule, and control all facets of life on earth. And look at some of His names. Some translations separate Wonderful Counselor into two different names, Wonderful and then Counselor. Whether you keep these as one or break them into two, it does not really matter. Just consider what they mean. **Wonderful**: Magnificent, Breathtaking, Brilliant. **Counselor**: Advisor, Mentor, Guide. **Mighty**: Powerful, Strong, Great. **Eternal**: Perpetual, Endless. **Prince**: Royalty, Superiority. An attempt to describe the indescribable. The one and only Son.

Get your armor on!

Therefore He is always able to save those who come to God through Him, since He always lives to intercede for them. For this is the kind of high priest we need: holy, innocent, undefiled, separated from sinners, and exalted above the heavens. He does not need to offer sacrifices every day, as high priests do—first for their own sins, then for those of the people. He did this once for all when He offered Himself. (Hebrews 7:25-27 NIV)

The essence of Christianity dwells in the person of the Son. The writer of Hebrews gives us some insight into that Person. He is always able to save (not just willing to but actually can and does save). He lives to intercede for us. The exact type of high priest we need – holy, innocent, undefiled, separated from sinners, exalted above the heavens. No need for continuous sacrifices as in the Old Testament times. Jesus did this once for all. One and done. No one took His life; He offered it. He was the supreme sacrifice! What a Son! What a Savior!

Get your armor on!

GOD THE SON

He is the image of the invisible God, the firstborn over all creation; because by Him everything was created, in heaven and on earth, the visible and the invisible, whether thrones or dominions or rulers or authorities—all things have been created through Him and for Him. He is before all things, and by Him all things hold together. He is also the head of the body, the church; He is the beginning, the firstborn from the dead, so that He might come to have first place in everything. (Colossians 1:15-18 NIV)

One of the most beautiful and comprehensive descriptions of the Son in Scripture! Look at all things He is:

1. Image of the invisible God. God in flesh – Immanuel.
2. Firstborn over all creation. This does not mean He was literally born. Consider the position of the firstborn son in any family during that time. The firstborn had all things passed down to him. He was the "favored" child because of his position of being the first. Jesus Christ has the position of the firstborn.
3. Creator of everything, in heaven and on earth, the visible and invisible. Genesis 1:1 says God created the heavens and earth. So how can Paul give Jesus credit for that creation if the Holy Trinity does not exist?
4. Before all things – with God in the beginning before the world began. Another piece of evidence to the Holy Trinity
5. Head of the body, the church. Good litmus test for any church. If Jesus is not the center, probably need to go elsewhere.
6. The Beginning. Everything starts and stops with Jesus.
7. Firstborn from the dead. He is the first to rise from the dead. We all will follow Him.
8. First place in everything. Pretty self-explanatory.

Give thanks to the Son for all that He is.

Get your armor on!

GOD THE SON

He is the radiance of His glory, the exact expression of His nature, and He sustains all things by His powerful word. After making purification for sins, He sat down at the right hand of the Majesty on high. So He became higher in rank than the angels, just as the name He inherited is superior to theirs. (Hebrews 1:3-4 NIV)

Here is more insight into the Son. I hope you are gaining some understanding of and a deeper perspective on just how unique and awesome the Son is. The Message translation says it this way, "[The] Son perfectly mirrors God, and is stamped with God's nature. He holds everything together by what he says—powerful words!" The Amplified translation says, "He is the sole expression of the glory of God, and He is the perfect imprint and very image of [God's] nature, upholding and maintaining and guiding and propelling the universe by His mighty word of power."

And there is more. After making provisions for our forgiveness of sin, He took His rightful position at the right hand of God and inherited His superior name. There is power in the name of Jesus. Use it but use it wisely!

Get your armor on!

GOD THE SON

Make your own attitude that of Christ Jesus, who, existing in the form of God, did not consider equality with God as something to be used for His own advantage. Instead He emptied Himself by assuming the form of a slave, taking on the likeness of men. And when He had come as a man in His external form, He humbled Himself by becoming obedient to the point of death—even to death on a cross. For this reason God also highly exalted Him and gave Him the name that is above every name, so that at the name of Jesus every knee should bow—of those who are in heaven and on earth and under the earth— and every tongue should confess that Jesus Christ is Lord, to the glory of God the Father. (Philippians 2:5-11 NIV)

This week we have been focusing on God the Son. I hope the past few verses have given you a bit of insight on just who the Son really is. Now that you know more about the Son, let's work on becoming more like Him. And what better way than starting with His attitude. You see, the Son was given the highest position in the Kingdom. But He did not consider that position something He had to hold on to for His own advantage. Instead, He gave up that position and took the position of a servant. Wow! The King of Kings and the Lord of Lords, equal with God, became a lowly servant in human likeness. He was humble and obedient while in human form. As a result of His obedience, He was given back His high position so that at some point in the future, every knee will bow and every tongue will confess that Jesus Christ is Lord! Strive to be more like the Son!

Get your armor on!

GOD'S JUDGMENT

And just as it is appointed for people to die once— and after this, judgment (Hebrews 9:27 NIV)

One quality of God that many do not want to accept or acknowledge is God's judgment. Up to now, we have reviewed many facets of God's characteristics, with most of them being the qualities we should strive to emulate. But let's not talk about God's judgment. Oh but we must! For without it, all other qualities are pointless. What difference does it make if we replicate God's characteristics if there is no judgment? Rest assured, we all will face judgment. Judgment for all the good and all the bad we have done. This verse is especially critical to those who believe in reincarnation. There is no grey matter in this verse. We live, we die once, and we face judgment. No do-overs. That is why it is so critical to live for Christ and Christ alone.

Get your armor on!

They will bring you consolation when you see their conduct and actions, and you will know that it was not without cause that I have done what I did to it." [This is] the declaration of the Lord GOD. (Ezekiel 14:23 NIV)

God has just pronounced His judgment on Israel. Notice the second section of the verse. "...you will know that it is not without cause..." God does not sit on His throne and eerily devise plans to punish His creation like some sinister ruler. He truly and dearly loves His children. However, He will not let continuous rebellion go unpunished. And He will not exact His punishment without cause. Normally when you get punished by your parents, you know why. You know you did wrong and expect to be punished. God is no different.

Get your armor on!

GOD'S JUDGMENT

Rise up, LORD! Do not let man prevail; let the nations be judged in Your presence. Put terror in them, LORD; let the nations know they are only men. (Psalm 9:18-19 NIV)

God's judgment is not relegated to man only. God also judges nations. For a quick lesson, just read Jeremiah 46-51. In those chapters, God pronounces judgment on 10 nations. Only one of those remains today – Egypt. That is why it is so critical to pray for our nation. The United States was founded on Judeo-Christian values. There have been stories upon stories about our founding fathers and their faith in our Lord and Savior Jesus Christ. Yet, we have drifted so far from those founding principles. It is sad when you think about it. Pray for our country. Pray for our country's leaders, even though we may disagree with them. There is still time. God has not turned His face from our nation...yet!

Get your armor on!

So then, each of us will give an account of himself to God. (Romans 14:12 NIV)

Ouch. This one hits deep to the core. Can you imagine standing before God and giving an account for all you have done, the good, the bad, and the ugly? There is some "behind the scenes" stuff I have done that I prefer remain unknown but to God and me. I did those things to serve others, not to get recognition. On the other hand, I know there are some things I have hidden way back in the closet that I do not want anyone to know about. Regardless, all bets are off and everything is put on the table. Do you believe if we lived this verse that we would live our lives differently? Sad to admit, but I think I would. Perhaps you would, too. Live for Christ, as if He was right there living it with you-because He is!

Get your armor on!

GOD'S JUDGMENT

The LORD is slow to anger and rich in faithful love, forgiving wrongdoing and rebellion. But He will not leave [the guilty] unpunished, bringing the consequences of the fathers' wrongdoing on the children to the third and fourth generation. (Numbers 14:18 NIV)

Most people only want to read the first part of this verse. They stop right after "rebellion". It is the rest of the verse that is so critical. God will not, cannot and will not leave the guilty unpunished. His righteousness and justice will not allow for it. The last part of this verse has also been taken out of context. Is God saying He will punish me for my father's sin? That flies directly in the face of personal accountability. Just as my father's salvation will not save me, neither will I be punished for my father's sin. Here is how I understand this part of the verse. If I fail to pass down to you and Scott/Sis the value of living for Christ, the consequences of that will be felt for generations to come. For an example, just look at Solomon's kids. I am sure you have seen it in some of your friends' lives as well. God is slow to anger. He is rich in faithful love. He is forgiving. But, He will not leave the guilty unpunished.

Get your armor on!

GOD KNOWS YOU

I chose you before I formed you in the womb; I set you apart before you were born. I appointed you a prophet to the nations. (Jeremiah 1:5 NIV)

Not only is He the creator of the universe; Not only does He hold the power of life and death in His hands; But God is a loving Father who knows us inside and out. These words were spoken to Jeremiah, but we can infer they were intended for all God's children. God was forming you while still in the womb. He was coloring your eyes and hair, framing your legs and arms, strengthening your bones, and yes, molding your "worms" as mom would say!! When He was forming you, He was also setting you apart for His work. Jeremiah's work was to be a prophet. What has God set you apart to be? We can spend from now to eternity trying to find out. That journey is called life. Live it to find out your work.

Get your armor on!

for you are all sons of God through faith in Christ Jesus. (Galatians 3:26 NIV)

How great it is to be called a son or daughter of God! Being a parent myself, I also know how proud it is to be a father. So I can only imagine how proud God is of His children. As a parent, we know our children. We know when they are in a good mood; we know when things are bothering them; sometimes, we just know to ask certain questions. I cannot really explain it. We just know. Think of that multiplied by 100, by 1,000, by a zillion kagillion. That is how much more God knows us, His children. Rest in the comfort of knowing we are His.

Get your armor on!

GOD KNOWS YOU

Your hands made me and formed me; give me understanding so that I can learn Your commands. (Psalm 119:73 NIV)

Imagine a potter molding a clay jar or bowl. He starts with a clump of clay, adds water, and slowly begins to spin the wheel. The clay begins to shape around his hands as he gently patterns the clump into the object he desires. This is exactly what the Lord does with us. He takes a clump of nothing and makes it into something pleasing. Bet you never thought of your life as a clump of nothing have you? But that is what we are without the Master's touch. Plus, He gave us understanding so we could learn His commands. He did not form us to have us sit on the shelf and look pretty. We must get out and learn His commands and share them with others.

Get your armor on!

But even the hairs of your head have all been counted. (Matthew 10:30 NIV)

OK, before we get into this verse, no funny wise cracks about your old man's bald spot!!! Ever try to count the number of hairs on your head? I know, I know, mine are getting easier to count by the day!! But think about it, to know the number of hairs on each person's head – that is over six billion people. To be able to know each person that intimately is pretty incredible. And to know our God knows that about us and then some! We truly do serve a wonderful heavenly Father.

Get your armor on!

GOD KNOWS YOU

LORD, You have searched me and known me. You know when I sit down and when I stand up; You understand my thoughts from far away. You observe my travels and my rest; You are aware of all my ways. Before a word is on my tongue, You know all about it, LORD. (Psalm 139:1-4 NIV)

For it was You who created my inward parts; You knit me together in my mother's womb. I will praise You, because I have been remarkably and wonderfully made. Your works are wonderful, and I know [this] very well. (Psalm 139:13-14 NIV)

Sis/Bubba, we have come to the last "verse of the day" for your freshman year. What a year it has been! Can you believe it? And what a verse to end on! After reading this, no wonder David was called a man after God's own heart. God knows us so well. He knows when we sit down; He knows when we stand up; He knows our thoughts; He knows when we travel and when we rest; He is intimately aware of all our ways. Before we even speak a word, He knows what we are going to say. I really love David's words in verses 13-14. God created our inward parts – those parts no one can see, like our heart, our soul, our mind, and our intentions. He knit us together. He joined our ligaments to the bones, weaved our body parts to be in perfect unity with one another. Cannot you see the imagery? We have been remarkably and wonderfully made. Praise be to the God and Father of our Lord and Savior Jesus Christ.

Get your armor on!

PRAYER (PART 2)

Devote yourselves to prayer; stay alert in it with thanksgiving (Colossians 4:2 NIV)

Well, Sis/Bubba, the first day of your sophomore year!!! Can you believe it? Seems just like yesterday we dropped you off for your freshman year.

I looked back and found that we had already had verses of the day focusing on prayer. But, since this is such a vital aspect of our Christian walk, I thought we could spend a couple of more weeks on the subject.

Three things I want to point out in Paul's instruction to the church in Colossians.

1) **Devote** yourselves to prayer. What does devote mean? To dedicate; to allocate; to assign. When we think of prayer, most times it is the last thing we do. Grabbing breakfast out of the pantry; grabbing your backpack as you head to school; as you drive to work. We think, 'Oh yeah, God, please watch over me today. Help me be a blessing to those I meet." Or something like that. OK, I have prayed today. But is that really prayer? Are we devoting ourselves to prayer? Absolutely not! If we truly devote ourselves to prayer, we will set aside an amount of time and actually get on our knees and pour our hearts out to God.
2) **Stay alert** in it. This does not mean pray as you go to sleep. Or, in most cases, start praying and then fall asleep. But be alert. Stay awake! Get out of the bed and on your knees. Put all distractions away and concentrate on your time alone with God.
3) **With Thanksgiving.** Do not forget to be thankful for all the many blessings God has given us. Even the little things. It tells God that you are actually paying attention to how He is taking care of you.

As you start each day, do not forget to devote yourself to prayer!

Get your armor on!

PRAYER (PART 2)

Pray constantly. (1Thessalonians 5:17 NIV)

Some translations say "pray without ceasing"; others say "never stop praying". Now are we to take this literally? I do not think so. However, we can have an attitude of praying constantly. Whether we are getting ready in the morning, walking (or riding our new cool looking bike with its little bell!) to class, driving to Bahama Bucks, or just relaxing on our patio, we can have an attitude of prayer, thanking God for the beauty of His creation, asking God to watch over us that we might be His Light, or asking God to help us be aware of other's needs. Whatever the case may be, wherever we may be, we can always be in an attitude of prayer. Prayer: it is how we get close to God. Do it constantly.

Get your armor on!

Until now you have asked for nothing in My name. Ask and you will receive, that your joy may be complete. (John 16:24 NIV)

Ever wonder why we end our prayers with the phrase "in Jesus' name"? Well, here is why! Jesus, Himself, told His disciples to ask in His name. Plus, if we are serious about our prayers, ending them with Jesus' name will remind us not to ask for things selfishly for our own benefit. The cool thing is, when we ask in Jesus' name, we will receive. Look back at the verse. Jesus says it right here – Ask and you WILL receive. He does not say maybe; if I feel like it; you have a good chance; perhaps you will. He says without a doubt, you will receive. Why? So that our joy will be complete. He gives us what we ask, in His name, because He wants to fill us with joy. Now that is the type of Savior I want to associate with!

Get your armor on!

PRAYER (PART 2)

Confess your sins to each other and pray for each other so that you may be healed. The prayer of a righteous man is powerful and effective. (James 5:16 NIV)

The Message translation starts this verse with "Make this your common practice:..". I like that. We would do well to make this verse a common, everyday practice. Confessing our faults to each other and praying for each other. Openly confessing our sins to an accountability partner will strengthen our resistance to Satan's temptations. Praying for each other will strengthen our relationships with one another. And here is the kicker – the prayer of a righteous person is powerful and effective. Who is a righteous person? One who is living right with God. So if we are living right with God, walking with Him daily, taking note of His Word, our prayers will become powerful, dynamic, useful, and effective.

If you have not developed your common practice, then I suggest you start today! Confess your faults to one another and pray for one another. Then get ready to be amazed!

Get your armor on!

PRAYER (PART 2)

Whenever you pray, you must not be like the hypocrites, because they love to pray standing in the synagogues and on the street corners to be seen by people. I assure you: They've got their reward! But when you pray, go into your private room, shut your door, and pray to your Father who is in secret. And your Father who sees in secret will reward you. When you pray, do not babble like the idolaters, since they imagine they'll be heard for their many words. Do not be like them, because your Father knows the things you need before you ask Him. (Matthew 6:5-8 NIV)

OK, I know this is a rather long reference, but I could not figure out where to stop. Plus, there is some really good stuff in here. While it is vitally important that we pray, we must be careful in how we pray and what we pray. Jesus referred to the religious leaders of the day as hypocrites because they loved to show off their prayers. These religious leaders wanted others to see how "religious" they were by praying in the streets. When we pray just so others can see us pray, then, as Jesus said, we have our reward. When we do pray, do not try to impress anyone with how long you can pray and how many big, fancy words you can use. Jesus is instructing us not to babble on like these hypocrites just rambling on without any meaning. Do not be so concerned about how long your pray. If you can get your point across in a few words, do not just keep praying to make the prayer last longer.

Here are the main points:

1) Do not show off with your prayers
2) Do not pray to be seen
3) Do not ramble on
4) Pray humbly
5) Pray sincerely
6) Pray from the heart

Get your armor on!

PRAYERS IN THE BIBLE

THE LORD'S PRAYER

This, then, is how you should pray: "Our Father in heaven, hallowed be your name, your kingdom come, your will be done on earth as it is in heaven. Give us today our daily bread. Forgive us our debts, as we also have forgiven our debtors. And lead us not into temptation, but deliver us from the evil one." (Matthew 6:9-13 NIV)

Jesus, speaking to His disciples, teaches us how to pray. Not that we should repeat these very words, but look at how He put together the proper structure of prayer.

1) "Hallowed be your name" – Sacred, holy, blessed is your name. Start your prayers by glorifying the One True God. Remember Who you are speaking to. He is the Almighty Creator God. Approach Him that way.
2) "Your will be done" – do not pray selfishly, for your own pleasures. Pray His ways become your ways; His wants become your wants.
3) "Give us today our daily bread" – pray for your specific needs of today. Remember the children in the wilderness on their way to the Promised Land. They were told to gather enough manna for that day. Anything more would be rotten the next day and could not be eaten. So here is where we pour out to God our daily requests.
4) "Forgive us" – all too often we do not include confession and forgiveness in our prayers. Here is where we confess our sins to God and ask forgiveness (I have a whole week of 'verses of the day' on forgiveness – stay tuned).
5) "lead us not into temptation" – while we are talking forgiveness, we might as well ask God to protect us from the evil one. When temptation comes our way, help us to draw on His strength, not our own, to overcome temptation. Remember, it is not a sin to be tempted. In fact, we ought to praise God that we are tempted. It tells us satan is scared of us so he tries to knock us off track.

So follow Jesus' example when we pray.

Get your armor on!

THE PRAYER OF JABEZ

Jabez cried out to the God of Israel, "Oh,that you would bless me and enlarge my territory! Let your hand be with me, and keep me from harm so that I will be free from pain." And God granted his request. (1 Chronicles 4:10 NIV)

You may recall that an entire book was written on this prayer. The prayer is composed of four parts:

1) Jabez asks God to bless him.
2) He asks God to enlarge his territory or increase his responsibility.
3) He prays that God will be with him and stay close to him.
4) He asks that God keep him from harm so that he will be free from pain.

Look at how the verse begins. Jabez was passionate in his plea to God: "He cried out to the God of Israel." God wants to hear that we need Him through passionate prayer.

Now look at what he prayed. His prayer reveals that Jabez understands what many people do not -- there is only one God and He should be the center of our focus. God wants to bless every life. But, we must first make the choice to invite God into our life and ask for His blessings. Jabez wants to succeed and increase his sphere of influence for God. The specific sphere of influence is not important. What is important is that when we want to reach for goals and accomplishments that we have God on our side. It is equally important to stay close to God and rely on His continued support and guidance throughout life. At the end of the verse it is clear that God approved of this faithful prayer by granting it.

One would be wise to follow the pattern of prayer set before us by Jabez!

Get your armor on!

THE PRAYER OF STEPHEN

While they were stoning him, Stephen prayed, "Lord Jesus, receive my spirit." Then he fell on his knees and cried out, "Lord, do not hold this sin against them." When he had said this, he fell asleep. (Acts 7:59-60 NIV)

Wow. I am not so sure I could duplicate Stephen's prayer. As he was breathing his last, he prayed for those who were killing him. And remember who was in the crowd, holding the coats of those throwing the stones? It was none other than the greatest apostle of Jesus – Paul. This takes Jesus' words to love your enemies to another level. But in reality, this is exactly what we are called to do. It is so easy to pray for those we love and those who love us. How difficult it is to pray for those we do not like! You know, I doubt Stephen knew the life in store for Paul when he prayed this prayer. But I have no doubt that God used this prayer to work in the life of Paul. What "enemy" might you need to pray for today? You never know, you could be praying for the next Paul.

Get your armor on!

PAUL'S PRAYER FOR THE COLOSSIANS

For this reason, since the day we heard about you, we have not stopped praying for you and asking God to fill you with the knowledge of his will through all spiritual wisdom and understanding. And we pray this in order that you may live a life worthy of the Lord and may please him in every way: bearing fruit in every good work, growing in the knowledge of God, being strengthened with all power according to his glorious might so that you may have great endurance and patience, and joyfully giving thanks to the Father, who has qualified you to share in the inheritance of the saints in the kingdom of light. (Colossians 1:9-12 NIV)

I just love Paul. I cannot wait to meet him face-to-face in Heaven. His prayers for his readers are so genuine. The cool thing about Paul is that he did not hide the fact he was praying for you. But he went a step further. He not only told people he was praying for them; he told them what he was praying for and why! Look at what he prayed for the Colossians. Here is the what: That God would fill them with the knowledge of His will through all spiritual wisdom and understanding. Here is the why: So that they would live a life worthy of the Lord; So that they would please Him in every way: So that they would bear fruit in every good work; So that they would grow in the knowledge of God; So that they would be strengthened by the power of God; So that they would have great endurance and patience; So that they would joyfully give thanks to the Father.

One "What" and seven "Whys". Purposeful prayer. Intentional prayer. Meaningful prayer. Follow Paul's example!

Get your armor on!

JESUS' PRAYER FOR ALL BELIEVERS

My prayer is not for them alone. I pray also for those who will believe in me through their message, that all of them may be one, Father, just as you are in me and I am in you. May they also be in us so that the world may believe that you have sent me. I have given them the glory that you gave me, that they may be one as we are one: I in them and you in me. May they be brought to complete unity to let the world know that you sent me and have loved them even as you have loved me. Father, I want those you have given me to be with me where I am, and to see my glory, the glory you have given me because you loved me before the creation of the world. Righteous Father, though the world does not know you, I know you, and they know that you have sent me. I have made you known to them, and will continue to make you known in order that the love you have for me may be in them and that I myself may be in them." (John 17:20-26 NIV)

I know this is long, but well worth the read.

In the verses preceding these, Jesus prayed for Himself, then His disciples. Here, He is praying for all future believers. He prays for unity of all believers so that the world may believe. You see, if we cannot live in unity with other believers, why in the world would a non-believer want to join God's family? Do not you see Jesus' passion for future believers? "May they be brought to complete unity to let the world know you sent me..." "Father, I want those you have given me to be with me where I am." "I...will continue to make you known in order that the love you have for me may be in them and that I myself may be in them."

Is it not great to know that our loving Father prayed for us, even before we were born!

Get your armor on!

WAYS OF MAN

There is a way that seems right to a man, but in the end it is the way of death. (Proverbs 16:25 NIV)

There are so many influences in our world today. Most all of them take the Word of God and twist it to fit a lifestyle rather than changing a lifestyle to fit the Word of God. And the crazy thing is, we (meaning the world in general, not specifically you and me) accept these teachings as right and true. Only problem is, in the end, they lead to death. Test every teaching against the Word of God. If it passes the test, then ok to believe in it. If it does not, run for the hills and have nothing to do with it.

Get your armor on!

The natural person does not accept the things of the Spirit of God, for they are foolishness to him, and he is not able to understand them because they are spiritually discerned. (1 Corinthians 2:14 NIV)

Remember from the first verse this week, we mentioned all the various thoughts and ideals and beliefs that exist today. Ever wonder why it is hard to carry on a conversation with a non-Christian? The "natural person" is a non-believer and does not accept the redeeming blood of Jesus. Spiritual things appear as foolishness to those who do not believe. To you and me, the Spirit of God reveals His character and His nature to us so that we can discern that which is spiritual. To the unbeliever, this all appears as garbage and worthless. So they are most willing to believe in anything that appears reasonable to them. It is unreasonable to us that God would become man and die for our sins. It is unreasonable to us that, though our sins can be as scarlet, we are made as white as snow. It is unreasonable for us to believe that we can receive forgiveness for any sin we have or will commit. God defies reason! Pray that you become spiritually discerned!

Get your armor on!

WAYS OF MAN

See to it that no one takes you captive through hollow and deceptive philosophy, which depends on human tradition and the basic principles of this world rather than on Christ. (Colossians 2:8 NIV)

The ways of man are based on hollow and deceptive philosophy. While they may appear reasonable and believable, they are, in fact, empty and void of anything worthwhile. We must guard ourselves against human tradition and the lies of this world and hold everything we hear and believe up to the standard set by Christ. I really like Paul's imagery here. "See to it that no one takes you captive..." You get the picture of an animal trapped in a cage with no way out and with no hope for survival. When we put our hope on human tradition and the basic principles of this world that is exactly where we will find ourselves.

Get your armor on!

This is what the LORD says: Cursed is the man who trusts in mankind, who makes [human] flesh his strength and turns his heart from the LORD. (Jeremiah 17:5 NIV)

Here is some wise advice from the prophet Jeremiah. There are a couple of notes in this verse. First, what does it mean to trust in mankind? Are we not to be trustworthy? Certainly! But...to put your faith in your fellow man, to put your belief system in something man-made, to follow the pattern of this world rather than that of Christ is futile. The prophet even says we are cursed if we do this. Secondly, what is the result of putting your trust in mankind? One's heart is turned from the LORD. Ouch. See, when we focus on the ways of man versus the ways of the LORD, our hearts will eventually turn from Him. Stay on course; do not exit the spiritual highway; keep your eyes on the road and on the prize!

Get your armor on!

WAYS OF MAN

It is better to take refuge in the LORD than to trust in man. (Psalm 118:8 NIV)

This verse goes along with yesterdays. Again, we are not being told here that man should not be trustworthy. We are. But we are not to put our hope in man. As the psalmist says, better to take refuge in the LORD. What does it mean to take refuge in the Lord? It is the Lord who is our shelter, our safe haven, our protection. He, and He alone, is our sanctuary. Remember in the Hunchback of Notre Dame, Esmeralda sought "sanctuary" in the church. She sought protection from the evil Frollo. Mankind cannot be all this to us. The things of this world cannot provide all this to us. Take refuge in the Lord, not in the ways of man.

Get your armor on!

WHAT IS SIN?

Now the works of the flesh are obvious: sexual immorality, moral impurity, promiscuity, idolatry, sorcery, hatreds, strife, jealousy, outbursts of anger, selfish ambitions, dissensions, factions, envy, drunkenness, carousing, and anything similar, about which I tell you in advance—as I told you before—that those who practice such things will not inherit the kingdom of God. (Galatians 5:19-21 NIV)

We talked a lot last week about the ways of man and how we are to differentiate ourselves from the world. I think the factor that is single handedly ruining our country is people do not call sin a sin anymore. We do not even know what sin is anymore. In the name of tolerance, we, the world, have turned a blind eye to sin. "As long as it does not affect me, you do what you want!" is the attitude that is tearing us apart from the inside out. Paul lists here a number of sins, fifteen to be exact. Then he adds the "and anything similar" to cover those he did not list specifically. What is the result of those who live like this? They will not inherit the kingdom of God. Pretty simple. Pretty black and white. Do not shy away from sin. Do not cover it up. Call it what it is.

Get your armor on!

WHAT IS SIN?

Therefore, put to death whatever in you is worldly: sexual immorality, impurity, lust, evil desire, and greed, which is idolatry. (Colossians 3:5 NIV)

In the verses preceding this one, Paul told the church in Colosse that they had been raised with Christ and to set their hearts and minds on things above where Christ is seated at the right hand of God. And because of their position in Christ, they should put to death whatever belongs to the earthly (worldly) nature. This list is pretty similar to the list from yesterday. Just like in class, when a teacher repeats something, better pay attention because you just might see it again on a test. Paul is telling us the same thing here. Apparently, these were rather common sins then as they are today. Paul is saying we should have nothing to do with them. Put them to death. Do not let them creep into your body. If your armor is securely fitted, they will not be able to enter.

So get your armor on!

But now you must also put away all the following: anger, wrath, malice, slander, and filthy language from your mouth. (Colossians 3:8 NIV)

I guess by now it is best I clue you in on my intent with these verses. Last week we talked about how the world views life. Care free; live as you want; do what you want; no consequences; no sin. We have become so "tolerant" that we have forgotten what sin is. I wanted to point out what the Bible calls sin. We should not be ashamed to point these sins out and call them for what they really are – SIN. We should not spend our time justifying why we do what we do; why we talk the way we do; why we reacted the way we reacted. All in an effort to make ourselves feel better. Sin is sin and there is no justification for it. Period; end of story.

Get your armor on!

So, for the person who knows to do good and does not do it, it is a sin. (James 4:17 NIV)

Up to now, I have shared with you what the Bible says is sin. What I call sins of Commission. Things we actually do that is sin. However, there are times we sin by doing nothing. What I call sins of Omission. James tells us here when we know to do good and do not do it, it is sin. If we know that we should react in love towards someone, but do not, we commit sin. Same as if we stole something from them. If your worst enemy fails and you react in joy rather than sadness, you sin. If a friend is in need and is hurting, but you ignore them, you sin. So sin is not always what we do, but sometimes what we fail to do.

Get your armor on!

For whoever keeps the entire law, yet fails in one point, is guilty of [breaking it] all. (James 2:10 NIV)

This one is an eye opener! One may argue that they live a pretty wholesome life. "Hey, I keep most of the 10 Commandments, most of the time," one may say. So does that make you perfect, holy, blameless? Absolutely not! For here, James tells us if we keep the whole law (obey God's commands, eliminating the sins of commission and omission), but fail in just one area, it is the same as if we broke all of the law! Wow! Now that would be pretty impossible to accomplish. Keep the whole law and not break any part of it. This is precisely why Jesus died for you and me. He knew there would be no way we could keep all the law and not break any one part of it. Right about now would be a good time to stop what you are doing and get on your knees and thank God for what He has done for you!

Get your armor on!

SIN'S RESULT

If we say, "We have no sin," we are deceiving ourselves, and the truth is not in us. (1 John 1:8 NIV)

If we say, "We have not sinned," we make Him a liar, and His word is not in us. (1 John 1:10 NIV)

I should probably clarify my rationale on these verses. I am not trying to point out any of your sins or make it appear as if you are living in continuous sin. My point is to provide you with ammunition from the Word. We have talked about man's evil ways and what sin is. Now we are addressing what the result of sin is. Failing to call sin a sin is one thing. We talked about that last week. But here we begin to see the consequences of becoming numb to sin. We deceive ourselves into thinking that sin does not exist and there are no consequences. All that does is prove we do not have or live by the truth. What is worse, we call God a liar for thinking we have not sinned. The NIV version of the last part verse 10 goes a bit further – "...and His Word has no place in our lives." How sad when we ignore the true Truth and Bread of Life.

Get your armor on!

you claim: I am innocent. His anger is sure to turn away from me. But I will certainly judge you because you have said: I have not sinned. (Jeremiah 2:35 NIV)

The fact that we may deceive ourselves into thinking we have not sinned does not change the fact that we have. Nor does it change the fact that God will judge us for our actions. We cannot escape. Do you think a police officer will not write you a ticket because you deny you were speeding? You can deny it all you want, but he has a radar gun as his guide and it shows you were doing 59 in a 45! God's radar gun says we all have sinned. Denying it does not change it.

Get your armor on!

SIN'S RESULT

"But the person, native or foreigner, who sins defiantly, deliberately blaspheming God, must be cut off from his people: He has despised God's word, he has violated God's command; that person must be kicked out of the community, ostracized, left alone in his wrongdoing." (Numbers 15:30-31 MSG)

I like the way The Message version translates this verse. Pretty harsh isn't it. If we keep living in our sin, denying we sin, what do you think should happen? This verse says we should be cut off from other believers, ostracized, left alone to continue in our sin. Yes, it may sound harsh, but that is how strongly God feels about those who defiantly continue in their sin. His holiness cannot tolerate deliberate sin and neither should we.

Get your armor on!

But your iniquities have built barriers between you and your God, and your sins have made Him hide [His] face from you so that He does not listen. (Isaiah 59:2 NIV)

This verse so clearly explains what happens when we sin. It creates a barrier between God and us. So much so that God hides His face from us. He cannot coexist with sin. And when we go to Him in prayer with unconfessed sin, He will not listen to us. This shows the importance of confession as part of our prayer life. Do not build that barrier but tear it down not only though confession, but more importantly through holy living.

Get your armor on!

SIN'S RESULT

But if you do not do this, you will certainly sin against the LORD; be sure your sin will catch up with you. (Number 32:23 NIV)

We might think we can get away with sin, especially, if we have not seen any consequences yet. But trust me, you will get caught. Your sins will be exposed sooner or later. If not exposed in this life, they will be exposed in the life after, when we stand before the judgment seat of Christ. Do not get too arrogant with your sin. Do not taunt God with your sin. It will catch up to you.

Get your armor on!

FORGIVENESS (PART 2)

But You are a forgiving God, gracious and compassionate, slow to anger and rich in faithful love, and You did not abandon them. (Nehemiah 9:17b NIV)

The last few weeks have been building to this week. We've learned about man's ways and twisted thinking, what sin is, and sin's result. All this give the appearance of leading to a dead end. And just when all is lost, God swoops in and saves us from ourselves with His forgiveness. We have talked about His forgiveness before, but this is such an important topic, I thought we could use a little refresher.

This verse is pretty self-explanatory and really provides insight into the character of God. What a beautiful description! Right away we see how forgiving He is. Look at the other descriptions. "Gracious and compassionate". Kindhearted and concerned. "Slow to anger". Patient. Long-suffering. Not complaining. Now look at the next description – "rich in faithful love". Do not think I can add anything else to this one. And above all, He did not, and will not, abandon His own. Thank you God for your loving kindness and your forgiveness.

Get your armor on!

You took away Your people's guilt; You covered all their sin. (Psalm 85:2 NIV)

I have said it before, but this verse is a good reminder. Not only does God forgive our sins, but He also removes the guilt of those sins from us. We do not need to beat ourselves up about our sins after we have truly confessed them to Him. Satan loves to dump the guilt on us and constantly remind us of the sin. So use this verse to shut him up. Jesus has taken away the guilt of our sin; He has covered **all** of our sins.

Get your armor on!

FORGIVENESS (PART 2)

And now do not be worried or angry with yourselves for selling me here, because God sent me ahead of you to preserve life. (Genesis 45:5 NIV)

This is from the story of Joseph. Recall his brothers sold him into slavery because of their jealousy. Here, he is forgiving his brothers for what they had done. He knew God had greater plans for his life and told his brothers so. This is a perfect picture of what Jesus has done for us. You see, Jesus was tortured on the cross because of our sins. We put Him there. In effect, Jesus is telling us not to be worried or angry with ourselves for putting Him on that cross. Why? The answer is because God sent Him ahead of us to preserve our lives. What a beautiful example of forgiveness!

Get your armor on!

How happy is the one whose transgression is forgiven, whose sin is covered! (Psalm 32:1 NIV)

I know this is going to sound rather silly, but we should be happy when we are tempted. Huh? Yes, that is right. Be happy when you are tempted for it tells us Satan is concerned and trying to knock us off course. When tempted, on occasion, we will fall into sin. But again, be happy because forgiveness is right around the corner. What can bring more joy than to be restored in relationship with your Creator! So do not worry, be happy!

Get your armor on!

FORGIVENESS (PART 2)

It is I who sweep away your transgressions for My own sake and remember your sins no more. (Isaiah 43:25 NIV)

Have you ever wondered why God offers such forgiveness? When you think about it, it really does not make a lot of sense. We keep on sinning and God just keeps on forgiving. Why? That is who God is. It is in His make-up, His character, His being. For His own name's sake, He offers forgiveness. It would go against His nature if He were not to offer forgiveness. And not only does He sweep them away, He remembers them no more! We often say we can forgive but cannot forget. But is that really forgiveness? Take a lesson from God. Remember your sins no more!

Get your armor on!

FORGET THE PAST

But Jesus said to him, "No one who puts his hand to the plow and looks back is fit for the kingdom of God." (Luke 9:62 NIV)

Now that we have forgiveness, we need to do as God does – forget the sin. Satan would like nothing else but to keep reminding us of our sin. His purpose is to keep the guilt continuously in our minds, thus making us less useful for God. I like the analogy Jesus uses here. A farmer guides the plow down the field. If he looks back to where he has been, the plow most likely will not go straight. You then end up with crooked rows. When we receive forgiveness and put our hands to the plow to move forward, but look back on our sinful nature, we end up crooked. So forget the sin and do not turn back.

Get your armor on!

If you died with Christ to the elemental forces of this world, why do you live as if you still belonged to the world? Why do you submit to regulations: "Do not handle, do not taste, do not touch"? (Colossians 2:20-21 NIV)

When we become a new creation in Christ, our old self is put to death and our new life has begun. We do not need to stay hooked on our old, elemental ways. Some in the Colosse church still wanted to live according to the laws and customs of their former way of life. Paul was encouraging these new Christians to forget those old laws and regulations for we now have new found freedom in Christ. So, put the past behind you.

Get your armor on!

FORGET THE PAST

But his wife looked back and became a pillar of salt. (Genesis 19:26 NIV)

Yesterday's verse was a word to put the past behind you. Here is an example of what happens when we try to look back at our former way of life. God told Lot and his family to get out of Sodom and Gomorrah for He was about to destroy the city because of its wickedness. But He warned them not to look back, for if they did, they would be turned into a pillar of salt. Now you may wonder what the big deal of looking back is. Why would God say such a thing? The key here is that when we leave our old life before Christ, we should not be tempted to look at what we left behind, but focus on that which is ahead. Old friends, old habits, old ways should no longer be a part of us. And we should not long for those days to return. Long only for the pure Word of God.

Get your armor on!

Therefore, no condemnation now exists for those in Christ Jesus, (Romans 8:1 NIV)

This verse is similar to the very first verse of this week. Again, Satan would love nothing more than for us to drown in our guilt of sin. And he will go to no lengths to remind us of our sin. However, as Paul tells the church in Rome, we have no condemnation if we are in Christ. No blame, no disapproval, no criticism, no conviction. In fact, it is quite the opposite. In Christ, we are commended, approved, rewarded, satisfied, content.

Get your armor on!

FORGET THE PAST

Brothers, I do not consider myself to have taken hold of it. But one thing I do: forgetting what is behind and strain towards what is ahead. I press on towards the goal to win the prize to which God has called me heavenward in Christ Jesus. (Philippians 3:13-14 NIV)

Wow! Paul just plain gets it! The "it" he refers to in verse 13 is perfection, what we will obtain when and only when we are with Christ in heaven. Paul did not claim to be perfect, yet. But what he did was forget what is behind: those things in his past that kept him from reaching perfection. And he strained towards what is ahead. His use of "straining" illustrates that it is not easy to do. In fact, it is hard work. But oh, the benefits!!! So forget what is behind and strain towards what is ahead.

Get your armor on!

FORGIVE OTHERS

And be kind and compassionate to one another, forgiving one another, just as God also forgave you in Christ. (Ephesians 4:32 NIV)

I hope you can see the progression we are making. We have looked at God's forgiveness and how we should forget the past once we have confessed our sin. Now we see the practical application of forgiveness. Pass it on to others. You want forgiveness? Give it and forgive like God. You are never more like God than when you forgive.

Get your armor on!

For if you forgive people their wrongdoing, your heavenly Father will forgive you as well. (Matthew 6:14 NIV)

This verse goes along with yesterday's verse. We should forgive as God forgives. Not that God's forgiveness is conditional, but why would we expect God to forgive us if we cannot forgive others? "Do as I say and not as I do" does not work in this case. Have compassion on others; forgive them when they wrong you. You would expect the same. And God certainly does!

Get your armor on!

FORGIVE OTHERS

Then Peter came to Him and said, "Lord, how many times could my brother sin against me and I forgive him? As many as seven times?" "I tell you, not as many as seven," Jesus said to him, "but 70 times seven. (Matthew 18:21-22 NIV)

You may have a friend or acquaintance that has rubbed you the wrong way...often...too often. You have forgiven that person once, twice, maybe even three times. You may ask, "How many more times should I forgive this person?" Seven is considered the perfect number. So Peter's assumption seems logical – forgive someone seven times. However, Peter did not yet have God's perspective; for Jesus said forgive 70 times seven. Now, did Jesus literally mean forgive someone 490 times? So on the 491st time, we should not forgive? I do not think so. I believe Jesus' use of 70 times seven means there is not a magical number. Does God keep track of how many times He has forgiven us? No. Neither should we keep track of how many times we have forgiven someone else. Keep on forgiving!

Get your armor on!

FORGIVE OTHERS

A person's insight gives him patience, and his virtue is to overlook an offense. (Proverbs 19:11 NIV)

Man, sometimes I wish this verse was not in the Bible. It is so hard to do. Plus, sometimes, I do not want to overlook an offense. I want to get even; I want to get back. It is our human nature to want and to do this. But we must look through God's eyes and see as He sees, do as He does. You certainly want God to overlook your offense to Him, right? Well, we need to do the same for others. It is another way of showing the world we are His!

Get your armor on!

Then Jesus said, "Father, forgive them, because they do not know what they are doing." (Luke 23:34 NIV)

Ok, what do you do when you forgive someone, yet that person just will not accept it? They still hold a grudge or still harbor anger against you. What do you do? The answer is unilateral forgiveness. God does not say that others will always accept your forgiveness. Others accepting our forgiveness is not our responsibility. Our responsibility is to forgive and let God take care of the rest. Here is a beautiful picture of unilateral forgiveness! Jesus, on the cross, is offering forgiveness to those who either do not want it, or will not accept it. What an example for the rest of us!

Get your armor on!

ROMAN ROAD TO SALVATION

as it is written: There is no one righteous, not even one; there is no one who understands, there is no one who seeks God. All have turned away, together they have become useless; there is no one who does good, there is not even one. (Romans 3:10-12 NIV)

Paul wrote the book of Romans mainly to share the path to Christ. Throughout the entire book, Paul lays out the plan of salvation. That is why you may have heard about "The Roman Road to Salvation." This week we will travel down that road to see how clearly Paul laid out the Gospel.

Paul quotes from several Old Testament verses, mainly Psalm 14 and 53. He points out that no one is righteous, not even one; no one does good, not even one. More to the point, we are sinners and helpless. Nothing we can do on our own changes that. We are a people without hope. Those that do not know God have become useless. How discouraging is that; to go through life with no hope; to be called useless. Quite a sobering thought. No surprise, we **need** Christ!

Get your armor on!

For all have sinned and fall short of the glory of God. (Romans 3:23 NIV)

We have already touched on man's sin nature. How we have all sinned and no one is righteous on their own merit. Paul states it pretty clearly here. There are two things to point out here. First, all have sinned. Paul does not leave anyone out here; there are no exceptions. Second, because of our sin, we fall short of God's glory. Think of your flag football team. If your quarterback always misses the receiver, you cannot reach the end zone. If all the passes fall short of the receiver, all the passes will be incomplete. That is what sin is like. Always missing the target; always falling short.

Get your armor on!

ROMAN ROAD TO SALVATION

For the wages of sin is death, but the gift of God is eternal life in Christ Jesus our Lord. (Romans 6:23 NIV)

So far, our journey down the Roman Road has been a little bumpy. No one is good enough; all have sinned; all is lost, or so it appears. This verse even starts out the same way. What sin earns is death. But there is a but. All is not lost because there is a but. "...but the gift of God is eternal life in Christ Jesus our Lord." While it may appear as if we have no hope, in actuality, God has provided the hope through His Son, Jesus Christ. Now, let's internalize this verse.

> For Jessica/Scott has earned death, but God has given Jessica/Scott eternal life in Christ Jesus our Lord.

Praise God for the but.

Get your armor on!

But God proves His own love for us in that while we were still sinners Christ died for us! (Romans 5:8 NIV)

We are finally beginning to see the light at the end of the tunnel in our walk through Romans! We started down the road with no hope. Think of it as walking through a thunderstorm. Winds blowing, eerie looking clouds hovering overhead. Now we see the sun peeking through the clouds. Blue sky appears behind the darkness. A ray of hope shines in the distance. Even while we were walking in hopelessness, Christ died for us. He did not wait until we showed some signs of dependency on Him; He did not wait until our hearts began to yearn for Him. No! While we were still stuck in our sinfulness, at our lowest point, Christ swooped down for the save. His love for us, His care for us, His desire for a relationship with us was proven when Christ remained on the cross and died. For you and me! Right about now would be a good time to get on our knees and thank Him for that supreme sacrifice!

Get your armor on!

if you confess with your mouth, "Jesus is Lord," and believe in your heart that God raised Him from the dead, you will be saved. With the heart one believes, resulting in righteousness, and with the mouth one confesses, resulting in salvation. (Romans 10:9-10 NIV)

For everyone who calls on the name of the Lord will be saved. (Romans 10:13 NIV)

We have finally reached the end of our Roman Road journey. And what a destination! We can summarize each stop along the way with these five words: Recognition, Acknowledge, Confession, Belief, and Calling. Recognize we are sinful and deserve death. Acknowledge there is nothing we, alone, can do to give us hope. Confess Jesus died for our sins. Belief that Jesus rose on the 3rd day (for if He had not, what kind of Savior would He be?). Call on the name of Jesus to save us from ourselves. Now you have a simple outline to share with those who do not know Christ. Now, go do it!

Get your armor on!

ASSURANCE OF SALVATION

And this is the promise that He Himself made to us: eternal life. (1 John 2:25 NIV)

We are progressing along a path of maturity in Christ, with the recognition of sin and sin's result, acknowledging God's forgiveness and that we should also forgive others, and once we ask for forgiveness, how we should forget the past and move towards Christ. Last week we traveled down the Roman Road to salvation. Now we will confirm our assurance of eternal life given through Christ.

First, look at the word promise. It means to guarantee, to certify, to pledge. Jesus has given us His word. Back in Biblical times, a man's word was his bond. Sadly, today it does not mean much. What has He promised us? Eternal life. What does that mean? It means everlasting, never ending, perpetual, endless, ceaseless, and timeless. This is what we have to look forward to: eternal life with Christ. Some will try to tell you that you can lose your salvation. But how can you if He has promised you eternal life? If we can lose it, it is not eternal now is it? Thank you, God, for your promise of eternal life!

Get your armor on!

For the promise is for you and for your children, and for all who are far off, as many as the Lord our God will call." (Acts 2:39 NIV)

Yesterday, we saw what God has promised to us. Who is us? The us is you, your children, and those generations to come (all who are far off). Basically, the "us" is anyone. Do not be confused by the words, "as many as the Lord our God will call" and think that if the Lord does not call, then we cannot be saved. The Lord's call is to everyone (read 2 Peter 3:9). This verse also explains how critical it is for us to pass down Christ to generations to come. How can they know if we do not teach them! So all of us who have called on Christ receive His promise of eternal life.

Get your armor on!

ASSURANCE OF SALVATION

But to all who did receive Him, He gave them the right to be children of God, to those who believe in His name, (John 1:12 NIV)

This verse fits hand in hand with yesterday's verse. Those who have called on Him receive His promise. Besides eternal life, His promise includes the right to be called children of God. Do you get it? We have been **given** the **right** to be called **His children**. Wow! Think about it. We ARE His children. This is just mind-boggling. Worship Him as your Father and we as His children.

Get your armor on!

But there's far more to life for us. We're citizens of high heaven! We're waiting the arrival of the Savior, the Master, Jesus Christ, who will transform our earthy bodies into glorious bodies like his own. He'll make us beautiful and whole with the same powerful skill by which he is putting everything as it should be, under and around him. (Philippians 3:20-21 MSG)

I really like the way the Message translation writes this verse. The opening sentence sets the tone for the entire verse. There is so much more to this life for us who believe in Christ. And it starts by becoming citizens of high heaven. Our anticipation of this citizenship is the arrival of our Savior, the Master, Jesus Christ Himself. When He arrives, He will transform us to be like Him – a glorious body, beautiful and whole! And just how can this be? It is by the power that enables Him to bring everything under His control. The God who is all powerful can do anything and everything. So it is of no surprise (or should be of no surprise) that He can and will transform us to be like Him. This is our assurance of our salvation: to be like Him!

Get your armor on!

ASSURANCE OF SALVATION

I have written these things to you who believe in the name of the Son of God, so that you may know that you have eternal life. (1 John 5:13 NIV)

How we can know we have eternal life? Read His Word. Why did the writers of Scripture write? For a number of reasons, but one of them was to provide us assurance of what we believe. John wrote his books to reassure us that we have eternal life in Christ. There is an old song by Russ Taff (he was part of the group called The Imperials from back in the 1970s and early 1980s). The song goes something like this, "Jesus said it, I believe it; I believe 'cause He said, and I know, yes I know, that I know He's gonna see me through." Jesus said it, John wrote it, I believe it 'cause He wrote it and I know, yes I know that I have eternal life!

Get your armor on!

CHRIST'S RETURN

Then I saw heaven opened, and there was a white horse! Its rider is called Faithful and True, and in righteousness He judges and makes war. His eyes were like a fiery flame, and on His head were many crowns. He had a name written that no one knows except Himself. He wore a robe stained with blood, and His name is called the Word of God. The armies that were in heaven followed Him on white horses, wearing pure white linen. From His mouth came a sharp sword, so that with it He might strike the nations. He will shepherd them with an iron scepter. He will also trample the winepress of the fierce anger of God, the Almighty. And on His robe and on His thigh He has a name written:KING OF KINGS AND LORD OF LORDS (Revelation 19:11-16 NIV)

This is probably one of the most descriptive references to the Second Coming of Christ in Scripture. Now to show you how important this is on the pages of Scripture, a total of 1,527 verses in the Old Testament refer to Christ's Second Coming. About 1 out of every 25 verses in the New Testament refers to the Second Coming of Jesus Christ. Next to the subject of faith, no subject is mentioned more often than the return of Christ. For every time the first coming of Christ is mentioned, the Second Coming is mentioned 8 times. The Lord Himself refers to His coming 21 times. Over 50 times we are exhorted to be ready for that great event. It is a major theme throughout the pages of Scripture. So get ready and be ready!

Get your armor on!

CHRIST'S RETURN

So now, little children, remain in Him, so that when He appears we may have boldness and not be ashamed before Him at His coming. (1 John 2:28 NIV)

Notice the verse did not say "if He appears" but "when He appears". The return of Christ is the most guaranteed event there is. We just do not know when it will be. That is why it is most critical for us to have boldness and not be ashamed before Him at His coming. What do we want Christ to find us doing when He returns? What, if in the middle of a heated conversation, you say something you should not, and that is the precise time Christ decides to return? What if, while sitting in the classroom, you glance at a neighbor's test, and that is the precise time Christ decides to return? What if, during the passion of the moment on a date, Christ returns? What if, while you are living a Godly life, being a positive witness for Him, Christ decides to return? We do not know when, but we do know He is coming back. Live boldly, live unashamed.

Get your armor on!

For the Lord Himself will descend from heaven with a shout, with the archangel's voice, and with the trumpet of God, and the dead in Christ will rise first. (1 Thessalonians 4:16 NIV)

Can you imagine the sight of this event? I picture the sun peeking through the clouds, perhaps just after a light rain storm. Bolts of light splintered through the breaks in the clouds. Then, the clouds separate and the sun bursts through and you have to squint your eyes it is so bright. Imagine, if you will, at this moment when the sun splits the sky, a trumpet sounding as loud as the loudest clap of thunder you have ever heard. BAM! Christ appears in the sky, ready to take His children home! Wow! What a sight that will be. Are you ready?

Get your armor on!

CHRIST'S RETURN

Dear friends, we are God's children now, and what we will be has not yet been revealed. We know that when He appears, we will be like Him, because we will see Him as He is. (1 John 3:2 NIV)

No more bone fragments in our pinkie; no more scars on our arms; no more screws in our broken arm; no more asthma, no more little aches and pains, sniffles, or runny noses. When that day comes, not if that day comes, we will be like Him – perfect, holy, blameless. If you are a child of God, you have nothing to fear of this day. Anticipate it; be anxious for it; be ready for it!

Get your armor on!

Then the sign of the Son of Man will appear in the sky, and then all the peoples of the earth will mourn; and they will see the Son of Man coming on the clouds of heaven with power and great glory. He will send out His angels with a loud trumpet, and they will gather His elect from the four winds, from one end of the sky to the other. (Matthew 24:30-31 NIV)

What will the sign of the Son of Man be? When will we see it? Answers to these questions are not known to man. And to be honest, what does it matter? The important thing is to be ready when this day comes. Cannot you see it! The Son of Man coming in the clouds of heaven with power and great glory. I imagine a sight so bright you will have to look away. It will be much more than a "beautiful postcard!" And then with a booming voice, like the sound of a loud trumpet, He will call His own to Him. We are His elect; we are His children, if we know Jesus Christ, His Son. Are you ready?

Get your armor on!

COUNT THE COST

As He was setting out on a journey, a man ran up, knelt down before Him, and asked Him, "Good Teacher, what must I do to inherit eternal life?" "Why do you call Me good?" Jesus asked him. "No one is good but One—God. You know the commandments: Do not murder; do not commit adultery; do not steal; do not bear false witness; do not defraud; honor your father and mother." He said to Him, "Teacher, I have kept all these from my youth." Then, looking at him, Jesus loved him and said to him, "You lack one thing: Go, sell all you have and give to the poor, and you will have treasure in heaven. Then come, follow Me." But he was stunned at this demand, and he went away grieving, because he had many possessions. (Mark 10:17-22 NIV)

We are continuing down our road to Christian maturity. We have seen sin and sin's result, forgiveness, how we not only receive it but also give it; we have seen our assurance of salvation and anticipate Christ's return. This next stop in our journey is a tough one, just as the rich young ruler found out. Following Christ is not always easy; it is not always the most popular thing to do; in some cases, it certainly is not what we want to do. The rich young ruler was only following Christ on the outside, for he treasured his possessions more than anything else. Jesus said for us to follow Him, we must forsake all else. There is an acronym for Faith. **F**orsaking **A**ll, **I** **T**ake **H**im. Following Christ may not always be the easiest thing to do, but it is always the right thing to do.

Get your armor on!

COUNT THE COST

"I have told you these things to keep you from stumbling. They will ban you from the synagogues. In fact, a time is coming when anyone who kills you will think he is offering service to God. They will do these things because they haven't known the Father or Me. But I have told you these things so that when their time comes you may remember I told them to you. (John 16:1-4a NIV)

Jesus is warning the disciples of pending persecution for acknowledging Jesus as the Savior. And persecuted they were. Peter was crucified; head downward during the persecution by Nero. Andrew died on a cross at Patrae, in Achaia, a Grecian colony. James was thrown from a pinnacle of the temple and then beaten to death with a club. Bartholomew was flayed alive in Albanopolis, Armenia. James, the elder son of Zebedee, was beheaded at Jerusalem. Thomas, the Doubter, was run through the body with a lance at Coromandel, in the East Indies. Philip was hanged against a pillar at Heropolis, a city of Phrygia, in Asia Minor. Matthew was slain by the sword, in Ethiopia, Abyssinia. Thaddeus was shot to death with arrows. Simon died on a cross in Persia (now Iran).

Many of these first disciples died at the hands of men who thought they were doing the right thing. These events were precisely what Jesus had predicted. So what are you willing to give to be a disciple? Are you willing to give it all just as these first disciples did? The cost is high, but the benefits are greater.

Get your armor on!

COUNT THE COST

Lot looked out and saw that the entire Jordan Valley as far as Zoar was well-watered everywhere like the LORD's garden and the land of Egypt. This was before God destroyed Sodom and Gomorrah. So Lot chose the entire Jordan Valley for himself. Then Lot journeyed eastward, and they separated from each other. (Genesis 13:10-11 NIV)

This is the story of Lot and Abraham as they journeyed from Egypt to Canaan. The two determined it was better for them to split ways. Lot looked around, to the east and to the west. He saw to the east the entire Jordan Valley; well-watered, green pastures as far as the eye could see, just like back in Egypt. Of course, he chose that route. And why not! It was easy. Planting crops would be easy because of the natural irrigation. There was plenty of pastures for his cattle to graze and be well fed. However, the easy route is not always the best route. For you see and it is mentioned here, this was before God destroyed Sodom and Gomorrah, wicked cities full of immoral and evil behavior.

The decision to live for Christ is much like the decision Lot had to make. Do you take the easy way out that leads to destruction? Or do you take the more difficult road that leads to fulfillment and eternal life? Time to decide!

Get your armor on!

COUNT THE COST

For it has been given to you on Christ's behalf not only to believe in Him, but also to suffer for Him, (Philippians 1:29 NIV)

Do not be surprised, brothers, if the world hates you. (1 John 2:13 NIV)

These two verses were just too good for me to exclude one, so you get a two-for-one special today! We have plenty of warnings in the New Testament that following Christ will not be easy. We will suffer for Him and the world will hate us. That is harsh treatment. One may think, "Why should I have to suffer to follow Christ? Should my life not be a bed of roses?" This type of thinking is straight from the pit of hell. It is a worldly and selfish viewpoint. All we have to do is look at Jesus. He never did anything wrong. He taught of love, peace and abundant, everlasting life. And what did He get for it? Crucifixion! Be bold! Be strong! Be of good courage! Because He has overcome the world! And because He has, we can too!

Get your armor on!

More than that, I also consider everything to be a loss in view of the surpassing value of knowing Christ Jesus my Lord. Because of Him I have suffered the loss of all things and consider them filth, so that I may gain Christ. (Philippians 3:8 NIV)

Do not you just love Paul! I tell you, the more I read his letters, the more I understand he just gets it. He had that eternal perspective, God's viewpoint. All that he gained while on earth was counted as loss compared to knowing Christ. What is more, he considered them "filth". He was more than willing to "suffer the loss" of all that he had, possessions, position, and power, so that he might gain Christ. Nothing else mattered to him but to know Christ more and more. That is what I call sacrifice. Paul counted the cost and came to the conclusion that it was more than worth it. What is your conclusion?

Get your armor on!

BE A DISCIPLE

Therefore, when many of His disciples heard this, they said, "This teaching is hard! Who can accept it?" (John 6:60 NIV)

From that moment many of His disciples turned back and no longer accompanied Him. (John 6:66 NIV)

These verses fit perfectly with last week's theme. Now that you have counted the cost, it is time to follow Christ and be His disciple. For some, the cost is too high for their liking and turn back to the offerings of this world. Jesus told His disciples that the harvest is plenty, but the workers are few, meaning there are many who need to know Christ, but only a few actually tell them about Him. A true disciple will follow Christ no matter how hard it is. Stand strong in His mighty power! Be a Disciple!

Get your armor on!

This is how we know we are in Him: the one who says he remains in Him should walk just as He walked. (1 John 2:5b-6 NIV)

Here is the litmus test for being Christ's disciple – to walk as Jesus walked. You want others to see Christ in you? Walk as Jesus walked! You want to pray like Jesus prayed? Walk as Jesus walked! You want to witness like Jesus witnessed? Walk as Jesus walked! Get the hint? You want to be a disciple of Christ? Walk as Jesus walked!

Get your armor on!

BE A DISCIPLE

So Jesus said to the Jews who had believed Him, "If you continue in My word, you really are My disciples. (John 8:31 NIV)

You have counted the cost of being Christ's disciple. You have determined that you will follow Christ even though the path is difficult. You have the example in Jesus. What next? Continue in My word! Notice Jesus said continue. He assumes you were already in the word when you decided to follow Him in the beginning. Now He says to persist, to go on, to keep on, to remain in His word. Crave His word; hide it in your heart; read it; meditate on it; memorize it. If you do, you really are His disciple.

Get your armor on!

By this all people will know that you are My disciples, if you have love for one another." (John 13:35 NIV)

Here is another "what next?" answer. Once you have decided to be a disciple of Christ, what next? Love one another. No one has ever seen God. No one has ever seen Christ. I disagree with both of those statements. We see God and we see Christ every time we show love towards another person. For it is the love of God living in us that is expressed outwardly towards others. You want to be a disciple of God? Show it, do not say it. Love one another.

Get your armor on!

BE A DISCIPLE

Summoning His 12 disciples, He gave them authority over unclean spirits, to drive them out and to heal every disease and sickness. (Matthew 10:1 NIV)

Ok, so I decide to be a disciple. Does it mean I join some secret society and have to go through all kinds of unique and guarded rituals? Does being a disciple give me any special powers? These are obviously rhetorical questions, but do point to some significance. For one, being a disciple of Christ should not be a secret! We are the live out our devotion to Christ so others can see!! Second, there are no rituals. There is no induction ceremony to attend or complete. And third, I would say yes, we are given special powers through His Spirit that He gives us. But these are not magical, mystical powers. So can we cast out unclean spirits? Can we heal disease and sickness? I say yes. However, I do not believe that power is through some broadway production show like Benny Hinn where he hits people over the head and "heals" them. I believe through our prayers and faith, we can heal disease and sickness, if God wills it. I believe through our encouragement and lifestyle, we can drive out unclean spirits. Not through some giant display of aura and sensation, but through daily, walking with Christ, living and loving as He did. Now that you are a disciple, go and live it so that others may see.

Get your armor on!

SPIRITUAL GIFTS

Yet grace was given to each of us individually in proportion to the measure of Christ's gift. (Ephesians 4:7 NIV)

And His gifts were some to be apostles, some prophets, some evangelists, some pastors and teachers. (Ephesians 4:10 NIV)

Since we have been discussing becoming a disciple of Christ, I want to focus the next two weeks on the topic of Spiritual Gifts. This is a subject of great confusion and misunderstanding, but it does not have to be. To start, we are going to visit several passages where spiritual gifts are listed. Here the apostle Paul lists a few gifts – apostles, prophets, evangelists, pastors, and teachers. One thing to take special note of: Each of us has been given a gift(s) as Christ has chosen. No believer can say they do not have a gift. Some believers will have more than one. Now, back to this list. Apostles are special messengers of Christ whom He sends for specific purposes. Prophets are not fortune tellers, but those inspired teachers who proclaim the truth in Christ. Evangelists are those who travel, preaching the gospel, like Billy Graham. Pastors (also called shepherds) are like Brother Mike, who lead a church. Teachers are not paid workers, but those who are gifted to teach a Bible Study class.

We will see several more lists of Spiritual Gifts in the next couple of days. Be seeking your gift.

Get your armor on!

SPIRITUAL GIFTS

A manifestation of the Spirit is given to each person to produce what is beneficial: to one is given a message of wisdom through the Spirit, to another, a message of knowledge by the same Spirit, to another, faith by the same Spirit, to another, gifts of healing by the one Spirit, to another, the performing of miracles, to another, prophecy, to another, distinguishing between spirits, to another, different kinds of languages, to another, interpretation of languages. But one and the same Spirit is active in all these, distributing to each one as He wills.
(1 Corinthians 12:7-11 NIV)

Here we have another list of Spiritual Gifts. A few things to note:

1) This is not an all-inclusive list. There are more gifts than listed here.
2) God distributes these gifts as He chooses (same concept from yesterday's verse)
3) Each gift has a purpose – "to produce what is beneficial"

Find your gift and start producing what is beneficial!

Get your armor on!

SPIRITUAL GIFTS

Now as we have many parts in one body, and all the parts do not have the same function, in the same way we who are many are one body in Christ and individually members of one another. According to the grace given to us, we have different gifts: If prophecy, use it according to the standard of faith; if service, in service; if teaching, in teaching; if exhorting, in exhortation; giving, with generosity; leading, with diligence; showing mercy, with cheerfulness.(Romans 12:4-8 NIV)

This is the last of the major "lists" of gifts found in the Bible. Some listed here that we have not seen before include service, exhortation, giving, leadership, and mercy. Not only does Paul mention what the gifts are, he provides the proper attitude in which they are to be used.

Here is a brief description of each of these gifts:

Service: the God-given ability to do for others whatever needs to be done, divine ability to carry the burdens or tasks of others without seeking notice or earthly reward.
Exhortation: the ability to motivate Christians to do the works of Christ.
Giving: being blessed by God with resources or time and being able to give them where and when they are needed with a cheerful heart.
Leadership: God-given insight into when something needs to be done, who can do it, how it can be completed, and how to lead those people to get it accomplished.
Mercy: A heart to care for and encourage those who are not able to care for themselves and whom no one else would care for. It is knowing who to help and when to help.

Now we have seen at least 18 different Spiritual Gifts in Scripture. I encourage you to search the internet for a Spiritual Gift survey and take the time to complete one. Though not scientific, it may give you a hint of what your gift(s) may be.

Get your armor on!

SPIRITUAL GIFTS

So Amos answered Amaziah, "I was not a prophet or the son of a prophet; rather, I was a herdsman, and I took care of sycamore figs. But the LORD took me from following the flock and said to me, 'Go, prophesy to My people Israel. (Amos 7:14-15 NIV)

You may think you have no special gifts or talents. You may think there is no way God can use you. You may think that you are not in any high position to be able to be used by God. That simply is a lie! Here is Amos, a lowly herdsman. Herdsman, by the way, were the lowest of lowly jobs back then. God took a herdsman and made him into a prophet. Do not believe that God could not do the same with you! You are a child of His. He loves you. He has gifted you to bring Him glory. Now go do it!

Get your armor on!

Much will be required of everyone who has been given much. And even more will be expected of the one who has been entrusted with more. (Luke 12:48 NIV)

You may read this verse and ask yourself, "What does this have to do with spiritual gifts?" Well, glad you asked. I think by now we should understand we have been given gift(s) as God sees fit. And we have been given the gift(s) to use for His benefit. So, now get to it! Use your gifts. They are not given to you to put on the shelf. You know how I like to personalize scripture. So let's read it this way,

> *"Much will be required of Jessica/Scott who has been given much. Even more will be expected of Jessica/Scott who has been entrusted with more."*

As you find your gifts, start putting them into practice.

Get your armor on!

SPIRITUAL GIFTS

To one he gave five talents; to another, two; and to another, one—to each according to his own ability. (Matthew 25:15 NIV)

I want to pick up where we left off last week regarding spiritual gifts. Rather than focusing on the list of gifts, let's talk about the various intricacies regarding our gifts. Say you have determined what your spiritual gift(s) is/are and you do not like what you have received. Maybe it is not a more visible (and in some people's opinion, more glamorous) gift. Or, perhaps you only received one and a friend has two or more. Do not question why God may have given one person a particular gift(s) and gave you only one gift or a completely different gift. God distributes the gifts just as He pleases. He knows what He is doing. Trust Him.

Get your armor on!

You are to instruct all the skilled craftsmen, whom I have filled with a spirit of wisdom, to make Aaron's garments for consecrating him to serve Me as priest. (Exodus 28:3 NIV)

This verse is of particular interest as we determine what our gift is and how to use it. As this verse points out, God may bless us with a specific gift to use at a specific time. Once that specific task is complete, the gift is removed and He blesses us with another one. Or, He may bless you with a gift to use for a period of time, and then give you a different one to use for a while, and so on. I can definitely see how God did not bless me with the gift of teaching until later in life – when I was ready for it. Through your journey of discipleship, be on the lookout for different gifts to use at different times. If one gift is removed, get ready, for God is about to gift you with another one!

Get your armor on!

SPIRITUAL GIFTS

If the foot should say, "Because I'm not a hand, I do not belong to the body," in spite of this it still belongs to the body. And if the ear should say, "Because I'm not an eye, I do not belong to the body," in spite of this it still belongs to the body. If the whole body were an eye, where would the hearing be? If the whole were an ear, where would be the sense of smell? But now God has placed the parts, each one of them, in the body just as He wanted. And if they were all the same part, where would the body be? Now there are many parts, yet one body. (1 Corinthians 12:15-20 NIV)

Here we see an example of the jealousy of spiritual gifts. This problem could tear at the very fabric of the church. Paul uses the analogy of the body. It fits perfectly within our discussion of Spiritual Gifts. We cannot all have the same gift. If all had the gift of mercy, then who would have faith? If all had the gift of giving, then who would teach? Granted, some gifts may be more visible, but all gifts are equally important. The key is to do what you can with what He has given you. Rejoice in the gift you have. Rejoice in the fact that God has blessed others with gifts that compliment yours. Rejoice that we can be many parts, but yet one body of Christ!

Get your armor on!

On that day many will say to Me, 'Lord, Lord, did not we prophesy in Your name, drive out demons in Your name, and do many miracles in Your name? Then I will announce to them, 'I never knew you! Depart from Me, you lawbreakers! (Matthew 7:22-23 NIV)

Be careful how you use your gifts! Early on in our review of spiritual gifts, Paul told us that spiritual gifts were to produce what was beneficial; for God's glory, not our own. In today's verse, Jesus warns us about the motives for using of our gifts. Some people on the Day of Judgment will come to Jesus, purporting that they did all things wonderful things, even claiming to use their gifts in Jesus' name. And what will be Jesus' response? "I never knew you! Depart from Me, you lawbreakers!" God gave us our gifts for one purpose and one purpose only – to make Him known. Do not use them for selfish reasons or to bring recognition your way. In the end, it will not get you anywhere.

Get your armor on!

Based on the gift they have received, everyone should use it to serve others, as good managers of the varied grace of God. (1 Peter 4:10 NIV)

Unlike what we saw yesterday, Peter tells us here the proper way to use our spiritual gifts. Use them to serve others. Be good stewards ("good managers") of the various gifts He has given you. Treat it much like a job. If you clean toilets for a living, clean them like no other person has ever cleaned a toilet before. Do not be ashamed to use your gifts, regardless of how important, unimportant, visible or behind the scenes you feel it is. Work at it as if working for the Lord. In fact, that is exactly what we are doing.

Get your armor on!

BEAR FRUIT

This same Good News that came to you is going out all over the world. It is bearing fruit everywhere by changing lives, just as it changed your lives from the day you first heard and understood the truth about God's wonderful grace. (Colossians 1:6 NLT)

I really like the way this verse is translated in the New Living Translation.

If you recall, we left off last semester talking about spiritual gifts. I want to continue focusing this semester on becoming a disciple. There are so many facets to growing as a disciple of Christ. It is not a destination, but a journey that will take a lifetime to fulfill and will not be complete until we see Jesus face-to-face.

The main point in this verse is to bear fruit. The Good News is the gospel of Jesus Christ. It bears fruit everywhere by the lives that are changed. Lives that were once without hope now have hope. Just as it has changed yours, you have the power within you to change others'. So go and bear fruit with the wonderful truth about God's grace.

Get your armor on!

BEAR FRUIT

But blessed are those who trust in the Lord and have made the Lord their hope and confidence. They are like trees planted along a riverbank, with roots that reach deep into the water. Such trees are not bothered by the heat or worried by long months of drought. Their leaves stay green, and they never stop producing fruit. (Jeremiah 17:7-8 NLT)

I love this picture painted by the prophet Jeremiah. If you trust in the Lord and have made the Lord your hope and confidence, look what type of tree you will become! Your roots will reach deep into the water. You will not be bothered by the heat or worried by long months of drought. Your leaves will stay green and you will never stop producing fruit. Of course, I want to focus on the last phrase – you will not stop producing fruit.

Would you want an apple tree that does not produce apples? Would you want a pear tree that does not produce pears? Both rhetorical questions, but you get the idea. Trees that do not produce fruit are useless. Just because you may have produced abundant fruit one season does not give you the right to take the next season off. You must continue producing fruit or risk becoming useless and of no value.

Get your armor on!

BEAR FRUIT

Then he took some of the land's seed and put it in a fertile field; he set it [like] a willow, a plant by abundant waters. (Ezekiel 17:5 NIV)

It had been planted in a good field by abundant waters in order to produce branches, bear fruit, and become a splendid vine. (Ezekiel 17:8 NIV)

Where was the seed planted? It was planted in a fertile field by abundant waters. Why there? It was planted there in order to produce branches, bear fruit and become a splendid vine.

Who should you hang out with? Where should you spend your Sundays? Where and with whom should you spend your free time? Who should be your closest friends? Only where and with whom a seed can be fed to produce branches, bear fruit, and become a splendid vine!

Get your armor on!

You'll recognize them by their fruit. (Matthew 7:16a NIV)

This one is pretty self-explanatory. How do you know what an apple tree looks like? How can you differentiate an orange tree from a pear tree? You know it by the fruit each tree bears. If there is no fruit, you do not know what kind of tree you are looking at. No one should ever have to ask if you are a Christian. They should be able to tell by the fruit that you bear.

Get your armor on!

BEAR FRUIT

But the seed in the good ground—these are the ones who, having heard the word with an honest and good heart, hold on to it and by enduring, bear fruit. (Luke 8:15 NIV)

This is taken from the parable of the seeds. Jesus names several types of seeds, where they fell, and their result. Those that fell on good ground bear fruit. Note that these seeds heard the Word with an honest and good heart. They acknowledged Jesus Christ, the true Word, with sincerity. Note also that their bearing of fruit did not come easy. But by holding on to the Word, and enduring whatever hardship they faced, they were able to bear fruit.

Bearing fruit is not always easy. Do not give up too easily, but hold on to the Word and endure. Then fruit will burst out from your branches in abundance.

Get your armor on!

LET YOUR LIGHT SHINE

For you were once darkness, but now [you are] light in the Lord. Walk as children of light — for the fruit of the light [results] in all goodness, righteousness, and truth. (Ephesians 5:8-9 NIV)

What a nice transition from last week to this week. Because we are the light in the Lord, we should walk as children of the Light. We do this by bearing fruit of goodness, righteousness, and truth. If we do bear this fruit of the Light, others will see our Light, be drawn to the Light, and become children of the Light as well. So let your light shine on!

Get your armor on!

You are the light of the world. A city situated on a hill cannot be hidden. (Matthew 5:14 NIV)

That's right – Jesus said you are the light of the world. Think of a house on the prairie, perched atop a hill. At night, when the lights are turned on inside the house, the house can be seen for miles. It is hard to hide it when the lights are turned on. In the same way, we are perched atop a hill with the true Light of the World inside us. When our light is shining, we cannot help but be noticed by others. So let your light shine so others may see!

Get your armor on!

LET YOUR LIGHT SHINE

Now this is the message we have heard from Him and declare to you: God is light, and there is absolutely no darkness in Him. If we say, "We have fellowship with Him," and walk in darkness, we are lying and are not practicing the truth. But if we walk in the light as He Himself is in the light, we have fellowship with one another, and the blood of Jesus His Son cleanses us from all sin. (1 John 1:5-7 NIV)

When you walk in dark room and turn the light on, the darkness goes away. Everything becomes visible because it is the light that makes things visible. Light and darkness cannot coexist. That is why we cannot have fellowship with God and walk in the darkness (continue in our sin). But if we walk in the true Light, we do have fellowship with Him. Not only do we have fellowship with Him, but also with one another. And not only with one another, but we receive an added bonus – forgiveness of sins. So why not walk in the light!

Get your armor on!

For God, who said, "Light shall shine out of darkness" —He has shone in our hearts to give the light of the knowledge of God's glory in the face of Jesus Christ. (2 Corinthians 4:6 NIV)

We live in a sinful world. But out of this sinful world, God brought forth the Light in the life of Jesus. And now that light lives in our hearts. But that light is not to be hidden. We are to shine that light of the knowledge of God's glory so that others can experience the benefits of the Light. If your batteries are running low, get them charged up so others can see the Light in you.

Get your armor on!

LET YOUR LIGHT SHINE

Do everything without grumbling and arguing, so that you may be blameless and pure, children of God who are faultless in a crooked and perverted generation, among whom you shine like stars in the world. (Philippians 2:14-15 NIV)

So how do we shine our light? I am sure you have had friends, classmates even, that all they do is complain. They can never be satisfied. Your professor can cancel class and they will complain that they got out of bed for no reason. They go through the cafeteria line and make a big fuss because the pizza dough is too hard. They drive to the mall and complain there was too much traffic. Their complaining drives you crazy and you do not even want to be around them. One way to let your light shine is to do everything without grumbling or complaining. You will set yourself apart by doing so. You will even shine like the stars! So quit complaining and start shining!

Get your armor on!

SEEK TO KNOW GOD

For you were once darkness, but now [you are] light in the Lord. Walk as children of light...discerning what is pleasing to the Lord. (Ephesians 5:8,10 NIV)

Now that you are letting your light shine (from last week's topic), it is time to discern what is pleasing to the Lord. Paul would not have told us to discern what is pleasing to the Lord if it were not possible to do. So we know we can discern this; it's just that we often simply do not do it. In order for us to discern what is pleasing to the Lord, we must seek after Him to know and understand His way and develop His perspective. I know this is so hard to do. That is why we must consciously make an effort each day to seek Him. Spend time each day in prayer. Spend time each day reading and memorizing His word. Spend time each day just sitting quietly, allowing God to speak to you. Seek to know God.

Get your armor on!

Who may ascend the mountain of the LORD? Who may stand in His holy place? The one who has clean hands and a pure heart, who has not set his mind on what is false, and who has not sworn deceitfully. He will receive blessing from the LORD, and righteousness from the God of his salvation. Such is the generation of those who seek Him, who seek the face of the God of Jacob. (Psalm 24:3-6 NIV)

This is what really separates a true disciple from a believer in Christ. A true disciple is one who actively, purposefully, and intentionally seeks to know who God is. A true disciple is one who has clean hands and a pure heart. In other words, a true disciple is unsoiled from the world. No dirt under the fingernails. A true disciple is one who has nothing but the best of intentions for others. What are the benefits of seeking God? You will receive blessing from the Lord and righteousness from God.

Get your armor on!

SEEK TO KNOW GOD

But the one who boasts should boast in this, that he understands and knows Me — that I am the LORD, showing faithful love, justice, and righteousness on the earth, for I delight in these things. (Jeremiah 9:24 NIV)

I am sure you have friends who have bragged about their material possessions or outlandish vacations. Or those who love to show off what their daddy just bought them. You may even be guilty of the same. I know I am! But God tells us if we are to boast, boast in the fact that we know and understand Him! He would not have said it if it were not possible to do. So do not let anyone tell you that you cannot possibly know and understand God. You can! When you seek to know Him, then you really have something about which to boast.

Get your armor on!

Search for the LORD and for His strength; seek His face always. (Psalm 105:4 NIV)

Self-explanatory. No commentary required. Do you not love it when God's word is so simply stated, leaving no room for debate!

Get your armor on!

SEEK TO KNOW GOD

I have not departed from the commands of His lips; I have treasured the words of His mouth more than my daily food. (Job 23:12 NIV)

Job was in the midst of experiencing the worst a man could experience. Everything was taken from him except his life: his family, his job, his wealth, his friends, and his heath. Even through all of this loss, there is one thing he refused to do - give up on God. Job continued to yearn for God's word, even more than daily food. For he knew only God's word would be able to sustain him during his most troubling times. Take a lesson from Job. Long after God's word. Treasure it more than daily food!

Get your armor on!

OBEY THE SPIRIT PROMPTLY

Then I heard the voice of the Lord saying: Who should I send? Who will go for Us? I said: Here I am. Send me. (Isaiah 6:8 NIV)

If we only had more people like the prophet Isaiah. The Lord is still calling out today: Who should I send? Who will go for Us? Unfortunately, not many Isaiahs exist anymore. Not many "disciples" are raising their hand, "Here I am. Send me." A true disciple looks for opportunities where the Lord is calling. A true disciple does not wait for someone else to do the Lord's work. A true disciple raises his hand and obeys the Spirit promptly. Will you respond with "Here I am. Send me"?

Get your armor on!

As He was walking along the Sea of Galilee, He saw two brothers, Simon, who was called Peter, and his brother Andrew. They were casting a net into the sea, since they were fishermen. "Follow Me," He told them, "and I will make you fish for people!" Immediately they left their nets and followed Him.(Matthew 4:18-20 NIV)

Focus on the last sentence in these verses. **Immediately**, they left their nets and followed Him. They did not ask: "Now what is it exactly you want me to do?" "Ok, but first tell me where you are going?" "Can I pray about that first?" "Will you give me a sign so I can know for sure you really want me to do this?" "Hold on there Jesus. You see, I have all these plans for my life right now. I have college, then I need to get a job, then I need to find a spouse, then I need to buy a home, then I need to have kids, then I need to build a career to provide for my family, then I need to plan for retirement, then... The "then's" never stop. Peter and Andrew and the other disciples did not come up with all these excuses. They **immediately** left their nets and followed Him. We would be wise to do the same. Obey the Spirit promptly.

Get your armor on!

OBEY THE SPIRIT PROMPTLY

Do not say to your neighbor, "Go away! Come back later. I'll give it tomorrow"—when it is there with you. (Proverbs 3:28 NIV)

Ok, I know you must be thinking, "What does this verse have to do with obeying the Spirit promptly?" I am glad you asked. Just as we are to treat our neighbors and pay our obligations, we must treat and pay God. When God presents an opportunity for you, do not dismiss it when you have the ability to do it right then. God never calls you to a task for which He has not already equipped you. Trust in Him to know He has already given you victory. Do not put it off until tomorrow. Obey the Spirit promptly.

Get your armor on!

The word of the LORD came to Jonah son of Amittai: "Get up! Go to the great city of Nineveh and preach against it, because their wickedness has confronted Me." However, Jonah got up to flee to Tarshish from the LORD's presence. He went down to Joppa and found a ship going to Tarshish. He paid the fare and went down into it to go with them to Tarshish, from the LORD's presence. (Jonah 1:1-3 NIV)

Here is a prime example of what happens when you do not obey the Spirit promptly. You know the story of Jonah, so we do not have to rehash it here. But why did Jonah run? He hated the people of Tarshish. He did not want them to experience God's mercy. He knew that if he went and preached against them, God's mercy would be showered upon them. God may call you to do something you do not like or do not want to do. That is not an excuse to not obey Him. Obey the Spirit promptly.

Get your armor on!

OBEY THE SPIRIT PROMPTLY

"Do whatever He tells you," His mother told the servants. **(John 2:5 NIV)**

This is taken from the story where Jesus performs His first miracle – turning the water into wine. Notice what Mary told the servants. Do whatever He tells you. This simple command demonstrates the amount of confidence she had in the Savior. True disciples have this same confidence. As I have said before, when God gives you a task, He has already given you the ability to accomplish it. Do not doubt yourself. Do whatever He tells you. Obey the Spirit promptly.

Get your armor on!

SPEAK THE WORD TRUTHFULLY

Let the message about the Messiah dwell richly among you, teaching and admonishing one another in all wisdom, and singing Psalm, hymns, and spiritual songs, with gratitude in your hearts to God. (Colossians 3:16 NIV)

Another title for this week's verses could be to Pursue the Word. Look what Paul is encouraging the Colossians to do – "Let the message about the Messiah dwell richly among you." Some translations say "Let the Word of God dwell in you richly..." I want you to focus on the word dwell. What does that mean? It means to reside, to stay, or to inhabit. When the Word stays with you, you can teach and encourage and support one another. The singing of Psalm, hymns, and spiritual songs convey the attitude of true fellowship with one another. And, speaking of attitude, you will have gratitude in your hearts to God for what He has done for you. See what happens when you pursue the Word. See what happens when you speak the Word truthfully.

Get your armor on!

You love evil instead of good, lying instead of speaking truthfully. You love any words that destroy, you treacherous tongue! This is why God will bring you down forever. He will take you, ripping you out of your tent; He will uproot you from the land of the living. (Psalm 52:3-5 NIV)

Ouch. This is some pretty severe action against an evil tongue. He will bring us down forever (which is a long time by the way). He will rip us out of our home or comfort zone. He will uproot us from the land of the living (in other words, we die). It shows just how serious God takes His word and our use of it. We are to speak truthfully or face similar punishment.

Get your armor on!

SPEAK THE WORD TRUTHFULLY

Be diligent to present yourself approved to God, a worker who does not need to be ashamed, correctly teaching the word of truth. (2 Timothy 2:15 NIV)

This is the main verse for AWANA – approved workman are not ashamed. If you are an AWANA, then, in my opinion, you are a disciple. If you are an approved workman, then your correctly teach the word of truth. If you correctly teach the word of truth, then you are a disciple. But you cannot teach what you do not know. Know God's word and you can correctly teach it. Correctly teach it and you can be an approved workman. Be an approved workman and become His disciple!

Get your armor on!

The prophet who has [only] a dream should recount the dream, but the one who has My word should speak My word truthfully, for what is straw [compared] to grain?" (Jeremiah 23:28 NIV)

Just like there is a difference between straw and grain, there is a difference between someone spouting nonsense about something and speaking His word truthfully. To be able to speak the Word truthfully, you must first know the Word. That is why having a defined scripture memory program is so vitally important to being a disciple. Buy an established program at a Christian bookstore or just start with your favorite book or chapter. Start somewhere, anywhere. Just start! Then, you can know His word and speak His word truthfully!

Get your armor on!

SPEAK THE WORD TRUTHFULLY

They questioned Him, "Teacher, we know that You speak and teach correctly, and You do not show partiality, but teach truthfully the way of God. (Luke 20:21 NIV)

The best compliment you can receive is one where people confess that you know, speak, and teach the way of God truthfully and without partiality. These people acknowledged this to Jesus because they saw Him live it out each day. You cannot teach what you do not live. Live correctly so you can speak and teach the word correctly.

Get your armor on!

PURSUE RIGHTEOUSNESS

Turn away from evil and do what is good; seek peace and pursue it. (Psalm 34:14 NIV)

What does it mean to pursue something? It means to follow, to chase, to hunt, to track, or to shadow. I like the phrase to shadow. Your shadow follows you around everywhere and conforms to you. It cannot do anything on its own. It only mimics what you do. We need to shadow Jesus Christ by turning from evil and doing what is good. We need to seek peace and chase after it. To pursue righteousness!

Get your armor on!

Blessed are those who hunger and thirst for righteousness, because they will be filled. (Matthew 5:6 NIV)

Note Jesus did not say they may be filled, or if they are lucky, they will be filled. Those who hunger and thirst for righteousness WILL be filled. But you have to want it, crave it, long for it, and hunger after it. Pursue righteousness and you WILL find it.

Get your armor on!

He made the One who did not know sin to be sin for us, so that we might become the righteousness of God in Him. (2 Corinthians 5:21 NIV)

I do not think we realize just what we have in our relationship with Christ. And I know we do not fully comprehend what He did to secure that relationship with us. He who knew no sin became sin for us. Why would He do that? We do that so we might become the righteousness in Him. We do that so we might be able to live moral, decent, and honest lives alongside Him. So because of what He has done for us, it is not too much to ask for us to pursue righteousness. Doing so means you are becoming a disciple.

Get your armor on!

PURSUE RIGHTEOUSNESS

The one who pursues righteousness and faithful love will find life, righteousness, and honor. (Proverbs 21:21 NIV)

You are what you pursue. Those who pursue righteousness will find love, life, and honor. Those who pursue wickedness will find hate, death, and disgrace. You do not have to ask me twice which I would rather have! Which will you pursue?

Get your armor on!

All the words of my mouth are righteous; none of them are deceptive or perverse. (Proverbs 8:8 NIV)

Wow. I wish I could say this describes me. Unfortunately, I cannot. However, that should not stop me from pursuing righteousness. The mark of a true disciple is one who knows his limitations and comprehends his humanity. He understands that he will never reach true righteousness until he stands face-to-face with Christ. Continue to pursue perfection until that day comes.

Get your armor on!

CHRISTIAN LIVING - THE DON'TS

And because they did not think it worthwhile to have God in their knowledge, God delivered them over to a worthless mind to do what is morally wrong. They are filled with all unrighteousness, evil, greed, and wickedness. They are full of envy, murder, disputes, deceit, and malice. They are gossips, slanderers, God-haters, arrogant, proud, boastful, inventors of evil, disobedient to parents, undiscerning, untrustworthy, unloving, and unmerciful. Although they know full well God's just sentence—that those who practice such things deserve to die —they not only do them, but even applaud others who practice them. (Romans 1:28-32 NIV)

Christian living is not always just about the things we cannot do. It is much more than that. We spent a week early on in our daily verses talking about those very things. However, the Bible clearly states actions and activities we should not be involved in as disciples of Christ. I want to take this week to discuss some of those things.

Today's society tolerates just about everything. There is no right or wrong. No morality. All actions are justified. And worse, some of these actions are even glorified and encouraged. But the Bible does point out there are actions that are evil and sinful. To be a true disciple, you will want to clear yourself from the activities listed here. Look back over the list carefully. Man, it is tough not to fall into temptation and commit one of these sins. But we must strive daily to remain faithful and committed to serving our Lord, even if it means going against the grain. Dare to be different! Dare to be a disciple!

Get your armor on!

And do not get drunk with wine, which [leads to] reckless actions, but be filled with the Spirit (Ephesians 5:18 NIV)

Many years ago, I prepared a lesson for my adult Bible Study class on this verse. During the preparation of that lesson, God laid on my heart this analogy. A slang word for alcohol is "spirits". You may have noticed advertisements on liquor stores that read "wine and spirits". You know, of course, when you received salvation in our Lord Jesus Christ, you received the Holy Spirit. So I will ask you what I asked the class that day, "With which spirit do you want to be filled?" For a disciple, the answer should be obvious!

Get your armor on!

Let us walk with decency, as in the daylight: not in carousing and drunkenness; not in sexual impurity and promiscuity; not in quarreling and jealousy. (Romans 13:13 NIV)

Ever walk through your apartment/dorm room in complete darkness and try not to run into things? It is a bit difficult. Going through life without Christ is very similar. You stumble around as if drunk; you have a tendency to knock things over; you may even find yourself in compromising situations that you never dreamed would happen. A true disciple walks with decency, as if walking in the daylight.

Get your armor on!

He will repay each one according to his works: eternal life to those who by patiently doing good seek for glory, honor, and immortality; but wrath and indignation to those who are self-seeking and disobey the truth, but are obeying unrighteousness; affliction and distress for every human being who does evil, first to the Jew, and also to the Greek; but glory, honor, and peace for everyone who does good, first to the Jew, and also to the Greek. (Romans 2:6-10 NIV)

If we truly believed this verse, I am sure most people would live differently. God will repay each of us according to our actions. This verse specifically points out those who are focused on self rather than the interest of others. Remember the words of Jesus, "For as much as you have done it unto the least of these, you have done it unto Me." True disciples keep their eyes off themselves and fixed on Jesus.

Get your armor on!

For there has already been enough time spent in doing the will of the pagans: carrying on in unrestrained behavior, evil desires, drunkenness, orgies, carousing, and lawless idolatry. (1 Peter 4:3 NIV)

Peter is encouraging his readers to no longer pursue human desires, but to do the will of the Father. He is basically saying, "Hey, enough of this useless and wasted energy following the desires of the world. Live to do the will of God." As we grow as a disciple, we should no longer desire to carry on in unrestrained behavior, acting as if our decisions have no consequences. We have spent enough time doing that. It is now time to grow up and become a dangerous disciple!

Get your armor on!

BE COMPLETE

Then David said to his son Solomon, "Be strong and courageous, and do the work. Do not be afraid or discouraged, for the LORD God, my God, is with you. He won't leave you or forsake you until all the work for the service of the LORD's house is finished. (1 Chronicles 28:20 NIV)

Do you ever get the feeling that the more you try to dig yourself out of a hole, the deeper into it you become? I know you have mid-terms this week and you feel buried under all the pressure and stress of school. In a bit different circumstances, Solomon felt the same way. He was about to take over as king in place of his father David. You can bet he felt a wealth of pressure. But look at how his father, David, encouraged him. Be strong and courageous. Do not be afraid or discouraged. Why? For the Lord God, MY GOD, is with you. He will not leave you until all the work for His service is completed. Claim this verse this week. Do not give up until the work is complete. For the Lord God, OUR GOD, is with you.

Get your armor on!

But endurance must do its complete work, so that you may be mature and complete, lacking nothing. (James 1:4 NIV)

James was telling the early churches to rejoice in times of trouble because adversity produces endurance. He then adds, endurance must do its complete work. The King James Version translates endurance as patience. I think patience is probably a better word. In other words, James is saying to be patient as you endure adversity. Because, if you are, you will become mature and complete, lacking nothing. Often times, we rush patience (an oxymoron). We do not wait long enough for the endurance to bring us to maturity and complete us. You want to "lack nothing"? You want to be mature? You want to be complete? Then you must wait for it. Do not rush patience. Be complete!

Get your armor on!

BE COMPLETE

"I have spoken these things to you so that My joy may be in you and your joy may be complete. (John 15:11 NIV)

The verse preceding this one tells us what things Jesus has spoken to us. Jesus tells us of His love for us and that if you keep His commands, we will remain in His love. And why is He telling us this? God so much wants us to feel the full joy He has planned for us. The only thing we need to do is keep His commands. Keep doing so we have complete, whole, and full joy. Is that so much to ask for such a return!!

Get your armor on!

But whoever keeps His word, truly in him the love of God is perfected. (1 John 2:5a NIV)

Today's verse fits well with yesterday's verse. Yesterday, we read where we keep His commands so that we may have complete joy. Here the Apostle John tells us by keeping His word, His love is perfected in us. Perfected can be translated as completed or to reached maturity. So how can we be complete? Keep His commands and keep His word. If I have said it once, I have said it a million times. You cannot keep what you do not know. Know His word; keep His word. Then you will be a complete disciple.

Get your armor on!

BE COMPLETE

I am sure of this, that He who started a good work in you will carry it on to completion until the day of Christ Jesus. (Philippians 1:6 NIV)

Have you seen those t-shirts that read, "Be patient with me, God isn't finished with me yet!" I bet the Apostle Paul had one of those shirts!! Do not lose hope when you feel frustrated, when you fall into temptation, or when you feel like the walls are caving in on you. God started something special in you from the day you were conceived. And you can bet He will carry it on to completion until the day of Christ Jesus. Let God complete His work in you!

Get your armor on!

FINISH WHAT YOU STARTED

Just one thing: live your life in a manner worthy of the gospel of Christ. Then, whether I come and see you or am absent, I will hear about you that you are standing firm in one spirit, with one mind, working side by side for the faith of the gospel,(Philippians 1:27 NIV)

Paul started this church in Philippi. He had seen them come to know Christ. He had seen them mature in their relationship with Christ. Now he was encouraging them to continue the journey; to live a life worthy of the gospel. Their continuing to do what they were taught to do would become known to Paul, whether or not he was physically there. What you do for Christ will be made known to people who are not even around you. See that you continue to live the way you were taught. See that you stand firm in one spirit, with one mind, working side by side for the faith of the gospel. See that you finish what you started.

Get your armor on!

But as for you, continue in what you have learned and firmly believed, knowing those from whom you learned, and that from childhood you have known the sacred Scriptures, which are able to instruct you for salvation through faith in Christ Jesus.(2 Timothy 3:14-15 NIV)

Paul sent this encouragement to Timothy. He was Timothy's mentor. Paul invested over 14 years of his life with Timothy. He knew Timothy probably better than Timothy knew himself. Take the advice of Paul. Continue in what you have learned. I have seen you grow and mature into the Christian young woman/man you are. From your childhood, you have known the sacred Scriptures. Finish what you have started.

Get your armor on!

FINISH WHAT YOU STARTED

Now I am giving an opinion on this because it is profitable for you, who a year ago began not only to do something but also to desire it. But now finish the task as well, that just as there was eagerness to desire it, so there may also be a completion from what you have. For if the eagerness is there, it is acceptable according to what one has, not according to what he does not have. (2 Corinthians 8:10-12 NIV)

Life is full of good intentions. We intend to get up early to study. We intend to read our Bible daily. We intend to live the example we ought to live. Good intentions and the desire to do good things are not good enough. We need to follow through with them. You may have started on the right foot but get distracted and stop. Follow through on those good intentions. You have begun to desire it; a true disciple will finish the task.

Get your armor on!

But I count my life of no value to myself, so that I may finish my course and the ministry I received from the Lord Jesus, to testify to the gospel of God's grace. (Acts 20:24 NIV)

I cannot wait to meet the Apostle Paul face-to-face. Just reading about his testimony makes me more in awe of his passion and desire for the gospel of Christ. He considered his life of no value so that he might finish the course – his ministry for the gospel. I know of no other Christian alive today with such focus and fervor. Strive to be like Paul. Strive to finish the course. Strive to finish what He has started in you!

Get your armor on!

FINISH WHAT YOU STARTED

And tell Archippus, "Pay attention to the ministry you have received in the Lord, so that you can accomplish it." (Colossians 4:17 NIV)

We do not know much about Archippus other than he was a fellow soldier for the gospel. What we do know is that the Lord gave him a specific task to do. Paul is encouraging him to finish the work he has received in the Lord. When the Lord gives you a task to do, He expects you to complete it. And you can be assured He has given you the ability to accomplish it. A true disciple does the same. Finish what you have started.

Get your armor on!

DEVELOP DISCERNMENT

A gentle answer turns away anger, but a harsh word stirs up wrath. (Proverbs 15:1 NIV)

The Lord gave us two ears and one mouth on purpose. We should always listen twice as much as we speak. I know it is hard to keep your mouth shut at times. Our nature is to respond immediately, especially when we feel attacked or are put on the defense. Next time you are faced with a situation like that, keep this verse in mind. A true disciple knows when to speak and when to listen. Develop discernment so you can turn away anger.

Get your armor on!

Carefully consider the path for your feet, and all your ways will be established. Do not turn to the right or to the left; keep your feet away from evil. (Proverbs 4:26-27 NIV)

College especially offers many opportunities to do fun things, to go to fun places, to meet fun people. But not all things, places, and people are always fun. You can easily find yourself in compromising situations. I am not suggesting you abandon "spur of the moment" decisions to join in on the fun. But I am suggesting you stop and carefully consider the path of your feet. Is this the right thing to do? What might happen if I do this or that? Do not turn to the right or to the left in compromise. Keep your eyes on the prize and your feet firmly rooted in the Word. Develop discernment!

Get your armor on!

DEVELOP DISCERNMENT

Guard your heart above all else, for it is the source of life. (Proverbs 4:23 NIV)

In ancient times, the heart was considered the center of one's being. It was more than a vital organ; it made up the entire person and was the source of life. We are to guard it above all else. A distinguishing characteristic of a disciple is one who has developed the talent to discern, not just right from wrong, but selecting from the better of two rights.

Get your armor on!

The highway of the upright avoids evil; the one who guards his way protects his life. (Proverbs 16:17 NIV)

Solomon's use of the highway analogy is a pretty good one. Consider your life as a highway consisting of numerous exits. Billboards are posted along the way offering a variety of opportunities that may take you off course. EXIT NOW! NEXT EXIT! TURN BACK, YOU MISSED US! A true disciple will develop discernment to consider which exits are the proper ones to take and which ones to pass on by.

Get your armor on!

Do not be conquered by evil, but conquer evil with good. (Romans 12:21 NIV)

What profound meaning in just a few simple words. Some translations will replace "conquered" with "overcome". Other synonyms include "get the better of" or "defeat". Do not let evil bring you down. Go back to the very first verse of this week's topic – "A gentle answer turns away anger." How do we overcome evil? Kill them with kindness!!! A true disciple will develop discernment to know when to kill them with kindness!

Get your armor on!

DEVELOP DISCIPLINE

Do not despise the LORD's instruction, my son, and do not loathe His discipline; for the LORD disciplines the one He loves, just as a father, the son he delights in. (Proverbs 3:11-12 NIV)

Have you ever heard your mom or me say, "This is going to hurt me more than it will hurt you"? I am pretty sure I have said it and I know for certain my parents said it to me. At the time, I did not believe them, because it really hurt!!! But discipline has its benefits. Look back at the verse. The LORD disciplines those He loves. Huh? I can testify that I certainly did not feel love when your Papa's belt hit my behind!! But your Papa was only doing this to teach me something. And it was a sign that he cared for me and loved me enough to teach me right from wrong. Loving discipline is missing in our society today. When you feel the pain of God's discipline, do not despise it; do not loathe it; but accept it as His love for you, the child He delights in.

Get your armor on!

So, because you are lukewarm, and neither hot nor cold, I am going to vomit you out of My mouth. (Revelation 3:16 NIV)

Ever been extremely hot and thirsty? You find a water fountain; bend down for a drink; anticipate a nice, cold, refreshing drink to flow into your veins. You take a giant gulp and SSSSPPPPEEEEWWWWWW!! Yuck. Warm water. Not refreshing at all. That is exactly how God treats those who are neither hot nor cold for Him. He would prefer to spew us out of His mouth, just like a gulp of warm water on a hot day. There is no fence riding with God. You are either for Him or against Him. A true disciple will develop discipline and avoid being lukewarm.

Get your armor on!

DEVELOP DISCIPLINE

"You must carefully follow every command I am giving you today, so that you may live and increase, and may enter and take possession of the land the LORD swore to your fathers. Remember that the LORD your God led you on the entire journey these 40 years in the wilderness, so that He might humble you and test you to know what was in your heart, whether or not you would keep His commands. He humbled you by letting you go hungry; then He gave you manna to eat, which you and your fathers had not known, so that you might learn that man does not live on bread alone but on every word that comes from the mouth of the LORD. Your clothing did not wear out, and your feet did not swell these 40 years. Keep in mind that the LORD your God has been disciplining you just as a man disciplines his son. (Deuteronomy 8:1-5 NIV)

OK, I know today's verse is pretty long. So take a moment to read back through it. The children of Israel wandered 40 years through the desert before they reached the Promised Land. They did so because they were not willing to trust God to deliver the land to them. Because of their lack of faith, God disciplined them – for 40 years!!! During that time, God fed them, clothed them, and kept them healthy. He brought them through the discipline so that they could experience the joy of the Promised Land. God will bring you through His discipline just the same. A true disciple will see through the discipline and experience the joy of God's blessed Promised Land!

Get your armor on!

DEVELOP DISCIPLINE

See how happy the man is God corrects; so do not reject the discipline of the Almighty. (Job 5:17 NIV)

I know during the strong arm of discipline, it is not very enjoyable. But trust me; after the discipline is over, you will be much better off. Remember, God's discipline comes in many forms and shapes. And it is a way for God to show just how much He cares for you. Go back to the first verse in this week's topics. God disciplines those He loves. God loves you; do not reject His discipline.

Get your armor on!

for the Lord disciplines the one He loves, and punishes every son whom He receives. Endure it as discipline: God is dealing with you as sons. For what son is there whom a father does not discipline? But if you are without discipline—which all receive —then you are illegitimate children and not sons. (Hebrews 12:6-8 NIV)

We have been focusing on the Lord's discipline all week, but have not spent much time on just what discipline is. Discipline is instruction designed to train in proper conduct or action. It is to train by instruction and exercise to bring about order and obedience. The Lord is trying to train us to obey His commands and act in accordance to His will. Without His discipline, we are like illegitimate children. No order; no obedience. You want order in your life? You want to be treated with respect? You want to be called a child of God? Develop discipline!

Get your armor on!

PUT OTHERS FIRST

Now we who are strong have an obligation to bear the weaknesses of those without strength, and not to please ourselves. Each one of us must please his neighbor for his good, in order to build him up. (Romans 15:1-2 NIV)

I can tell this is going to be a tough topic this week. Why? I do not do this very well. Your mom, on the other hand, has this one down pat! Paul is writing to established Christians, those strong in their walk with the Lord. It is we who are to bear the weaknesses of those who are new in Christ. That does not mean we are to tolerate their sin, but we are to be patient with them as they learn to walk with Christ. They may still hold on to certain sinful habits. Do not condemn them, but lovingly rebuke them and show them how to live the Christian lifestyle. We are to be attentive to their needs until they can stand on their own. We are to build them up so they, in turn, can do the same for someone else.

Get your armor on!

Do nothing out of rivalry or conceit, but in humility consider others as more important than yourselves. Everyone should look out not [only] for his own interests, but also for the interests of others. (Philippians 2:3-4 NIV)

Again, this is one tough charge! This is so hard to do. Do not misinterpret the meaning here. We are not to forsake our well-being for the well-being of others. But we should be intently aware of the interests of others. All too often, we are so focused on ourselves, that we completely miss opportunities to be a blessing to others – whether by meeting their physical needs, saying an encouraging word, or providing a compliment. Do not consider yourself too important that you cannot stop and serve others.

Get your armor on!

PUT OTHERS FIRST

For by the grace given to me, I tell everyone among you not to think of himself more highly than he should think. Instead, think sensibly, as God has distributed a measure of faith to each one. (Romans 12:3 NIV)

Wow, this one hits below the belt. Paul tells us not to think more highly of ourselves than we ought to, but to think sensibly. I am sure you have met people and all they do is talk about them. They have done this; they have done that; they were the best at this; they were the best at that. Gag! Enough already!! God's Word says enough of that, start thinking sensibly, prudently, wisely, logically. When disciples do that, we show our maturity in Christ.

Get your armor on!

No one should seek his own [good], but [the good] of the other person. (1 Corinthians 10:24 NIV)

Here is another verse that many take totally out of context. Paul is not telling us we should neglect our well-being to take care of others. Or if we enjoy in the pleasures God has blessed us with that we are going to hell. That is not it at all. The point is that we should not be so caught up in ourselves that we forget about others. God may have abundantly blessed you. So instead of accumulating things, why not, out of that abundance, bless someone else by meeting their needs. That is what a true disciple does! Now go and do the same.

Get your armor on!

PUT OTHERS FIRST

For I have no one else like-minded who will genuinely care about your interests; all seek their own interests, not those of Jesus Christ. (Philippians 2:20-21 NIV)

What a compliment! Paul is referring to Timothy. He tells the church at Philippi that Timothy is the only one who genuinely cares about others. Too many are self-seeking, looking only after their own interests, not that of Jesus Christ. Timothy, on the other hand, was truly interested in meeting other's needs. You may ask, "How does Paul know that?" Remember, Paul spent over 14 years mentoring Timothy. He knew Timothy. It had to be obvious through his actions that Timothy genuinely cared for others. I pray that you may receive similar compliments and that others will see that you genuinely care for them.

Get your armor on!

RESPECT OTHERS

just as I also try to please all people in all things, not seeking my own profit, but the profit of many, that they may be saved (1 Corinthians 10:33 NIV)

Here is a distinguishing characteristic of a true disciple. What is your motive behind doing something good? Paul was not doing these things so that he would receive the accolades. He was doing good things for the benefit of others. He did not limit what he was doing to a select group of friends or to a particular neighborhood, ethnicity, or people group. He treated all people, regardless of race, color, religion, or creed, with the same respect and for the same reasons – so that they may see Jesus through him. I pray others see Jesus in you.

Get your armor on!

Pursue peace with everyone, and holiness—without it no one will see the Lord. See to it that no one falls short of the grace of God and that no root of bitterness springs up, causing trouble and by it, defiling many. (Hebrews 12:14-15 NIV)

It is hard to be on good terms with everyone. Some people just flat out rub me the wrong way. Regardless of the way I feel towards another, I should always seek peace with them and treat them with respect. Otherwise, no one will see the Lord in me! In addition, it will only cause trouble and allow a root of bitterness to grow. Through some Roundup® weed killer on that root of bitterness! Respect others!

Get your armor on!

RESPECT OTHERS

Salt is good, but if the salt should lose its flavor, how can you make it salty? Have salt among yourselves and be at peace with one another." (Mark 9:50 NIV)

Salt adds flavor to most any food. But if the salt has lost its flavor, how can it spice up the food? Let's not take this verse too literally and start throwing salt on everyone. But in that sense, do not lose your flavor and thus pass up the chance the spice up someone's day. Say hello; give that complement; hold the door for someone. Sprinkle the salt! Respect others.

Get your armor on!

If possible, on your part, live at peace with everyone. (Romans 12:18 NIV)

If you jump directly to the last phrase, I bet you are thinking, 'Yeah right! That's impossible!" Well, you are right. Some people just do not make it easy for you to live in peace with them!! But look again at middle phrase – on your part. You cannot control other people's reaction or attitude. But you can control yours. Do not let someone else's action control your reaction. If possible, on your part, live at peace with everyone.

Get your armor on!

So then, we must pursue what promotes peace and what builds up one another. (Romans 14:19 NIV)

You know, if we put into practice what we focused on last week (put others first) and this week (respect others), just think of how much better our world would be. So then, why do not we do this? I do not know. So, starting today, let's pursue what promotes peace and what builds up one another. Do not be quick to criticize. Do not be quick to judge. Do not be quick to read ulterior motives into things. Pursue what promotes peace. Pursue what builds up one another. Respect others and they will respect you.

Get your armor on!

LOVE IN ACTION

But be doers of the word and not hearers only, deceiving yourselves. (James 1:22 NIV)

This verse can really apply to most any action. It is one thing to say it and a completely different thing to actually do it. I'll give you a page out of my college minister's book on love. You open it up and it reads like this, "Do it!" The end. You want to learn how to put love into action. Do it! Quit talking about it and starting doing it.

Get your armor on!

For I was hungry and you gave Me something to eat; I was thirsty and you gave Me something to drink; I was a stranger and you took Me in; I was naked and you clothed Me; I was sick and you took care of Me; I was in prison and you visited Me. "Then the righteous will answer Him, 'Lord, when did we see You hungry and feed You, or thirsty and give You something to drink? When did we see You a stranger and take You in, or without clothes and clothe You? When did we see You sick, or in prison, and visit You?' "And the King will answer them, 'I assure you: Whatever you did for one of the least of these brothers of Mine, you did for Me. (Matthew 25:34-40 NIV)

Yesterday, you were challenged to put love into action by actually loving others. So how do you do that? Take some advice from Jesus Himself. When we have loved on the least of God's children, it is the same as if we have loved on God. Show love to those who are unlovable. Show love to those who are stand-offish. Show love to those who may dress, talk, or act different from you.

Get your armor on!

LOVE IN ACTION

If I speak the languages of men and of angels, but do not have love, I am a sounding gong or a clanging cymbal. If I have [the gift of] prophecy, and understand all mysteries and all knowledge, and if I have all faith, so that I can move mountains, but do not have love, I am nothing. And if I donate all my goods to feed the poor, and if I give my body to be burned, but do not have love, I gain nothing. Love is patient; love is kind. Love does not envy; is not boastful; is not conceited; does not act improperly; is not selfish; is not provoked; does not keep a record of wrongs; finds no joy in unrighteousness, but rejoices in the truth; bears all things, believes all things, hopes all things, endures all things. (1 Corinthians 13:1-7 NIV)

You want to know what love looks like? Read these verses again. You can acquire all the wealth in the world; you can possess all the faith in the world; you can have the most talent in all the land; you can help little old ladies cross the street. But without love, it is all worthless. It is just a bunch of senseless noise. I doubt you will be able to emulate all of these love characteristics, but you can certainly select one and improve upon it. So, go ahead, what are you waiting on? Pick one and start loving today!

Get your armor on!

LOVE IN ACTION

This is how we have come to know love: He laid down His life for us. We should also lay down our lives for our brothers. (1 John 3:16 NIV)

Do you really think the Apostle John meant for us to die for one another? I do not think so. This goes back a few weeks ago when we were discussing putting others first. We do so not to the neglect of ourselves, but so that we do not focus too much on "me" and forget about others. Jesus showed perfect love – He died in our place. Mere man cannot do that. But we can, in a way, die to ourselves and our wants/needs in order to meet the needs of others. Just as Jesus' love was one of action and initiative, do not wait for someone else to show you love before you love them in return. You take the first step!

Get your armor on!

No one has ever seen God; but if we love one another, God lives in us and his love is made complete in us. (1 John 4:12 NIV)

Love should be the motivating factor behind any action. Whatever we do, whether talking, thinking, or actually doing, we should do so motivated by love for others. Do not be fake. People can see right through you. True, no one has ever physically seen God. But when you put love into action, others will see Christ in you. Show Christ to others. Put love into action.

Get your armor on!

LOVE OTHERS

"You have heard that it was said, Love your neighbor and hate your enemy. But I tell you, love your enemies and pray for those who persecute you, so that you may be sons of your Father in heaven. For He causes His sun to rise on the evil and the good, and sends rain on the righteous and the unrighteous. For if you love those who love you, what reward will you have? Do not even the tax collectors do the same? And if you greet only your brothers, what are you doing out of the ordinary? Do not even the Gentiles do the same? (Matthew 5:43-47 NIV)

I know you have heard this before, but it never gets old. It is easy to love those who are lovable. But Jesus said if you do that, what reward will you have? Do the unbelievers not do the same? How are you differentiating yourself from them if you just do what they do? Oh, but by loving your enemies or those who are not so lovable, then we stand out in the crowd. Then others will take notice. Then we will be children of our Heavenly Father.

Get your armor on!

"I give you a new commandment: love one another. Just as I have loved you, you must also love one another. (John 13:34 NIV)

The 11th Commandment. This one does not leave much room for misinterpretation or misunderstanding. Since Jesus loved us, we also ought to love one another. No qualifiers. No ifs. No buts. Simply, love one another.

Get your armor on!

LOVE OTHERS

The one who does not love does not know God, because God is love. (1 John 4:8 NIV)

Dear friends, if God loved us in this way, we also must love one another. No one has ever seen God. If we love one another, God remains in us and His love is perfected in us. (1 John 4:11-12 NIV)

Here is how we can tell who is a disciple of God and who is not. If we do not love, we do not know God. And we are not talking about surface love. Casual love only goes so far and then fades away. No, we are talking about deep, compassionate, loving type love that transcends all boundaries and has no end. By ourselves, we cannot show this type of love. That is why I love the last phrase of v12. If we start showing love, God will start loving through us and His love will be made perfect in us so that we WILL be able to love others deeply. Break through the surface. Love others!

Get your armor on!

Little children, we must not love in word or speech, but in action and truth; (1 John 3:18 NIV)

We spoke about surface love yesterday. The Apostle John is referencing that type of love here. Love that only goes as far as a word and an ear, but stops just short of actually doing something. You want to love others – SHOW IT! People do not care how much you know until they know how much you care! Start loving others.

Get your armor on!

LOVE OTHERS

For the entire law is fulfilled in one statement: You shall love your neighbor as yourself. (Galatians 5:14 NIV)

The Golden Rule. It is arguably the most essential basis for a disciple of Christ. A key element of the Golden Rule is that a person attempting to live by this rule treats all people with consideration, not just members of his or her group. Before you use the excuse that "so-and-so is not my neighbor", think again. Jesus explained who our neighbor was in the parable of the Good Samaritan. Our neighbor is basically everyone. So let's start fulfilling the entire law – Love Others.

Get your armor on!

STAND FIRM

Therefore as you have received Christ Jesus the Lord, walk in Him, rooted and built up in Him and strengthened in the faith, just as you were taught, and overflowing with thankfulness. (Colossians 2:6-7 NIV)

We have focused this entire semester on being a disciple of Christ. I hope and trust our verses have made an impact and changed your perspective. Now that we know what to do, we must do it, being rooted and built up in Him, strengthened in the faith, just as you were taught, and overflowing with thankfulness. Stand firm Sissy Girl / Bubba!

Get your armor on!

But now He has reconciled you by His physical body through His death, to present you holy, faultless, and blameless before Him — if indeed you remain grounded and steadfast in the faith, and are not shifted away from the hope of the gospel that you heard. (Colossians 1:22-23 NIV)

Picture yourself standing on the beach, waiting for the waves to roll in. Wiggling your toes in the sand, the water crashes against the shore, reaching higher than your ankles. Then, as soon as the water came, it recedes back into the ocean. As it does, the sand moves under your feet. Not very stable ground is it? Being a disciple of Christ, the ground you stand on is firm. Water may come and go, but the ground remains solid. It is not shifted away like sand at the beach. Remain grounded and steadfast in the faith. Stand Firm!

Get your armor on!

STAND FIRM

Therefore, brothers, stand firm and hold to the traditions you were taught, either by our message or by our letter. (2 Thessalonians 2:15 NIV)

Your mother and I have tried to raise you and your brother/sister with an understanding and love for our Lord Savior Jesus Christ. Others around you, either at AWANA, in your Bible Study classes, or through the numerous sermons from the pastor, may have picked up where we might have failed. So either by our words or actions, or the words and actions of others, you were taught what it meant to be a disciple of Christ. So hold firm to those traditions as you were taught. Stand Firm.

Get your armor on!

If you do not stand firm in your faith, then you will not stand at all. (Isaiah 7:9b NIV)

While standing on one leg, try to move around a bit; bend over; put your socks on; tie your shoes. It is hard to do without losing your balance. That is what it is like going through life without faith in Christ. You may be able to stand there for a while, but eventually, you will lose your balance. The prophet Isaiah tells us to stand firm on our faith. Otherwise, we will not be able to stand at all. Stand Firm, Sissy Girl/Bubba Boy!

Get your armor on!

STAND FIRM

And I pray that you, being rooted and established in love, may have power, together with all the Lord's holy people, to grasp how wide and long and high and deep is the love of Christ, and to know this love that surpasses knowledge—that you may be filled to the measure of all the fullness of God. (Ephesians 3:17b-19 NIV)

Today, I want you to take a field trip. Walk around campus and find the largest tree you can find. Then just sit at its base, staring at its thick trunk, glancing up at its broad branches. Think about the power of that tree. Think how deep in the ground its roots must reach. It is practically an immovable object. When we are immersed in God's love, Paul tells us we have power. His love is like those far reaching roots dug deep in the ground. It holds us firm when the winds of life crash against us. That is what keeps us on firm ground, stable, practically immovable. Stay rooted and established in His love. Then, as His disciple, you will be able to stand firm.

Get your armor on!

THE CHURCH

The stone that the builders rejected has become the cornerstone. (Psalm 118:22 NIV)

I wanted to start this semester by covering a very important topic – the Church. Satan has made every attempt to water down church and make it unnecessary, old fashioned, and a thing of the past. I must admit he has done a pretty good job. However, as long as the Spirit of God remains in the hearts of men and women, he is fighting a losing battle! Can I get an AMEN!

So what is the church exactly? Where does it get its origin? What is the foundation of the church? What is the purpose of church? Why should I attend church? We will explore the answers to these questions in the coming weeks.

First and foremost, the church has at its foundation Jesus Christ. In ancient building, the cornerstone, also called the capstone, was the largest stone placed at the corners of each building. If that stone was not large enough or strong enough, the entire building would fall. All other stones had to be properly aligned with the cornerstone or the building would fall. A good litmus test for you whenever you are looking for a church home – Who or what is their cornerstone? If the church does not speak of Jesus Christ, then go somewhere else. Jesus is the cornerstone; He is the capstone. Without Him, the church will fall.

Get your armor on!

THE CHURCH

And I also say to you that you are Peter, and on this rock I will build My church, and the forces of Hades will not overpower it. (Matthew 16:18 NIV)

Yesterday, we read where Jesus was the foundation of the church. So what is Jesus saying here to Peter? Is Peter the foundation of the church? Is Jesus contradicting Himself? Of course not! In the verses directly preceding this one, Peter makes the declaration that Jesus is "the Messiah, the Son of the Living God." It is on this foundation that the church is built. As long as the church declares Jesus as "the Messiah, the Son of the Living God", the church will live and no power can overcome it! But when we stop making this declaration, we are doomed to failure. So make sure your worship includes this declaration – "Jesus, you are the Messiah, the Son of the Living God!"

Get your armor on!

And He put everything under His feet and appointed Him as head over everything for the church, which is His body, the fullness of the One who fills all things in every way. (Ephesians 1:22-23 NIV)

So just who put Jesus at the crowned head of the church? God did! God placed everything under His feet and appointed Him head over everything for the church. All activities, all Bible studies, all worship within the church should be done with the intent to promote Christ. If a church has all of this, but misses out on the opportunity to share Christ with others, then all is worthless. The church has lost its way. Make sure any activity within the church is done so with the intent to share the good news of Jesus Christ. Why? It is because He has been appointed to the exalted position as head over everything for the church.

Get your armor on!

THE CHURCH

He is also the head of the body, the church; He is the beginning, the firstborn from the dead, so that He might come to have first place in everything. (Colossians 1:18 NIV)

Jesus is not only the foundation of the church; He is also the head of the church. You can look at this in two ways. Jesus is in charge of the church. He is the control center, just like the head is to a human body. Your brain tells the rest of the body what to do. Jesus is the brain of the church. Secondly, you can look at Jesus being the head as in the crown jewel of the church. You hear all about the paparazzi's fuss over the royal couple Prince William and Kate. Why? It is because of their royalty. Jesus should be the fuss of the church because of His royalty. He is the head; He is the crown jewel of the church.

Get your armor on!

Husbands, love your wives, just as also Christ loved the church and gave Himself for her, to make her holy, cleansing her in the washing of water by the word. He did this to present the church to Himself in splendor, without spot or wrinkle or any such thing, but holy and blameless. (Ephesians 5:25-27 NIV)

Jesus is the cornerstone of the church; He is the foundation of the church; He is the head; He is the crown of worship. These are all attributes of what Jesus is to the church. But what is the church to Jesus? The same as a bride is to the husband. Christ so loved the church that He gave Himself for her. And why did He do this? He did so to make her holy; to present her to Himself in splendor, without spot or wrinkle, but holy and blameless. Wow! Now that is love!

If Christ so loved the church as to give Himself for her, then what should our response be to the church? Rhetorical question – you know the answer!

Get your armor on!

THE CHURCH

For as the body is one and has many parts, and all the parts of that body, though many, are one body— so also is Christ. (1 Corinthians 12:12 NIV)

Let's continue this week with our discussion of the Church, shall we? And let's make a distinction between the universal church and the local church. When I say universal church, I do not mean one church for the entire population. I mean, collectively, all believers make up the church. It is not intended to be one common denomination for all believers. The local church is local body of believers within your community. Members of God's universal church should seek membership and fellowship in a local church.

So the universal church is the one body mentioned in this verse. The many parts are the local churches spread all over the world. However, remember the litmus tests for the church that we discussed last week: they must promote and worship Jesus Christ as God revealed in man, the Savior of the World.

Get your armor on!

Now you are the body of Christ, and individual members of it. (1 Corinthians 12:27 NIV)

So just who or what is the church? Simply put, you are! We call an erected building a church. We go to that building to worship and conduct Bible studies. We say Christ "dwells" within the sanctuary. But really, those four walls of the church building in no way can contain the power that is Jesus Christ. We are the church! Our bodies hold within us the power of the Spirit. See Ephesians 2:22.

I remember a few years ago teaching a group of 8th grade boys. We were talking about the church. I told them about a little chant – "Don't go to church; Be the Church!" I know it is a bit corny, but very applicable. So I challenge you the same as I did those 8th grade boys – do not go to church; Be the Church!

Get your armor on!

for the training of the saints in the work of ministry, to build up the body of Christ (Ephesians 4:12 NIV)

This verse provides the purpose of church. So we can be trained in the work of the ministry; to build up the body of Christ. Remember in high school, at swim meets / tennis matches, you had team members cheering you on. You cheered for your team mates. Why? Your cheering showed your support for them. Your cheering attempted to give them that extra boost of encouragement to push just a little harder. Did it make you or them swim faster / play better? Perhaps. But you can be rest assured, it made them feel a part of a team. That is what church is all about. To make you feel a part of the team; that you are not alone in this world attempting to make a difference all by yourself. Get involved in a local team! You will be glad you did.

Get your armor on!

So the church throughout all Judea, Galilee, and Samaria had peace, being built up and walking in the fear of the Lord and in the encouragement of the Holy Spirit, and it increased in numbers. (Acts 9:31 NIV)

See what happens when a team sticks together? Yesterday's focus was being a member of a local team. This verse tells us what happens when that team sticks together. They had peace, were being built up in fear (reverence) of the Lord, and encouraged by the Holy Spirit. But the important part is they increased in number. When the church, that is you and me, begins to show itself to the rest of the world, others begin to take note and want what we have. The end result – we grow in numbers. The journey is not about what you take to heaven, but who you take with you!

Get your armor on!

THE CHURCH

Saul agreed with putting him to death. On that day a severe persecution broke out against the church in Jerusalem, and all except the apostles were scattered throughout the land of Judea and Samaria. (Acts 8:1 NIV)

There is one thing to note about the church. Satan has been trying to destroy it from the very first day of existence. This verse is a harsh reminder that we Christians must never give up. The pastor may leave; the various ministers may leave; a group within the church may disagree with a decision made. Attacks can come from any one, in any direction, about anything. We must expect them and be prepared when they come. Pastor Mike tells us deacons that we carry 2 buckets with us at all times, one filled with water, the other with gasoline. When we hear of something negative and destroying the body, put it out with water. When we hear of some great and mighty workings of our Lord, throw gasoline on it to make it spread! So pick up your buckets and allow God's discernment to guide you on which to use when!

Get your armor on!

WHY DO CHURCH?

He came to Nazareth, where He had been brought up. As usual, He entered the synagogue on the Sabbath day and stood up to read. (Luke 4:16 NIV)

The "He" here is Jesus. The key phrase here is "As usual..." As usual, Jesus attended church. If the Son of Man felt it necessary to attend church, why should it be any different for us? In the famous words of Forrest Gump, "That's all I got to say about that!

Get your armor on!

Pure and undefiled religion before our God and Father is this: to look after orphans and widows in their distress and to keep oneself unstained by the world. (James 1:27 NIV)

The church is to be about the business of ministering to those in need. This includes not only sharing the gospel, but also providing for physical needs (food, clothing, shelter) as necessary and appropriate. Hence, "look after the orphans and widows." The church is also to equip believers in Christ with the tools we need to overcome sin and remain free from the pollution of the world. This is done by biblical teaching and Christian fellowship. Hence, "keep oneself unstained by the world." So be about the business of the church. Minister to others and equip yourself to remain free from sin's pollution. Do church!

Get your armor on!

WHY DO CHURCH?

And let us be concerned about one another in order to promote love and good works, not staying away from our meetings, as some habitually do, but encouraging each other, and all the more as you see the day drawing near. (Hebrews 10:24-25 NIV)

On the same theme as yesterday, we "do" church in order to meet the needs of the body. Here, we see another reason to "do" church – to promote love and good works and encourage one another. We cannot do this if we stay away from our meetings, as some do. That is why regular church attendance is so vitally important. Promote love and good works. Encourage one another. Do church!

Get your armor on!

But encourage each other daily, while it is still called today, so that none of you is hardened by sin's deception. (Hebrews 3:13 NIV)

Ever had anyone do you wrong? You get mad, upset, ticked off. The more time that passes, the more ticked you become and the more difficult it becomes to reconcile with that person. You become "hardened by sin's deception." Regular church attendance will not allow that sin to harden. The conviction of the Word will soften you, or it should! So be encouraged. Get softened. Attend church regularly.

Get your armor on!

Now, my brothers, I myself am convinced about you that you also are full of goodness, filled with all knowledge, and able to instruct one another. (Romans 15:14 NIV)

Paul is convinced the Roman Christians are able to instruct one another. He had taught them the gospel. They were full of goodness, filled with all knowledge by the Holy Spirit. Now it was just a matter of doing it. We have what these early Christians had. We, too, are full of goodness, being filled with all knowledge by the Holy Spirit. Now we just need to go about instructing one another through regular church attendance. So what are you waiting for?

Get your armor on!

PREDESTINATION

The Lord does not delay His promise, as some understand delay, but is patient with you, not wanting any to perish, but all to come to repentance. (2 Peter 3:9 NIV)

The idea or concept of predestination has been hotly debated throughout generations. Before the debate can be discussed, we must first clearly define predestination. In the context of this week's verses, I am using the term to mean God has pre-ordained those who will come to know Him and those who will be condemned to hell. If we take that point of view, then the above verse is contradictory. For how can God desire all to come to repentance if He has already condemned some of us to eternal punishment? Further to this point of view, what, then, is the purpose of evangelism? What is the purpose of the Great Commission? Why teach, baptize, and obey if we are predestined?

Look at John 3:16 – "For God so loved the world that He gave His only begotten Son, that whosoever believes in Him..." Who is the "whosoever"? Anyone. How can it be anyone if God predestines those who believe?

Predestination falls flat on the basis of who God is. The logic just does not hold up.

Get your armor on!

PREDESTINATION

But we must always thank God for you, brothers loved by the Lord, because from the beginning God has chosen you for salvation through sanctification by the Spirit and through belief in the truth. (2 Thessalonians 2:13 NIV)

When we see verses that reference being chosen or predestined, we must read them in their proper context. As in the above verse, "from the beginning God has chosen you for salvation..." Many people will stop here and use this verse as justification for predestination. However, we must continue to read the verse. Paul is telling the church in Thessalonica that from the very beginning, God chose us to be saved by the Spirit through belief in the Son. God chose the ***way*** we would be saved, not ***who*** would be saved.

Get your armor on!

for He chose us in Him, before the foundation of the world, to be holy and blameless in His sight. In love He predestined us to be adopted through Jesus Christ for Himself, according to His favor and will, (Ephesians 1:4-5 NIV)

Again, we must read these verses in their entirety and in proper context. Yes, God chose us. But continue to read. He chose us to be holy and blameless in His sight through the works of His Son. Yes, He predestined us. But continue to read. He predestined us to be adopted as His sons through the works of His Son. And just so we cannot take credit for ***how*** we are saved, Paul adds, "...according to His favor and will." It is only because of His pleasure and will that we ***can be*** saved.

Get your armor on!

PREDESTINATION

Many are called but few are chosen. (Matthew 22:14 NIV)

This may take a while, so stick with me. This chapter includes the parable of the Wedding Feast. The king, God, prepares a wedding ceremony for his son, Jesus. The parable lists four groups of people who fail to come to a saving knowledge of Christ. The first are those who are invited but ignore the invitation (v 2-3). You invite them to church but they will not come. Secondly we see those who make light of the invitation (v 4-5). Yes, they may come to church once in a while, but they focus too much on the worries of this world and fall away, having never come to know Christ. Thirdly, we see those who lash out in anger against the gospel (v 6). These hate God and everything for which He stands. Obviously, they are not saved. And lastly, group four, those who come to church but remain unconverted (v 10). They attend church, appear religious, but are never saved. How do we know they were never saved? Read verse 11. The king, God, returns, sees a guest who does not have the proper wedding garments, and throws him out. The wedding garments represent the righteousness of Christ which is put on at conversion. Galatians 3:27 says, "For all of you who were baptized into Christ have clothed yourselves with Christ." We have put on the wedding garments representing the salvation we now have through Christ. This guest did not have on the wedding garment, was not saved, and therefore cast out of the presence of God.

Now, look at verse 14. Why does Jesus end the parable with this phrase? Think about his audience. The Roman Empire was in charge. To build the Roman army, all men were called. However, only those found proper were chosen to join. If you did not meet the qualifications, you were not chosen to be part of the army.

Yes, many are called by the preaching of the Gospel into the outward community of the church. But few are chosen to dwell with God in glory because they have not come to the master of the feast for a wedding garment, salvation through Christ.

Get your armor [and garment] on!

PREDESTINATION

As it is written: Jacob I have loved, but Esau I have hated. (Romans 9:13 NIV)

Many include divine election with predestination. I do not believe you can or should combine the two. Refer back Genesis 25 where the story of Jacob's and Esau's birth occurs. Rebekah is told that the oldest son, Esau, will serve the youngest son, Jacob. So if predestination does not exist, then why, before the boys were ever born, did God say Esau would serve Jacob? Here is where divine election comes into play. Scripture does not say Esau was condemned to hell. However, I do believe through God's divine election, Jacob was chosen to continue the lineage of blessing. Before time began, God devised a plan to bless all nations through Abraham, Isaac, Jacob, on down through David, and eventually pointing to Jesus. Why did not God choose Esau? I honestly do not know. But I do know God is sovereign! He has His reasons. Why did God choose Abraham from the start? Why did God choose David to be king instead of Jonathan? Why did God choose Paul to preach to the Gentiles? Why did God choose Billy Graham to be one of the greatest evangelists of the 20th Century? I do not know. But just because He chose these men does not mean He condemns all others. He just had a divine purpose for each of these men to fulfill. Has God called you for a divine purpose? I bet He has! Better not waste the opportunity.

Get your armor on!

MAKE THE MOST OF EVERY OPPORTUNITY

About midnight Paul and Silas were praying and singing hymns to God, and the prisoners were listening to them. (Acts 16:25 NIV)

We are given abundant opportunities to make Christ known. It is our responsibility to take advantage of those opportunities. Here we see an example of Paul and Silas doing just that. Having just been thrown into prison without even a fair trial, they could have complained, especially Paul. He was a Roman citizen. If he had made that known, he would have been immediately released. But what did they do? They remained in prison and were praying and singing hymns to God. HUH? Yes, they were conducting their own little church service, right there in prison. Truly, they were making the most of every opportunity. Go and do likewise.

Get your armor on!

Walk in wisdom toward outsiders, making the most of the time. (Colossians 4:5 NIV)

Remember Paul wrote this letter to Christians in the church of Colosse. So the "outsiders" were non-Christians. When we approach non-Christians, we need to use God's wisdom for words to say, how to react, and what to do so that we may make the most of the time. We will never know if we will get another opportunity. So make the most of the time while you still have it.

Get your armor on!

MAKE THE MOST OF EVERY OPPORTUNITY

Pay careful attention, then, to how you walk—not as unwise people but as wise—making the most of the time, because the days are evil. (Ephesians 5:15-16 NIV)

You have heard this before, but people are watching you, especially non-Christians. They would love nothing more than to catch you in a sin. And believe me, they will point it out loud and clear when they do. That is why it is so important to be very careful how you live. What you say; How you react; Where you go; How you spend your free time; How you spend your money. So be wise, not unwise, making the most of the time.

Get your armor on!

Mordecai told [the messenger] to reply to Esther, "Do not think that you will escape the fate of all the Jews because you are in the king's palace. If you keep silent at this time, liberation and deliverance will come to the Jewish people from another place, but you and your father's house will be destroyed. Who knows, perhaps you have come to the kingdom for such a time as this." (Esther 4:13-14 NIV)

I want to focus on the very last sentence. "Who knows, perhaps you have come to the kingdom for such a time as this." We never know how the mighty hand of God works. People cross your path; you are put in certain situations. You wonder, "Why in the world did that happen? You may never know that God did not put you in a situation "for such a time as this." So always be aware and always make the most of every opportunity.

Get your armor on!

MAKE THE MOST OF EVERY OPPORTUNITY

Then Mary took a pound of fragrant oil—pure and expensive nard—anointed Jesus' feet, and wiped His feet with her hair. So the house was filled with the fragrance of the oil. (John 12:3 NIV)

Considering the opportunity, Mary certainly made the most of it. And she was loudly criticized for it. She took fragrant oil, about an annual salary's worth, and poured it all over Jesus' feet. Jesus looked favorably on her act, but the disciples did not. We may have an opportunity that arises and it may not be popular. You may even be criticized for it. However, Jesus knows your heart. You carry through with what you know is right and do not worry about what others may say.

Make the most of every opportunity.

Get your armor on!

NEVER GIVE UP

In fact, all those who want to live a godly life in Christ Jesus will be persecuted. (2 Timothy 3:12 NIV)

You have heard it happen to others. Perhaps you have experienced it firsthand. All is going well when all the sudden – BAM! Your world is turned upside-down. Nothing seems to work. Nothing seems to go your way. You want a re-do. You want to start over. You want to give up. Jesus warned us of those days. Paul warned Timothy, too. If you are living godly, you will face persecution. You will have rough days ahead. But keep your eyes on the prize! Do not let Satan win. Never give up!

Get your armor on!

Then some Jews came from Antioch and Iconium, and when they had won over the crowds and stoned Paul, they dragged him out of the city, thinking he was dead. After the disciples surrounded him, he got up and went into the town. The next day he left with Barnabas for Derbe. (Acts 14:19-20 NIV)

Paul was preaching the gospel. The Jewish leaders did not care for what he had to say. So they convinced the crowd and turned them against Paul. They then dragged Paul out of the city, stoned him, and left him for dead. And what does Paul do? He gets up and goes back in the city?!?!? Never mind these people just tried to kill him. Paul was one determined man. He did not give up. He kept pursuing the gospel with every ounce in his body. Now go and be a Paul!

Get your armor on!

strengthening the hearts of the disciples by encouraging them to continue in the faith, and by telling them, "It is necessary to pass through many troubles on our way into the kingdom of God." (Acts 14:22 NIV)

What a comfort to have a strong Christian support group around you. For when we are down, they can lift us up. This is exactly what Paul and Barnabas were doing. Encouraging the new disciples to continue in their faith and to let them know they should expect troubles for the kingdom of God. Even though troubles will come, and they will, we should not allow them to get us off course. Keep pursuing the faith! Never give up!

Get your armor on!

but He with an oath made by the One who said to Him: The Lord has sworn, and He will not change His mind, You are a priest forever. (Hebrews 7:21 NIV)

The "He" refers to God and the "You" refers to Jesus. But if you continue to read, Paul tells us that through Christ, we are all priests. And the same can be said of us, "[We] are a priest forever." Once we are accepted into the family of God, we cannot be removed. So, let's personalize the verse.

"but God with an oath made by Jesus who said to Jessica/Scott. The Lord has sworn, and He will not change His mind, Jessica/Scott is a priest forever."

With that in mind, never give up!

Get your armor on!

NEVER GIVE UP

... God's gracious gifts and calling are irrevocable. (Romans 11:29 NIV)

When God gives you a spiritual gift, He does not ask for it back. When God calls you to a task, He has already given you the ability to accomplish it. He will not say, "Oops, sorry about that. I meant to give that to someone else." "Oops, sorry, I meant to call someone else to do that." NO! He gives you specific gifts to use for His purpose. He calls you to do specific tasks for His purpose. It is up to us to take full advantage and use them or do them. Do not let anything stand in your way. Never give up!

Get your armor on!

THE BATTLE IS THE LORD'S

David said to the Philistine, "You come against me with a dagger, spear, and sword, but I come against you in the name of the LORD of Hosts, the God of Israel's armies— you have defied Him. Today, the LORD will hand you over to me. Today, I'll strike you down, cut your head off, and give the corpses of the Philistine camp to the birds of the sky and the creatures of the earth. Then all the world will know that Israel has a God, and this whole assembly will know that it is not by sword or by spear that the LORD saves, for the battle is the LORD's. He will hand you over to us." (1 Samuel 17:45-47 NIV)

We all have struggles. Difficulties arise all around us at times. And it seems like when it rains, it pours! When we attempt to fix things ourselves, it just makes matters worse. It is during these struggles that we must remember who is on our side. Look at David's comments to Goliath. Man, what confidence! Remember, David was a scrawny teenager. Goliath was a mammoth of a man, 8 to 9 feet tall. How did he have such confidence? He knew God was on his side. He knew the battle was not his to fight. David turned everything over to the Lord and let Him fight. You will be wise to do the same.

Get your armor on!

and he said, "Listen carefully, all Judah and you inhabitants of Jerusalem, and King Jehoshaphat. This is what the LORD says: 'Do not be afraid or discouraged because of this vast multitude, for the battle is not yours, but God's. (2 Chronicles 20:15 NIV)

The enemies of Israel began to maneuver and position themselves to attack. As typical, the children of Israel overreacted and just knew this was the end. Then King Jehoshaphat voiced this prayer. If you read further in this chapter, you will find that Israel was victorious and they did not even have to raise a finger! When it appears as if the entire world is against you, remember this verse. Do not be afraid or discourage because of this vast multitude, all the problems or difficulties you may be experiencing. The battle is not ours to fight, but the Lord's.

Get your armor on!

Do not be afraid of them, for the LORD your God fights for you. (Deuteronomy 3:22 NIV)

Moses was passing the reins to Joshua. As he did so, he gave Joshua this encouragement. Speaking of his enemies, Moses told Joshua not to be afraid of them. Why? Because the Lord your God fights for you. Man, if we only lived like we really believed that! We are not to go through life afraid of anything. We are not to go through life timid and weak. Be bold! Be strong! Be courageous! Remember who is on your side!

Get your armor on!

But Moses said to the people, "Do not be afraid. Stand firm and see the LORD's salvation He will provide for you today; for the Egyptians you see today, you will never see again. The LORD will fight for you; you must be quiet." (Exodus 14:13-14 NIV)

Moses is speaking to the children of Israel right before they crossed over the Red Sea. Pharaoh's army was quickly approaching. The children of Israel were trapped against the sea. Can you imagine the chaos? Imagine the screaming, the running around, the arms flailing, the crying. But look what Moses tells them. "You must be quiet." Yes, he says the Lord will fight for you. But I want to focus on the "be quiet" part. Amidst the chaos, sometimes we just need to be quiet and let the Lord handle things.

Get your armor on!

There has been no day like it before or since, when the LORD listened to the voice of a man, because the LORD fought for Israel. (Joshua 10:14 NIV)

In the verses preceding this one, Joshua had just lead Israel against five Ammonite kings. That is five to one and the one won. Overcoming such overwhelming odds, Joshua was at a loss for words. All he could think was he had never seen anything like it. When we let the Lord fight for us, great things are bound to happen. We, too, might claim we have never before seen anything like it. Put God to the test; let Him show His great and mighty power. Pray you get the opportunity to claim, "I have never before seen anything like this."

Get your armor on!

IMPORTANCE OF BAPTISM

Wash yourselves. Cleanse yourselves. Remove your evil deeds from My sight. (Isaiah 1:16 NIV)

Let's make one thing very clear – there are no saving graces within the baptismal waters. Salvation is not dependent upon whether or not you have been baptized. It is an outward expression of an inward conversion. And do not go too far on the other side to say there is no compelling reason to be baptized. It is the first step of obedience after conversion.

Origins of baptism date back to the Old Testament, most always in reference to being cleansed, as in today's verse. David's prayer in Psalm 57 after being caught in adultery with Bathsheba references the same.

Think of it this way. Your hands are dirty. You wash them with water to get them clean. It is very easy to see that your hands were once dirty, but now they are clean. Baptism is that outward evidence that you have been cleaned on the inside. Therefore, baptism is the ***<u>sign</u>*** of conversion, not the ***<u>means</u>*** of conversion.

Get your armor on!

not by works of righteousness which we have done, but according to His mercy He saved us, through the washing of regeneration and renewing of the Holy Spirit, (Titus 3:5 NIV)

Here we see more symbolism that relates baptism to the washing away of sins and cleansing from sin's grip. This is not a literal washing and cleansing because it references the work done by the Holy Spirit. It is not done by any of our "works of righteousness." We are saved by grace through faith in Christ Jesus, not by faith ***<u>and</u>*** something else. If that were so, it would mean that faith in Christ is not enough to save a person but the person must perform a ritual in order to be saved. Now how ridiculous is that?

Get your armor on!

IMPORTANCE OF BAPTISM

Then Peter said to them, "Repent, and let every one of you be baptized in the name of Jesus Christ for the remission of sins; and you shall receive the gift of the Holy Spirit. (Acts 2:38 NIV)

And he brought them out and said, "Sirs, what must I do to be saved?" So they said, "Believe on the Lord Jesus Christ, and you will be saved, you and your household." (Acts 16:30-31 NIV)

Remember, interpretation of Scripture should not be relegated to just one verse, but developed throughout Scripture as a whole. That is why we have two verses today. Many choose only to look at Acts 2:38 to say baptism is necessary for salvation. However, Peter was not telling his audience that they could not be saved without baptism. He was telling them that their genuine repentance, which accompanies salvation, would be evidenced by their baptism.

But let's put logic to the test. If baptism is a requirement for salvation, then why did Paul, in Acts 16:31, state only that the jailor needed to believe? If baptism is so vitally important for salvation, would you not think it would be listed everywhere salvation was mentioned?

Get your armor on!

And Jesus said to him, "Assuredly, I say to you, today you will be with Me in Paradise. (Luke 23:43 NIV)

Just as many use Acts 2:38 as the requirement for baptism, this verse is probably the most compelling piece of evidence to the contrary. Here, there was neither the necessity nor the opportunity for baptism. The thief was killed that day along with Jesus. There was no way for him to be baptized. The cleansing power of Christ's blood, to which baptism points, was sufficient to assure him of his entrance into eternity. So there was no reason from him to be baptized.

Get your armor on!

IMPORTANCE OF BAPTISM

Corresponding to that, baptism now saves you—not the removal of dirt from the flesh, but an appeal to God for a good conscience—through the resurrection of Jesus Christ, (1 Peter 3:21 NIV)

All this talk about how baptism does not save you. Then, why is baptism important? Look at what the apostle Peter tells us. Baptism is a covenant sign, a public declaration of a person's identification with Christ and it symbolizes identification with his death, burial, and resurrection. It is the symbolism of baptism that is important. It does not wash away your sins, as water removes dirt from the flesh, but it does appeal to God for a good conscience. It is the right thing to do, following salvation.

Get your armor on!

DANGERS OF DOUBT

Now Ahab told Jezebel everything Elijah had done and how he had killed all the prophets with the sword. So Jezebel sent a messenger to Elijah to say, "May the gods deal with me, be it ever so severely, if by this time tomorrow I do not make your life like that of one of them." (1 Kings 19:1-2 NIV)

Doubters come in two forms. A willing doubter is someone who doubts but is willing to learn, to have their mind changed, to grow and expand. A willful doubter is just that-full of will. He's already made up his mind. Jezebel was a willful doubter. She had just heard of the mighty hand of God burning the sacrifice before the prophets of Baal in Chapter 18. And she continues to deny His power. Do not be a Jezebel. Do not be a willful doubter.

Get your armor on!

Moses said to the LORD, "O Lord, I have never been eloquent, neither in the past nor since you have spoken to your servant. I am slow of speech and tongue." The LORD said to him, "Who gave man his mouth? Who makes him deaf or mute? Who gives him sight or makes him blind? Is it not I, the LORD? Now go; I will help you speak and will teach you what to say." But Moses said, "O Lord, please send someone else to do it." (Exodus 4:10-13 NIV)

Ah, Moses. You just have got to love him, do not you? Never mind he was speaking to the Lord through a burning bush; never mind God had just performed a couple of miracles right in front of his eyes; never mind God just told him He would teach him what to say. Still Moses made excuses. He doubted his own ability to do what God called him to do. More significantly, he doubted God's ability to use him, even going as far as to say, "O Lord, please send someone else..." Do not let the dangers of doubt creep in on you. When God calls you to do something, do it! He has already given you the ability to do it.

Get your armor on!

DANGERS OF DOUBT

Abraham fell facedown; he laughed and said to himself, "Will a son be born to a man a hundred years old? Will Sarah bear a child at the age of ninety?" (Genesis 17:17 NIV)

Abraham just found out the news that Sarah was to have a baby. And what was his response? He laughed at God. However, he had a pretty good reason to laugh. Sarah was 90 years old. Who ever heard of a 90 year old woman having a baby? Do not ever underestimate the power of God. When He tells you something is going to happen, it will. Do not doubt. Just believe.

Get your armor on!

So the other disciples told him, "We have seen the Lord!" But he said to them, "Unless I see the nail marks in his hands and put my finger where the nails were, and put my hand into his side, I will not believe it." (John 20:25 NIV)

Doubting Thomas. You know this is the origin for that saying. He just could not bring himself to believe in the resurrection of our Lord. It was beyond his comprehension. I am not sure I would not have said the same thing if the disciples had told me. What is not listed here is Jesus' words to Thomas when Thomas finally believed. You believe because you have seen. More blessed are those who believe without seeing. Today, Jesus does not visibly appear before our eyes so that we can believe. However, just like you cannot see the wind, you can see the effects of it to know it is there. Similarly, you can see the effects of the presence of the Lord! Now that you have seen, go and do as He directs.

Get your armor on!

DANGERS OF DOUBT

Gideon replied, "If now I have found favor in your eyes, give me a sign that it is really you talking to me. (Judges 6:17 NIV)

Have we not all pulled a Gideon? I mean, we want extra assurance that God is directing us one way or another. You know this story. Gideon put his fleece out for a sign from God, not only once, but twice. Why did not he believe after the first sign? The same can be asked of us. When you feel the presence of the Holy Spirit directing you, trust it, believe it, do it.

Get your armor on!

DANGERS OF COMPLACENCY

But I have this against you: you have abandoned the love [you had] at first. Remember then how far you have fallen; repent, and do the works you did at first. Otherwise, I will come to you and remove your lampstand from its place—unless you repent. (Revelation 2:4-5 NIV)

This is John's letter to the church in Ephesus. Jesus Christ was their first love. You remember the spiritual mountain top you ascend to when you attended church camp or a weekend retreat? A few days after you return, you descend back into the normal daily grind called life. The light that burned so bright at camp is now a slight flicker. Sometimes that fizzle is due to our complacency. We get back into our comfort zone and are satisfied with the status quo. If we stay in our comfort zone, God will come to us and remove our lampstand – our light, our way. Do not let that happen. Do not get complacent.

Get your armor on!

Woe to those who are at ease in Zion and to those who feel secure on the hill of Samaria—the notable people in this first of the nations, those the house of Israel comes to. (Amos 6:1 NIV)

Therefore, they will now go into exile as the first of the captives, and the feasting of those who sprawl out will come to an end. (Amos 6:7 NIV)

Here is a description of the pride and security for which God will reckon. Many fancy themselves as people of God, living in sin and in conformity to the world. Call them "careless Christians". They are "at ease" and "feel secure" but danger is right around the corner. It is those who will be the first to go into exile; the first to be captives. That is what complacency becomes. It numbs the spirit to our surroundings. It makes us comfortable. It creates a false sense of security. Before long, Satan has us where he wants us. Be alert. Be watchful. Complacency will kill you.

Get your armor on!

DANGERS OF COMPLACENCY

For the waywardness of the inexperienced will kill them,
and the complacency of fools will destroy them.
(Proverbs 1:32 NIV)

Let's take a closer look at the definition of complacency. According to Webster's, complacency is self-satisfaction especially when accompanied by unawareness of actual dangers or deficiencies; an instance of usually unaware or uninformed self-satisfaction. Read the second part again – uninformed self-satisfaction. I think this is what the writer of Proverbs is trying to tell us. The uninformed self-satisfiers, whom he calls "fools", will be destroyed. It is these individuals who are so blinded by their attitude of complacency, that they cannot see the dangers right in front of them. Do not let that kind of attitude sink in on you. Be aware of the danger of complacency.

Get your armor on!

I know your works, that you are neither cold nor hot.
I wish that you were cold or hot. So, because you are
lukewarm, and neither hot nor cold, I am going to vomit
you out of My mouth. Because you say, 'I'm rich; I have
become wealthy, and need nothing,' and you do not know
that you are wretched, pitiful, poor, blind, and naked,
(Revelation 3:15-17 NIV)

Complacency breeds mediocrity. Mediocrity breeds lukewarmness. God hates lukewarmness. You are neither hot nor cold for Him. You are just going through the motions, taking no stand for Christ. Think of it this way. You are enjoying an afternoon in the sun. Sweat builds up. Your mouth becomes dry. You need a good drink of ice cold water! You find a water fountain and anticipate a refreshing drink. You take the largest gulp your mouth can hold. SSSPPPPEEEEWWWWW!!!! Warm water! Yuck! Same feeling God has for those who are complacent for His name.

Get your armor on!

DANGERS OF COMPLACENCY

And at that time I will search Jerusalem with lamps and punish the men who settle down comfortably, who say to themselves: The LORD will not do good or evil. (Zephaniah 1:12 NIV)

Some think that because they have not experienced God's judgment yet, that they may not ever. There could be no conclusion further from the truth. "At that time" is only known by God. When that time comes, He will search and punish those who are complacent, doing their own thing, thinking no punishment will come their way. Keep your guard up. Do not be complacent.

Get your armor on!

DANGERS OF COMPROMISE

King Solomon loved many foreign women in addition to Pharaoh's daughter: Moabite, Ammonite, Edomite, Sidonian, and Hittite women from the nations that the LORD had told the Israelites about, "Do not intermarry with them, and they must not intermarry with you, because they will turn you away [from Me] to their gods." Solomon was deeply attached to these women and loved [them]. He had 700 wives who were princesses and 300 concubines, and they turned his heart away [from the LORD]. (1 Kings 11:1-3 NIV)

Solomon was the wisest man to ever live. In his early years, he was a close to God, like as his father, David. However, as Solomon aged, things began to change. He began to compromise. The Lord had told him not to intermarry with other nations. But Solomon was "deeply attached" and "loved" these women. More likely, it was lust, not love, he felt. And look at the last phrase of verse 3 – "they turned his heart away from the Lord." That is what happens when we compromise.

Get your armor on!

In the fifth year of Israel's King Joram son of Ahab, Jehoram son of Jehoshaphat became king of Judah, replacing his father. He was 32 years old when he became king; he reigned eight years in Jerusalem. He walked in the way of the kings of Israel, as the house of Ahab had done, for Ahab's daughter was his wife. He did what was evil in the LORD's sight. (2 Kings 8:16-18 NIV)

Jehoram was not too far removed from David's reign, about 116 years after David. We see here the lasting impact from Solomon's mistake that we read about yesterday. In the subsequent verses to these, Jehoram led his troops into battle, only to have them tuck tail and run away. No wonder Jehoram's reign was short lived, only 8 years. Rarely does compromise affect you only in the short term. It can have lasting effects for generations to come!!

Get your armor on!

DANGERS OF COMPROMISE

Daniel determined that he would not defile himself with the king's food or with the wine he drank. So he asked permission from the chief official not to defile himself. (Daniel 1:8 NIV)

Babylonian King Nebuchadnezzar had just seized Israel. He was looking for a few good men he could train in the ways of Babylon and eventually serve on his court. Daniel was selected as one of those men. However, Daniel was determined not to compromise. He took quite a stand, for to deny the king was almost certain suicide. Be determined just as Daniel was. Do not compromise!

Get your armor on!

Then, willing to gratify the crowd, Pilate released Barabbas to them. And after having Jesus flogged, he handed Him over to be crucified. (Mark 15:15 NIV)

Here we see how compromise can be influenced by others. Pilate knew Jesus was innocent. He knew the right thing to do was to release him. However, influenced by the crowd, Pilate compromised and gave Jesus over to be crucified. Stand by your convictions. Do not let the "crowd" wrongly influence you to go against what you know is right. Do not be a "pleaser" and fall to compromise.

Get your armor on!

DANGERS OF COMPROMISE

For though they knew God, they did not glorify Him as God or show gratitude. Instead, their thinking became nonsense, and their senseless minds were darkened. Claiming to be wise, they became fools and exchanged the glory of the immortal God for images resembling mortal man, birds, four-footed animals, and reptiles. Therefore God delivered them over in the cravings of their hearts to sexual impurity, so that their bodies were degraded among themselves. They exchanged the truth of God for a lie, and worshiped and served something created instead of the Creator, who is blessed forever. (Romans 1:21-25 NIV)

Here we see firsthand the dangers of compromise. Paul is referring to mankind in general. Though God has been revealed to man in His creation, man has refused to see Him. Instead, their thinking has become nonsense. Claiming to be wise, they became fools. Instead of worshipping the Creator, they worshipped the created. They exchanged the truth for a lie. This is exactly what happens when we compromise. God's word warns us of this danger. Take heed!!

Get your armor on!

MAKING THE RIGHT DECISIONS

The LORD God took the man and placed him in the Garden of Eden to work it and watch over it. And the LORD God commanded the man, "You are free to eat from any tree of the garden, but you must not eat from the tree of the knowledge of good and evil, for on the day you eat from it, you will certainly die." (Genesis 2:15-17 NIV)

Now why would God create the perfect environment and then put a condition on living in it? Because He wanted man to be obedient. If God did not give man the ability to choose, then we would be merely puppets in His hands. But with that free choice, there are consequences, both good and bad. Here we see consequences for wrong decisions – death! Now do not take this the wrong way. Not all bad decisions lead to death. I just wanted you to know that our decisions do have consequences and to be mindful of them while making your decisions.

Get your armor on!

The people refused to listen to Samuel. "No!" they said. "We must have a king over us. Then we'll be like all the other nations: our king will judge us, go out before us, and fight our battles." (1 Samuel 8:19-20 NIV)

Probably worse than making a wrong decision is making a decision for the wrong reasons. Samuel tried to convey to the nation that choosing a king was not the desire God had for them. But they refused to listen. And look at their reasoning, "Then we will be like all other nations." They only wanted to be like other nations. So when making decisions, stop for a second and check your motives. Are you making a decision to be like others? If so, then you probably know what you should do.

Get your armor on!

MAKING THE RIGHT DECISIONS

Then the men [of Israel] took some of their provisions, but did not seek the LORD's counsel. So Joshua established peace with them and made a treaty to let them live, and the leaders of the community swore an oath to them. (Joshua 9:14-15 NIV)

Our freedom to make decisions is not a license to live free from God. In this instance, Joshua failed to consult God and made a bad decision. In the end, he was obligated to hold himself and his people to his commitment to the Gibeonites – a commitment that prevented Israel from fully conquering Canaan. As in yesterday's verse, seek the counsel of others. But more importantly, seek the counsel of our Lord, no matter how large or small the decision may be.

Get your armor on!

From the Issacharites, who understood the times and knew what Israel should do (1 Chronicles 12:32 NIV)

This verse underscores two essential components of effective decision making: awareness and decisiveness. Good decisions require adequate information and careful analysis of all of the pertinent facts. Although there is a place for spontaneity, important decisions generally should not be rushed. But, once made, such decisions should be decisively communicated and implemented. Like the men of Issachar, leaders need to understand the times and be well aware of the cultural climate in which they live and work, so that they may become transformers rather than conformers.

Get your armor on!

MAKING THE RIGHT DECISIONS

a wise man will listen and increase his learning, and a discerning man will obtain guidance (Proverbs 1:5 NIV)

Sometimes the right decisions require input from others. You will be wise to seek out the counsel of others when making certain decisions. However, you must use discernment in who you ask. You do not want someone who will just agree with you, regardless of the situation. You need to make sure you ask someone who will be impartial and objective. Listen and increase your learning!

Get your armor on!

ABSOLUTE TRUTH

Jesus told him, "I am the way, the truth, and the life. No one comes to the Father except through Me. (John 14:6 NIV)

I want to focus on the truth part of this verse. Just what is truth? Truth is defined as "the state of being in accord with fact or reality" but can also mean "constancy or sincerity in action or character." Some will argue that there is no absolute truth; there are only perceptions and opinions. I say that is a bunch of bologna!

You want to know absolute truth? Then get to know the One who has absolute knowledge.

You want the truth about the beginning of the world and the purpose we are on earth? Talk to the One who was there!

You want to understand what standards must be followed as human beings? Talk to the One who has defined reality!

The ultimate proof that there is absolute truth will not come through some clever philosophical argument. It will come from a personal encounter with the One who declared: "I am the Truth."

Get your armor on!

ABSOLUTE TRUTH

You are a king then?" Pilate asked. "You say that I'm a king," Jesus replied. "I was born for this, and I have come into the world for this: to testify to the truth. Everyone who is of the truth listens to My voice." (John 18:37-38 NIV)

Jesus believed in absolute truth. He believed in absolute truth so strongly that He came to this world, lived and died to bear witness to that truth. Yes, there is such a thing as absolute truth, regardless of what society may say about it. You want to know absolute truth? Listen to the voice of Jesus through His Word!

Get your armor on!

When the Counselor comes, the One I will send to you from the Father —the Spirit of truth who proceeds from the Father—He will testify about Me. (John 15:26 NIV)

We have learned that there is such a thing as absolute truth. We have learned that absolute truth comes from Jesus Christ. Now, where can we find this absolute truth? Through His Holy Spirit. This verse tells us that the Holy Spirit will reveal the things of God to us, thus teaching us the truth. Therefore, believers can learn the truth through the Spirit of Truth who lives within them.

Get your armor on!

ABSOLUTE TRUTH

We are from God, and whoever knows God listens to us; but whoever is not from God does not listen to us. This is how we recognize the Spirit of truth and the spirit of falsehood. (1 John 4:6 NIV)

Abraham Lincoln once used the following to teach some people about truth. He asked, "*How many legs would a sheep have if you called its tail a leg?*" Quickly they answered, "*Five*!" The President then said, "*No, it would only have four legs. Calling a tail a leg does not make it one.*"

Just because people may say there is no such thing as absolute truth does not make it so. Those who deny absolute truth belong to the spirit of falsehood. Those who listen to God possess the Spirit of truth. So, the things of God are true whether we accept them or not! Thank God for the truth!

Get your armor on!

Truthful lips endure forever, but a lying tongue, only a moment. (Proverbs 12:19 NIV)

The truth stands forever because its foundation is indestructible. Speaking the truth and living the truth will establish credibility and a good reputation among your fellow man. However, a lying tongue is but for a moment for soon it will be discovered. You will lose your good reputation and all credibility with your fellow man. If you have no absolutes, you live as you please. However, it does not change the fact that the Bible is still true, Jesus is still the only way to God, and that He is the absolute truth.

Get your armor on!

TOLERANCE

If anyone comes to you and does not bring this teaching, do not take them into your house or welcome them. Anyone who welcomes them shares in their wicked work. (2 John 1:10-11 NIV)

According to Wikipedia, tolerance is the practice of permitting a thing of which one disapproves. Do you understand that definition? Permitting something of which you disapprove. If we disapprove of it, then why let it go on? Because we are so afraid of offending someone? Well, John was not afraid. He tells us that if someone comes to us with a different teaching than "Jesus Saves", we should not have anything to do with them. Of course, we should attempt to correct them in Christian love, but we should not fellowship with them, welcome them in our house, and hang out with them as if we were best friends. For if we do, we share in their wicked work! Do not let tolerance pull you down.

Get your armor on!

In the temple courts he found people selling cattle, sheep and doves, and others sitting at tables exchanging money. So he made a whip out of cords, and drove all from the temple courts, both sheep and cattle; he scattered the coins of the money changers and overturned their tables. (John 2:14-15 NIV)

Why was Jesus so angry with these people to create such a scene? I mean were not these people there to provide a need (animals for sacrifices) for those coming to the temple? Yes, they did provide a need, but with the wrong motives. They were not there to worship at the temple, but to make a profit from others. Jesus knew their hearts and was not so tolerant. Do not let tolerance stop you from pointing out wrong behavior.

Get your armor on!

TOLERANCE

When they kept on questioning him, he straightened up and said to them, "Let any one of you who is without sin be the first to throw a stone at her." (John 8:7 NIV)

Just yesterday, we saw where Jesus was not so tolerant of the money changes at the temple. Here, we see just the opposite. He is quite tolerant. Or is he? In the subsequent verses, Jesus did not condemn the woman. He was not tolerant of her sin either. He told her to go and sin no more. To me, that is not tolerance, but calling sin a sin and dealing with it straight up. Not trying to justify it; not trying to excuse it; not blaming someone else for it, but dealing with it head on!

Use Jesus' example of how to be merciful and gracious without being tolerant of sin.

Get your armor on!

Gracious words are a honeycomb, sweet to the soul and healing to the bones. (Proverbs 16:24 NIV)

I really like the flow of these verses this week. We read where we were not to be tolerant of a people preaching a different salvation. We read two examples of Jesus showing lack of tolerance of sin: one in which He was not so gracious, and the other where He displayed much grace and mercy. I said yesterday that you need to discern the moment and deal with sin in the appropriate manner. This verse tells us why. Because gracious words are sweet to the soul and provide healing to the bones. Some instances, we need to just flat out deal with sin directly. Others, we need to use sweet words of honeycomb to point out sin.

Get your armor on!

TOLERANCE

I urge you, brothers and sisters, to watch out for those who cause divisions and put obstacles in your way that are contrary to the teaching you have learned. Keep away from them. (Romans 16:17 NIV)

While the Apostle Paul did not specifically state it here, I am sure he intended the brothers and sisters to do so with Christian love and compassion. But this is clear instruction on what to do with those who cause division and teach that which is contrary to the Bible. We are to be on the lookout for them and steer clear from them. We are not to sit back and let them continue to teach false doctrine under the guise of "do what you want as along as it does not offend someone else" or "it is ok for you to believe one thing and ok for me to believe something totally different." True, it is appropriate at times to be tolerant. But someone teaching false doctrine that contradicts Scripture is not one of those times!

Get your armor on!

BE INTENTIONAL

Practice these things; be committed to them, so that your progress may be evident to all. (1 Timothy 4:15 NIV)

I find myself sometimes going through each day and get lost in the routine. I drive the same route to and from work. I normally park in the same spot. Greet people in the hallways with a shallow "Good morning, how are you?" but with no intentions of really finding out how they are. But that is not how we are to be at all. We need to have a goal in mind. A purpose. A reason. An aim. Take from the instructions Paul was giving Timothy. Do not just go through the motions. Be intentional about everything you do! It will be evident to all!

Get your armor on!

if you seek it like silver and search for it like hidden treasure, then you will understand the fear of the LORD and discover the knowledge of God. (Proverbs 2:4-5 NIV)

Do you wake each morning anticipating what the day may hold? Or do you dread dragging yourself out of bed to take on the challenges of another day? I bet if we treated each new day like we were in search of silver or hidden treasure, we would approach the day differently. I challenge you to take on each new day in search of hidden treasure, found only in God's Word. In doing so, you will discover the knowledge and presence of God. A true gold rush indeed!

Get your armor on!

BE INTENTIONAL

I love those who love me, and those who search for me find me. (Proverbs 8:17 NIV)

This verse goes hand-in-hand with yesterday's verse. We need to take on the challenges of each new day and be intentional about seeking God. Do not just open the Bible and start reading. Do not just get on your knees and start talking. Do not just attend church and sit quietly in the pews. Develop / create / follow a Bible reading plan. Write down specific prayer requests to offer up to our Lord. Go to church with the anticipation and expectation of meeting our Savior one-on-one. Be intentional!

Get your armor on!

For it would have been better for them not to have known the way of righteousness than, after knowing it, to turn back from the holy commandment delivered to them (2 Peter 2:21 NIV)

We all know those who were once on fire for Christ, only to have the flame fizzle. I can recall some college friends who, as freshman, would go dorm to dorm witnessing for Christ. But by their sophomore year, you would not see them darken the doorway to church. According to this verse, it would have been better had they not known the way of righteousness! Ouch! That is why being intentional is so vitally important to a consistent walk with Christ. Leave nothing to chance. Be intentional!

Get your armor on!

BE INTENTIONAL

"Be very strong, and continue obeying all that is written in the book of the law of Moses, so that you do not turn from it to the right or left (Joshua 23:6 NIV)

So be very diligent to love the LORD your God for your own well-being. (Joshua 23:11 NIV)

This is Joshua's farewell speech to the nation of Israel. Good advice today as it was thousands of years ago. You want to be successful in life? You want to live at peace with the world? Notice I did not say "in peace" but "at peace" – there is a difference! Then be intentional about your relationship with Christ. Continue to obey all that is written in His Word. Keep your focus. Do not turn to the right or to the left. Be very diligent to love the Lord. Be intentional in your walk with God!

Get your armor on!

FRUIT OF THE SPIRIT

So, my brothers and sisters, you also died to the law through the body of Christ, that you might belong to another, to him who was raised from the dead, in order that we might bear fruit for God. (Romans 7:4 NIV)

We have previously talked about bearing fruit. But I want to concentrate on the Fruit of God, more precisely, the Fruit of the Spirit. This week we will list the various fruit of God before we dive into the individuals types of fruit. Matthew 7:16 tells us we will be recognized by our fruit. It is the fruit that distinguishes (or should distinguish) us from non-Christians. So as we walk through the Fruit, be thinking what fruit distinguishes you.

Get your armor on!

But the fruit of the Spirit is love, joy, peace, forbearance, kindness, goodness, faithfulness, gentleness and self-control. Against such things there is no law. (Galatians 5:22-23 NIV)

Here is probably the most comprehensive listing of Fruit of the Spirit in all of scripture. Nine different kinds of fruit, yet all rolled together to form the Fruit of the Spirit. It is like a mixed berry fruit smoothie!! And it is a wonderful picture of the church as well. All kinds of people with different backgrounds and cultures, combined together in perfect unity to make up the church.

Get your armor on!

FRUIT OF THE SPIRIT

Finally, brothers and sisters, whatever is true, whatever is noble, whatever is right, whatever is pure, whatever is lovely, whatever is admirable—if anything is excellent or praiseworthy—think about such things. (Philippians 4:8 NIV)

Characteristics of the Fruit of the Spirit. That is what Paul is describing for us. If we want to know what the Fruit of the Spirit looks like, think of something true or noble. If you want to know if you have acted in line with the Fruit of the Spirit, ask yourself were your actions admirable. Were your intentions pure? Once you know what the Fruit of the Spirit looks like, then concentrate on those things, "think about such things." And do such things.

Get your armor on!

And now these three remain: faith, hope and love. But the greatest of these is love. (1 Corinthians 13:13 NIV)

So is there one Fruit of the Spirit that is more important than another? A bit like the question, "Is one spiritual gift more important than another?" My initial reaction would be to say, "No." However, after reading this verse, one might say, "Yes. Love." Some commentaries say the fruit of the Spirit is simply love and all others are an outflow of it. Paul says of all the fruit and virtues of Christ, the greatest is love. For you cannot have any other fruit without it.

Get your armor on!

FRUIT OF THE SPIRIT

And over all these virtues put on love, which binds them all together in perfect unity. (Colossians 3:14 NIV)

So what makes the Fruit of the Spirit stick together? What is it that causes this inconceivable mixture of thought, opinions, and viewpoints come together as one? Simply put: LOVE. It is the glue, the cement, the adhesive that brings all things of God together.

Get your armor on!

PURE JOY

Rejoice in the Lord always. I will say it again: Rejoice! (Philippians 4:4 NIV)

So just what does it mean to rejoice in the Lord? As Christians, it is our privilege to rejoice in what God has done for us. Not at certain times of the year, but at all times! Even in times of affliction, distress, and persecution, we can rejoice in the character, consistency, and promises of God. We should be always happy for there is always cause to rejoice in Christ.

Get your armor on!

I tell you, in the same way, there will be more joy in heaven over one sinner who repents than over 99 righteous people who do not need repentance. (Luke 15:7 NIV)

I tell you, in the same way, there is joy in the presence of God's angels over one sinner who repents." (Luke 15:10 NIV)

Pure joy from the mouth of Jesus! Can you not see it? All of heaven breaking out in joyous celebration over one person, just one person, who comes to know Christ. That is the pure joy we need to be conscience of and long for.

Get your armor on!

PURE JOY

They read the book of the law of God, translating and giving the meaning so that the people could understand what was read. (Nehemiah 8:8 NIV)

Then all the people began to eat and drink, send portions, and have a great celebration, because they had understood the words that were explained to them. (Nehemiah 8:12 NIV)

They had not celebrated like this from the days of Joshua son of Nun until that day. And there was tremendous joy. (Nehemiah 8:17b NIV)

Man, what a celebration! What was the cause of the celebration? It began with the reading of God's word. But not only the reading, but also the understanding of it. People spontaneously broke out in celebration because the Word of God was read and explained to them. And because of such, there was not just happiness, not just pleasure, but tremendous joy! Nothing would bring your **F**ather and **f**ather more joy than for you to break out in tremendous joy over the reading and understanding of God's Word!

Get your armor on!

PURE JOY

Then the people rejoiced because of their leaders' willingness to give, for they had given to the LORD with a whole heart. King David also rejoiced greatly. (1 Chronicles 29:9 NIV)

Yesterday, we saw where the reading and understanding of God's word set off a celebration. So what set off this celebration? It was an offering taken from the people of Israel to build the temple. Because the people gave from their whole heart. They did not give with restrictions. They did not give begrudgingly. They did not give expecting something in return. They did not give and then complain how the money was used. They gave from their whole heart, with only pure motives. And because they did so, they experienced pure joy.

You want to experience pure joy? Give with your whole heart!

Get your armor on!

This is the day the LORD has made; let us rejoice and be glad in it. (Psalm 118:24 NIV)

Today is January 20, 2012 / January 24, 2014. You only have one of today. You will never ever get another January 20, 2012 / January 24, 2014. So why would you not want to rejoice in it? Do not concentrate so much on yourself and fail to recognize that God made this day for you – just for you! So get out there and rejoice! Find pure joy in what God has made and given you today.

Get your armor on!

PATIENCE

From ancient times no one has heard, no one has listened, no eye has seen any God except You, who acts on behalf of the one who waits for Him. (Isaiah 64:4 NIV)

I am not one to talk about patience very well as I do not always exhibit this Fruit of the Spirit. So do as I say and not as I do this week! This verse should give us encouragement to really strive to be patient. Look at the last phrase. The "You" is God. It is He who acts on behalf of those who wait for Him. When you do not receive what you want, do not get mad at God. He knows you either do not need what you ask of Him or you do not need it now. So wait patiently for Him to work.

Get your armor on!

The LORD is good to those who wait for Him, to the person who seeks Him. It is good to wait quietly for deliverance from the LORD. (Lamentations 3:25-26 NIV)

The problem with patience is that we want it right now! I really like the last sentence of this verse. How does one wait quietly for the Lord? It means to have undistracted focus, total concentration, undivided attention. Position yourself so that you can hear God's communication to you. Separate yourself, turn from the noise of the world. And then... wait.

Get your armor on!

I wait for the LORD; I wait, and put my hope in His word. (Psalm 130:5 NIV)

As you wait on the Lord, do not expect to see writing on the wall. God's leading and direction takes many forms. God leads through others and through our circumstances. Most importantly, He leads us through His Word. God will never be inconsistent with His Word. His Word is truly hope we can bank on!

Get your armor on!

PATIENCE

Wait for the LORD; be courageous and let your heart be strong. Wait for the LORD. (Psalm 27:14 NIV)

Waiting for God is not a seasonal or sporadic thing, neither is it unique. It is something that should be a part of us, as embedded in the life as breathing. At times, you may be breathing pretty hard, but you do not stop breathing! In the same way, do not give out on God. It may get hard, but keep on waiting. Continue to be strengthened by His promises. Wait for the Lord!

Get your armor on!

Be silent before the LORD and wait expectantly for Him; do not be agitated by one who prospers in his way, by the man who carries out evil plans. Refrain from anger and give up [your] rage; do not be agitated—it can only bring harm. For evildoers will be destroyed, but those who put their hope in the LORD will inherit the land. (Psalm 37:7-9 NIV)

Sometimes, we might get agitated by others who may have received a blessing while we sit patiently waiting for ours. Others may be getting engaged and married. Others may have received job offers. You wonder, "Is this ever going to happen to me?" "Why is this not happening to me, too? What have I done wrong?" As this verse tells us, do not get angry. Do not get agitated. It can only bring harm. Rejoice with others while you wait for yours. Eventually, you will inherit the land!

Get your armor on!

GOODNESS

For it is God's will that you, by doing good, silence the ignorance of foolish people. (1 Peter 2:15 NIV)

You have heard the saying, "Kill them with kindness." That is basically what Peter is saying in these verses. When people say bad things about us, perhaps spread false rumors about us, or assume our motives are insincere, it hurts. However, God's will is that we silence these foolish people. And we do that by doing what is good. Living in a way that refutes these false accusations. Others will know the ignorance of foolish people because our lifestyle will prove otherwise. So go and "do good" to silence foolish people.

Get your armor on!

For it is better to suffer for doing good, if that should be God's will, than for doing evil. (1 Peter 3:17 NIV)

What have your mother and I always told you. If you do something against our wishes, we better here it from you rather than from someone else. You may be punished either way, but the punishment will be worse if we hear it from someone else. In the same sense, if I am going to suffer, I would rather suffer from doing good than from doing evil. And we certainly know the suffering from doing evil is much worse!

Get your armor on!

So we must not get tired of doing good, for we will reap at the proper time if we do not give up. Therefore, as we have opportunity, we must work for the good of all, especially for those who belong to the household of faith. (Galatians 6:9-10 NIV)

Jessica Biel got her big break playing a real wholesome character on *7th Heaven*. Tired of that wholesome character, she posed semi-nude for a magazine. I get really frustrated when I see actors and actresses go to the extreme on a movie roll to "prove" they are not goodie two-shoes. What is wrong with wholesome characters? We should never tire of doing good, because we will reap a harvest in the proper time if we do not give up. Note here "proper time." Only God knows the proper time so keep looking for opportunities to do good.

Get your armor on!

You see that a man is justified by works and not by faith alone. (James 2:24 NIV)

James was explaining how works and faith fit together. Works does not justify you in righteousness to God. But works does provide evidence of that justification. Because of our faith, we should want to do good things. The good we do will provide the evidence that we belong to God. Others should see Christ in us through the good we do. Of the Fruit of the Spirit, this is one that should be quite evident to others.

Get your armor on!

GOODNESS

Show family affection to one another with brotherly love. Outdo one another in showing honor. (Romans 12:10 NIV)

Let's think broader than our immediate family. Think of your church family; your sorority / architecture family; your Baylor / OU family. We should show family affection to all of them. And I really like the second phrase – outdo one another. Just think of what our community would look like if we all had this attitude – to outdo one another. And think of the impact for Christ this attitude would have!

Get your armor on!

FAITHFULNESS

Now faith is the reality of what is hoped for, the proof of what is not seen. (Hebrews 11:1 NIV)

Faith: belief in, devotion to, or trust in somebody or something, especially without logical proof

Faith is difficult for "modern day" thinkers. These so called thinkers want physical proof and scientific evidence before they will believe in something. What they fail to see is we live by faith every day. Faith in the metal properties that allow a chair to hold you up. Faith in the electrical properties that allow you to flip the switch and the light comes one. Faith in the mechanical properties that allow your car to start each morning.

One may argue, "But I have physical evidence that these properties work. Where is the physical evidence that some spirit loves me and died for me?" Why it is right before your very eyes! It is life itself! It is the change in a person's heart. It is the unexpected check in the mail to cover a recent doctor bill. It is the encouragement your professor gives you after a tough test. It is the forgiveness a friend gives you for a wrong. Those are the proofs of what is not seen!

Hope for what is real! Prove what is not seen! Have faith!

Get your armor on!

FAITHFULNESS

So faith comes from what is heard, and what is heard comes through the message about Christ. (Romans 10:17 NIV)

So just how does one obtain faith? Where does it come from? I can tell you from experience that you do not wake up one day and all the sudden have abundant faith. Absolutely not! Faith is developed over time. And, if we are being honest with one another, faith really never stops growing. But back to the original question. Where does it come from? Plain and simple – from reading God's Word! You develop faith by reading God's Word and learning from experiences of both the ancient prophets in the Old Testament and the early apostles in the New Testament. Part of the purpose behind the "verse of the day" is to show you just how great Scripture is and how it applies to daily life.

I know you are busy with classes, homework, projects. Life. But make time to read God's Word. Make time to develop strong faith. Seed it; feed it; water it; read it!

Get your armor on!

FAITHFULNESS

A woman suffering from bleeding for 12 years had endured much under many doctors. She had spent everything she had and was not helped at all. On the contrary, she became worse. Having heard about Jesus, she came behind Him in the crowd and touched His robe. For she said, "If I can just touch His robes, I'll be made well!" Instantly her flow of blood ceased, and she sensed in her body that she was cured of her affliction. (Mark 5:25-29 NIV)

"Daughter," He said to her, "your faith has made you well. Go in peace and be free from your affliction. (Mark 5:34 NIV)

You have probably heard of this story many times. Key things to learn here in this classic demonstration of faith.

1. The woman had been dealing with this for years – 12 to be exact.
2. She had consulted many others who did not have an answer.
3. Not only did she not get better, she actually got worse.
4. She recognized the One who could heal her.
5. She knew if she could just get near Jesus, she would be healed.

So what does this tell us about faith?

1. It takes a while to perfect.
2. It does not come from others.
3. Things may not improve overnight. We must persevere.
4. Faith only comes from the One.
5. To receive it, we only need to be near Jesus.

Get your armor on!

FAITHFULNESS

For we walk by faith, not by sight. (2 Corinthians 5:7 NIV)

This goes back to the first verse of this week – Hebrews 11:1, "...the proof of what is not seen." The whole essence of faith is believing what is not seen. Doubting Thomas was commended for seeing and believing. However, Jesus added that more blessed are those who have not seen and yet still believe. We must exercise our faith to believe God even when we cannot see where He is leading us. The words of an old time hymn come to mind:

Have faith in God when your pathway is lonely.
He sees and knows all the way you have trod;
Never alone are the least of His children;
Have faith in God, have faith in God.

Get your armor on!

Now without faith it is impossible to please God, for the one who draws near to Him must believe that He exists and rewards those who seek Him. (Hebrews 11:6 NIV)

This is a rather blunt statement, but could not be stated more true. Without faith, it is impossible to please God. If we are to draw near to Him, we must believe that He is; that He exists. And that He rewards those who diligently seek after Him. Not sure I can or should add any more commentary.

Get your armor on!

THANKSGIVING

Give thanks in everything, for this is God's will for you in Christ Jesus. (1 Thessalonians 5:18 NIV)

Really? Give thanks to God in everything?

If you have food in your fridge, clothes on your back, a roof over your head and a place to sleep you are richer than 75% of the world.

If you have money in the bank, your wallet, and some spare change you are among the top 8% of the world's wealthy.

If you woke up this morning with more health than illness you are more blessed than the million people who will not survive this week.

If you have never experienced the danger of battle, the agony of imprisonment or torture, or the horrible pangs of starvation you are luckier than 500 million people alive and suffering.

If you can read this message you are more fortunate than 3 billion people in the world who cannot read it at all.

It all depends on your perspective. Give thanks to God in everything!

Get your armor on!

Enter his gates with thanksgiving, and his courts with praise! Give thanks to him; bless his name! (Psalm 100:5 NIV)

When we go to God in prayer, one of the first things we should do is give thanks. When we enter His presence, thanksgiving should be on our minds. Give thanks to Him; bless His name! He wants it; He deserves it; we owe it to Him.

Get your armor on!

THANKSGIVING

giving thanks always for everything to God the Father in the name of our Lord Jesus Christ, (Ephesians 5:20 NIV)

Two key words in this verse: "always" and "everything". Thanksgiving should always be on our minds when we approach our Lord and Savior. When we wake in the morning; when we go to sleep at night; walking to class; walking to the cafeteria; when you pass a test; when you fail a test (just do not tell your father!!); sitting at a stop light; sitting in traffic; when we drop that last bite of candy on the ground; when we spill coffee on our new shirt; when we stub our toe; or when we hit our funny bone (which is not very funny!). I could go on and on, but I think you get the point. Always and for everything, we should give God thanks.

Get your armor on!

When they had pasture, they became satisfied;
they were satisfied, and their hearts became proud.
Therefore they forgot Me. (Hosea 13:6 NIV)

We must never forget to give thanks. This verse is very clear what happens when we do. When we become satisfied with what the Lord gives us, our hearts become proud. When we become proud, thinking what we have is earned or the result of our work instead of His, we forget God. My prayer is that we never forget to give Him thanks for what He has done and will do for us!

Get your armor on!

THANKSGIVING

Then I brought the leaders of Judah up on top of the wall, and I appointed two large processions that gave thanks. (Nehemiah 12:31a NIV)

The children of Israel had just completed the rebuilding of the Wall of Jerusalem. This was a significant event, for the wall meant security and protection. To commemorate this event, Nehemiah appointed two large processions, or choirs, to give thanks. You see, Nehemiah knew the importance of giving thanks back to God. If you read further in this chapter, you will see that the entire nation rejoiced and could be heard from "far away" (v 43).

My prayer for you is that others will hear from far away the rejoicing you have when giving thanks to God!

Get your armor on!

SELF-CONTROL

Instead, I discipline my body and bring it under strict control, so that after preaching to others, I myself will not be disqualified. (1 Corinthians 9:27 NIV)

Self-control is the ability to control one's emotions, behaviors, and desires in order to obtain some reward, or to avoid some punishment.

In the preceding verses, Paul uses the illustration of an athlete to show he/she must bring his/her body under strict control in order to perform at their highest level of ability. That includes a strict diet to eat only those foods which will enhance their performance. It includes a strict training regimen so their muscles and joints can endure the stress placed on them during competition.

We should treat out spiritual health no different. Notice how Paul used the words "discipline my body." Life is hard. We face constant temptations that, if we partake, will disqualify our witness. In order to withstand, we must bring ourselves under strict control. Exercise self-control so as to make yourself qualified!

Get your armor on!

A man who does not control his temper is like a city whose wall is broken down (Proverbs 25:28 NIV)

This one hits home to me because I do not always keep my temper under control. But think about the importance of walls during ancient times. Their purpose was to provide security and protection from outside forces. A city with fortified walls was safe from invasion and its citizens were secure. So it is with one who exercises self-control. One who fails to do so is like a city with broken down walls – wide open for invasion from Satan's arrows. Remember to use our shield of faith which allows us to fend off the flaming arrows of the evil one!

Get your armor on!

SELF-CONTROL

Now one day he went into the house to do his work, and none of the household servants were there. She grabbed him by his garment and said, "Sleep with me!" But leaving his garment in her hand, he escaped and ran outside. (Genesis 39:11-12 NIV)

But the LORD was with Joseph and extended kindness to him. He granted him favor in the eyes of the prison warden. (Genesis 39:21 NIV)

Here we see the story of Joseph and Potiphar's wife. She had her eye on Joseph and wanted to have an affair with him. Joseph was tending to his own business when out of nowhere came temptation. Now think about it. No one else was in the house. Joseph had a willing partner. Who would know? No one would find out. But Joseph would have no part in it. He exercised self-control and got out of Dodge!

And what did it get him? Thrown in jail!! Exercising self-control will not always end nicely. But look at vs 21. The Lord was with Joseph and extended kindness to him. Know this, when we are in God's will, doing as He requires, maintaining self-control over our bodies, we are right where God wants us to be.

Get your armor on!

SELF-CONTROL

but hospitable, loving what is good, sensible, righteous, holy, self-controlled (Titus 1:8 NIV)

Paul is outlining for Titus qualities to look for when appointing elders to the church. Even though this list is intended for leaders in the church, it most certainly applies to any self-proclaimed Christian.

I am sure you have wondered how certain people reached levels of leadership. If you have not seen it yet, you will. It is imperative that we, as Christians, work to prove ourselves hospitable, loving what is good, sensible, righteous, holy, and self-controlled. Why? To be appointed as a leader? Well, not necessarily. That might be a side result. But the key is to show the rest of the world what and who a Christian is. The world has seen way too many high profile Christian "leaders" who have fallen flat. Non-believers use these examples as justification for their continued sin. It is time for us to stand up, practice what is righteous and holy and act with self-control.

Get your armor on!

SELF-CONTROL

For this very reason, make every effort to supplement your faith with goodness, goodness with knowledge, knowledge with self-control, self-control with endurance, endurance with godliness, godliness with brotherly affection, and brotherly affection with love. (2 Peter 1:5-7 NIV)

Here we see the natural progression of those who display the Fruit of the Spirit and how each one is interwoven with the other. Since we are focusing on self-control this week, follow the progression of that part of the Fruit. With self-control comes endurance, which leads to godliness, which leads to brotherly affection, which ends with love.

If we are truly seeking God, exercising control over our bodies, keeping our temper under wraps, fleeing temptation even when no one else is around, displaying self-control to non-believers, we will see progress towards godliness. That godliness will spill over to brotherly affection for others, showing concern for their well-being, and ultimately in the display of the "greatest of these which is love."

This cannot happen unless you start with self-control.

Get your armor on!

GIVING

Each person should do as he has decided in his heart—not reluctantly or out of necessity, for God loves a cheerful giver. (2 Corinthians 9:7 NIV)

The pastor of the church I attended in college once shared the following story. He was giving a series of sermons on tithing. After about the third or fourth sermon, an elderly lady approached him after the service. She said in a huff, "All you do is talk about give, give, give. Do not you have anything else better to talk about?" To that, the pastor replied, "Well, I cannot think of a better definition of Christianity!"

This hits many right between the eyes! We might write a check out of sense of obligation. We might put a few dollars in the offering plate, while keeping a wad of cash in our pocket. While writing a check, we might daydream about other things you can buy with this money. If that is your attitude, God would prefer you keep your money. Remember, God so loved the world that He gave!

Get your armor on!

"Every tenth of the land's produce, grain from the soil or fruit from the trees, belongs to the LORD; it is holy to the LORD. (Leviticus 27:30 NIV)

You may wonder where we got the idea of tithing, giving 10% to the church. Literally, the word tithe means a tenth. And we see mention of the tithe way back in the Old Testament. This verse says the tithe does not even belong to us; it belongs to God! So, it really is not ours to in the first place.

So get your checkbook out and your armor on!

GIVING

Honor the LORD with your possessions and with the first produce of your entire harvest; then your barns will be completely filled, and your vats will overflow with new wine (Proverbs 3:9-10 NIV)

Giving is an act of worship. We are committing to God that we trust His provision. I can tell you, when you and Jessica/Scott were babies, some months were difficult. I remember telling your mother to wait to go to the grocery store. I delayed paying certain bills for a few days. One thing we never wavered was making our tithe contribution. And you know what? You never missed a meal. You always had clean clothes. God provided for us just as He tells us here. Make the commitment now to honor God with the first produce of your entire harvest – all that you earn. See if this verse does not play out for you as it has for your mother and me.

Get your armor on!

then Yahweh your God will choose the place to have His name dwell. Bring there everything I command you: your burnt offerings, sacrifices, offerings of the tenth, personal contributions, and all your choice offerings you vow to the LORD. (Deuteronomy 12:11 NIV)

While I do believe God commands us to bring a tithe, it certainly does not have to stop with a 10th. There is no law that says you cannot give more than that. But the key to me in this verse is that we are to give a 10th to the local church ("the place to have His name dwell"). After that, we can give our personal contributions to other worthy causes.

Get your armor on!

GIVING

In every way I've shown you that by laboring like this, it is necessary to help the weak and to keep in mind the words of the Lord Jesus, for He said, 'It is more blessed to give than to receive.'" (Acts 20:35 NIV)

You may know of friends who do not tithe. You may know of friends who do not lift a finger to help anyone in need. As the old saying goes, it is the 20% of the church that does 80% of the work. And we 20 percenters get a bit tired of doing all the work. When I get discouraged, this verse always brings me back to earth. Remember back to the first verse of this week – the best definition of Christianity is GIVE!

Get your armor on!

Give generously to him and do so without a grudging heart; then because of this the Lord your God will bless you in all your work and in everything you put your hand to. (Deuteronomy 15:1 NIV)

Giving is such an important topic that I thought we would take two weeks to look at it. Besides, the Bible has so many good verses on giving that I could not stop with just five!

How are we to give? Without a grudging heart. What is a grudging heart? One that is reluctant, unwilling, complaining. That is not how God desires us to give. He wants us to give with a whole heart. Pure in motives. Not expecting any congratulations, no recognition, no plaques in your honor, nothing in return. But from your whole heart, give. Go and do likewise and enjoy the blessings that will flow.

Get your armor on!

GIVING

"Jesus looked at him and loved him. 'One thing you lack,' he said. 'Go, sell everything you have and give to the poor, and you will have treasure in heaven. Then come, follow me.'" (Mark 10:21 NIV)

We saw yesterday what happens when we give out of pure motives. Today shows the opposite. The rich young ruler came to Jesus proud of his accomplishments and wealth. But Jesus knew his heart. He was not willing to give. The verse that follows tell us the young man walked away stunned and grieving, for he had many possessions and did not want to part with them. We must have a heart willing to give or our gift will not mean much.

Get your armor on!

Do not be deceived: God cannot be mocked. A man reaps what he sows. Whoever sows to please their flesh, from the flesh will reap destruction; whoever sows to please the Spirit, from the Spirit will reap eternal life. (Galatians 6:7-8 NIV)

This verse can be applied to more than the area of giving. It goes back to the intent of the giver. It is a matter of the heart. If you give out of spite or guilt, then do not expect to see much in return. In fact, this verse tells us to expect destruction. But if you give joyfully and in worshipful response to our Loving Lord, then from the Spirit we will reap the blessings of God's presence in our lives. In short, you reap what you sow. So sow (and give) to please the Spirit.

Get your armor on!

GIVING

"Will a man rob God? Yet you are robbing Me!" You ask: "How do we rob You?" "By not making the payments of the tenth and the contributions. You are suffering under a curse, yet you—the whole nation—are still robbing Me. Bring the full tenth into the storehouse so that there may be food in My house. Test Me in this way," says the LORD of Hosts. "See if I will not open the floodgates of heaven and pour out a blessing for you without measure. (Malachi 3:8-10 NIV)

You may remember Mom and me telling you and Jessica/Scott the story of us being robbed about a month after our wedding. We had taken a trip to Galveston with some friends. When we returned home, we notice the door to the garage was opened. We walked in the house and noticed the back door was wide open. The house looked like a scene out of a movie. Dresser drawers left opened; clothes thrown on the bed. We felt violated.

We know exactly how God feels when we fail to give. In this verse, we are told that failing to give is the same as robbing God. I really like the encouragement right after the chastisement. We are told to test God through our giving. When we have the proper attitude in giving, we will see the floodgates open and the abundant blessings poured out without measure! Do not you get it? Without measure! That means we will not be able to quantify the amount of blessings we will receive. To that, I say where can I give?

Get your armor on!

GIVING

We want you to know, brothers, about the grace of God granted to the churches of Macedonia: During a severe testing by affliction, their abundance of joy and their deep poverty overflowed into the wealth of their generosity. I testify that, on their own, according to their ability and beyond their ability, they begged us insistently for the privilege of sharing in the ministry to the saints, and not just as we had hoped. Instead, they gave themselves especially to the Lord, then to us by God's will. (2 Corinthians 8:1-5 NIV)

Here is the prime example of having the proper motives when it comes to giving. The Macedonian church was hit hard by affliction and deep poverty. Yet when it came time to collect an offering for Paul and other traveling evangelists, their poverty was turned into wealth – the wealth of their generosity in giving. And look again. They begged to give even more! How could they have given so much out of extreme poverty? Read verse 5 – "they gave themselves especially to the Lord." And therein lays the heart of giving. Giving yourself first to God, then to others.

Get your armor on!

HUMILITY

And all of you clothe yourselves with humility toward one another, because God resists the proud but gives grace to the humble. Humble yourselves, therefore, under the mighty hand of God, so that He may exalt you at the proper time. (1 Peter 5:5b-6 NIV)

As we enter this week's theme, let's make clear what we are talking about when we mention humility. Humility does not mean weakness. Being humble does not mean you allow others to walk all over you. Here is a good definition: a modest opinion or estimate of one's own importance in comparison to God. Oh, we might hold a fancy titled position at some Fortune 500 company; we might be viewed as having some important position within the community; we might even be president of the church choir or even chairman of the deacons. But when we compare ourselves to the standard of God, we realize just how low in importance we rank.

So let's not think too highly of ourselves. But keep our God perspective in mind. When we do that, He will lift us up in the proper time!

Get your armor on!

But He gives greater grace. Therefore He says: God resists the proud, but gives grace to the humble. (James 4:6 NIV)

Why would God resist the proud? Let's unpack what proud means and stands for. To be proud means to have a pleasure or satisfaction over something regarded as highly honorable or creditable to oneself or to show a high opinion of one's own dignity, importance, or superiority. Being proud is all about "ME." Totally the opposite of God. No wonder God resists the proud.

Put on humility and then get your armor on!

HUMILITY

This grace was given to me—the least of all the saints—to proclaim to the Gentiles the incalculable riches of the Messiah, (Ephesians 3:8 NIV)

I chose this verse as an example of what humility looks like. Paul was arguably the greatest evangelist aside from Christ. Yet look at what he calls himself – the least of all the saints. Paul did not expect a great deal of fanfare. He did not expect people to look up to him. And he certainly did not expect people to bow down to him. He just went about his business the best way he knew how. And while he was at it, he showed the rest of us how to do the same.

Get your armor on!

The fear of the LORD is what wisdom teaches, and humility comes before honor. (Proverbs 15:33 NIV)

Focus on that last phrase for a moment – "humility comes before honor." Remember, humility does not refer to weakness. It just means we have a modest viewpoint of our self-importance. When we determine that we really are not that important and that the world can go on without us, then we will have a place of honor before God. Now go back to the first part of the verse. Fear, meaning reverent respect, of the Lord is what wisdom teaches. We must recognize that we need Him to help us through life. Keeping proper perspective of who God is and who we are can only lead to success! Maybe not in the world's eyes, but certainly in God's eyes.

Get your armor on!

HUMILITY

When pride comes, disgrace follows, but with humility comes wisdom. (Proverbs 11:2 NIV)

This verse sums up humility and pride quite simply. An attitude of "ME first" can only lead to disgrace. When you think of yourself more highly than you ought, you set yourself up for disappointment because those expectations cannot and will not be met. But the attitude of humility will never bring disappointment for that attitude does not expect any praise or commendation; it does not think of itself as being higher in importance than anyone else.

Seek humility. Then, get ready for God to rain His blessings upon you.

Get your armor on!

OBEDIENCE

Therefore, I urge you, brothers, in view of God's mercy, to offer your bodies as living sacrifices, holy and pleasing to God--this is your spiritual act of worship. (Romans 12:1 NIV)

We have so many ways to express our worship to the Lord Almighty. Did you know that obedience to God is an act of worship? Paul is urging his readers in this verse to be obedient and goes as far as to say it is our spiritual act of worship. Other translations say that obedience is our "reasonable act of worship." I like that reasonable part – sensible, practical. It makes sense to be obedient. So go and makes sense of the day – be obedient.

Get your armor on!

But Samuel replied: "Does the LORD delight in burnt offerings and sacrifices as much as in obeying the voice of the LORD? To obey is better than sacrifice, and to heed is better than the fat of rams. (1 Samuel 15:22 NIV)

Why do you go to church? Why do you pray? Why do you give? Why do you have a quiet time? Why do you read your Bible? Too many Christians cannot tell you why. We just do them because that is what we are to do. This verse tells us the Lord does not delight in His children just going through the motions. In this case, offering burnt offerings and sacrifices because that is what you are to do. No, God delights much more in simple obedience. Obedience that comes from the heart. Deep down, honest, true, authentic, sincere, unconditional obedience.

Get your armor on!

OBEDIENCE

Now that you know these things, you will be blessed if you do them. (John 13:17 NIV)

God never expects or commands us to do something beyond our ability. We might believe it is impossible to do; but you know, with God, nothing is impossible. So here, the words of Jesus tell us now that we know what to do, we will be blessed if we do them. We all know how to be obedient; it just is not easy. But we know the blessings that will come by doing so. So you want to be blessed today? Be obedient. Now that you know what to do, go and do it.

Get your armor on!

Whoever has my commands and obeys them, he is the one who loves me. He who loves me will be loved by my Father, and I too will love him and show myself to him." (John 14:21 NIV)

How can we tell a person loves Jesus? Simply watch their lives. You can tell. Those who are obedient to His commands demonstrate God's love for everyone to see. When we are obedient, another cool thing occurs. God reveals Himself to us. You want to get close to God? Obey His commands.

Get your armor on!

Be strong and very courageous. Be careful to obey all the law my servant Moses gave you; do not turn from it to the right or to the left, that you may be successful wherever you go. (Joshua 1:7 NIV)

As the baton was passed from Moses to Joshua, we see these encouraging words. Be careful to obey all the law (the Bible). Do not turn from it to the right or to the left (do not take any exits – stay on the highway). For when you do, you will be successful. Be strong and very courageous! Be bold! Do not back down. Even when you are all alone. Remain obedient!

Get your armor on!

SERVE OTHERS

Whatever you do, do it enthusiastically, as something done for the Lord and not for men, knowing that you will receive the reward of an inheritance from the Lord. You serve the Lord Christ. (Colossians 3:23-24 NIV)

We all cannot be the smartest student in the classroom; the stud athlete on campus, the man with the corner office. Some of us have to do the grunt work! So, if you are a grunt, then be the best grunt you can be! Be enthusiastic about the job you do. Be proud of the job you do. Know that the job you do is a reflection of your relationship with Christ. If all you do is complain and act jealous towards those "above" you, what kind of reflection is that? Serve others and in so doing, you will serve the Lord Christ.

Get your armor on!

Serve with a good attitude, as to the Lord and not to men (Ephesians 6:7 NIV)

Ah, motives. They get us every time! You can serve others and still not be blessed. Why? Because you do so with the wrong attitude. You do it to be noticed. You do it to store up "points" to exchange with God later when you need (or more likely WANT) something. God cuts right to the point. Serve with a good attitude as if you were actually serving the Lord, not man. Because, in effect, that is exactly what you are doing when you serve!

Get your armor on!

SERVE OTHERS

Do what you have learned and received and heard and seen in me, and the God of peace will be with you. (Philippians 4:9 NIV)

So how do we serve others enthusiastically with proper attitude? Well, you pick out someone to emulate. This is what Paul is telling the church in Philippi. Hey gang, do what you have learned from me and seen me do. You know, I have always told you kids that you can say anything you have heard me say. You can do anything you have seen me do. If I have said it or done it, then I cannot fault you for doing the same. Puts a ton of pressure on me to make sure I live out my faith. Now go and do likewise!

Get your armor on!

You call Me Teacher and Lord. This is well said, for I am. So if I, your Lord and Teacher, have washed your feet, you also ought to wash one another's feet. For I have given you an example that you also should do just as I have done for you. (John 13:13-15 NIV)

We saw Paul's example yesterday. Here we see Jesus'. To wash one's feet was considered to be the lowliest of lowliest jobs. Remember, people then walked barefoot or with sandals. Your feet got really dirty. It was customary for a slave to wash the feet of the home owner and his guests when they entered the house. Here, Jesus just finished washing the disciples' feet as an example of just what a servant's hearts was all about. Then he said we should do just as He has done for us. Serve others!

Get your armor on!

SERVE OTHERS

For even the Son of Man did not come to be served, but to serve, and to give His life—a ransom for many." (Mark 10:45 NIV)

You may have realized by now that the world does not revolve around you. We are not the center of the universe unlike what we might think!! We are not put on this earth to see how much stuff we can collect or to see who has the most friends on Facebook. Really, we are not that important. The Son of Man was one name used to describe Jesus. In other words, even the Most High God did not come ***to be served***, although he, more than anyone else, deserved to be served. No. He came ***to serve*** and to give His life as a ransom for the rest of us. Here is the ideal description of a Christian – one sent to serve others!

Get your armor on!

SET THE EXAMPLE

He was a scribe skilled in the law of Moses, which Yahweh, the God of Israel, had given. The king had granted him everything he requested because the hand of Yahweh his God was on him (Ezra 7:6 NIV)

Now Ezra had determined in his heart to study the law of the LORD, obey it, and teach its statutes and ordinances in Israel. (Ezra 7:10 NIV)

The "he" in these verses is Ezra, a priest and scribe for King Artaxerxes. I find it interesting to note the king recognized the hand of God was on Ezra. And then in verse 10 we read Ezra was determined to study the law of the Lord (the Bible), obey it, and teach it. So do you believe the hand of the Lord was on Ezra because of the decision he made in his heart? I do. And the Lord will do the same for you if you make it a priority to study God's Word, obey it, and teach it! Set the example by knowing God's Word.

Get your armor on and use the Sword of the Spirit!

When Daniel learned that the document had been signed, he went into his house. The windows in its upper room opened toward Jerusalem, and three times a day he got down on his knees, prayed, and gave thanks to his God, just as he had done before. (Daniel 6:10 NIV)

You know the story here. King Darius had just been tricked into signing a decree that no one would petition any god except the king. Daniel had a habit of conducting his quiet time by an opened window for all to see. He did not let some silly decree stop him. He continued to conduct his quiet time just as he always had. Daniel set the example for the rest of us. Do not succumb to peer pressure or let the trappings of this world stop you from doing what you know to do. Follow Daniel's lead and set the example!

Get your armor on!

SET THE EXAMPLE

It is not that we do not have the right to support, but we did it to make ourselves an example to you so that you would imitate us (2 Thessalonians 3:9 NIV)

Paul is referencing the fact that when he visited the Thessalonica church, he did not mooch off them. Instead, he worked hard and paid for his food and housing. Sure, he had a right to receive support from the congregation. But more importantly, he set the example of hard work while doing ministry so as not to be a burden. Others were acting irresponsibly, taking advantage of the hospitality of others. Paul even said in the next verse that those not working should not eat! Take a page from Paul's book. Set the example so that others would imitate you.

Get your armor on!

He did what was right in the LORD's sight as his father Uzziah had done. In addition, he did not enter the LORD's sanctuary, but the people still behaved corruptly. (2 Chronicles 27:2 NIV)

Sometimes you can do all the right things and people will still mess up. King Jotham did that very thing. He did what God wanted him to do. He followed the example set by his father, King Uzziah. Jotham tried to set the proper example. Still, the people behaved corruptly. That is where man's free will comes into play. You are accountable for you. You set the proper example for others to follow. If they do not follow, that is not your fault.

Get your armor on!

and you became imitators of us and of the Lord when, in spite of severe persecution, you welcomed the message with joy from the Holy Spirit. As a result, you became an example to all the believers in Macedonia and Achaia. For the Lord's message rang out from you, not only in Macedonia and Achaia, but in every place that your faith in God has gone out. Therefore, we do not need to say anything, (1 Thessalonians 1;6-8 NIV)

Wow! What a compliment! The news of the attitude, behavior, and witness of the Thessalonica church had spread to the entire region. There was no reason for Paul to mention it to others because they had already heard. They had set the example. You see what happens when you do the right things? Word spreads. Others hear of your "joy from the Holy Spirit" and the "Lord's message [rings] out from you." You can receive no greater compliment.

Get your armor on!

INWARD BEAUTY

Your beauty should not consist of outward things like elaborate hairstyles and the wearing of gold ornaments or fine clothes. Instead, it should consist of what is inside the heart with the imperishable quality of a gentle and quiet spirit, which is very valuable in God's eyes. (1 Peter 3:3- NIV)

We get way too caught up in this world trying to look like the next hot model or some picture in a magazine. Do not we know by now those pictures are so airbrushed it is impossible for a normal person to look like that! Instead, our beauty should be what is inside the heart. The imperishable qualities of a gentle and quiet spirit are what we should strive for. God could care less what you look like on the outside. He looks into the heart to see the true you. Let others see the true you too!

Get your armor on!

We all, with unveiled faces, are looking as in a mirror at the glory of the Lord and are being transformed into the same image from glory to glory; this is from the Lord who is the Spirit. (2 Corinthians 3:1 NIV)

When you look in the mirror, who do you see? Do you like what you see? We all stand before God with unveiled faces. That is, no covering to hide our sin. He sees us as we truly are. I pray that others see you for who you truly are as well – a blessed child of God, being formed in His image day by day.

Get your armor on!

INWARD BEAUTY

"Woe to you, scribes and Pharisees, hypocrites! You are like whitewashed tombs, which appear beautiful on the outside, but inside are full of dead men's bones and every impurity. In the same way, on the outside you seem righteous to people, but inside you are full of hypocrisy and lawlessness. (Matthew 23:27-28 NIV)

Jesus has a knack for not beating around the bush, but getting right to the heart of the matter, literally. For it is the heart that is the center of the matter. Do not be like the scribes and Pharisees. They put on a show for all to see. Jesus saw right through them. His analogy of a whitewashed tomb is quite fitting. On the outside it looks great, but the inside is full of stench and rotting bones. When you put on a show for others to see, you are just fooling yourself. Do not be fooled. Let your inward beauty shine!

Get your armor on!

Charm is deceptive and beauty is fleeting, but a woman who fears the LORD will be praised. (Proverbs 31:30 NIV)

This is going to make you laugh. Your mother will see some hot model on a commercial or in my Sports Illustrated magazine. The first words out of her mouth are, "Just wait until you have two babies! Your stomach will not look so flat!" Outward beauty is, in fact, fleeting. Here one day and gone the next, only to be replaced by the next best thing or someone. Do not take this to extreme, but we should not be so concerned about our outward appearance. Yes, we need to take care of our bodies. After all, we are the temple of the Lord. We should not be so concerned about what others think of our clothes, new hair style, how white our teeth are, the color of our eyes, how nice we wear our make-up, how manly our 3-day shadow is. The emphasis should be on the fear of the Lord. The reverent respect and awe of our Savior, Jesus Christ. That is where true beauty lies.

Get your armor on!

INWARD BEAUTY

Surely You desire integrity in the inner self, and You teach me wisdom deep within. (Psalm 51:6 NIV)

Words from David, a man after God's own heart. This psalm was written after Nathan confronted David regarding his affair with Bathsheba. On the outside, no one could see any problems with David. But David knew on the inside, what he had done was wrong. You can put on a good front for others to see. But God desires integrity in the inner self. The self that is revealed when no one is looking. Let others see your inward beauty!

Get your armor on!

INTEGRITY

Better a poor man who lives with integrity than someone who has deceitful lips and is a fool. (Proverbs 19:1 NIV)

Integrity: firm adherence to a code of especially moral or artistic values **: incorruptibility**, an unimpaired condition **: soundness**, the quality or state of being complete or undivided **: completeness**, state of being without restriction.

I want to key on the three words I have bolded. **Incorruptibility** – without fault. Not that we are perfect by any means, but we strive to be. No one will be able to bring a charge against us. We treat others fairly and honestly, with decency. **Soundness** – showing good judgment. Not that we always make the right decisions, but that we use a common sense approach to all decisions, bathing them in prayer. **Completeness** – having all things necessary to accomplish whatever task is ahead.

We are told to desire integrity more than any riches of this world. Would you not rather be poor according to the world's viewpoint, but possess incorruptibility, soundness, and completeness, than have all the possessions this world can offer, knowing you acquired those things deceitfully? Desire to live with integrity. More precious than the rarest of gems.

Get your armor on!

INTEGRITY

Man cannot be made secure by wickedness, but the root of the righteous is immovable. (Proverbs 12:3 NIV)

Your mom and I took Biscuit for a walk the other day. Along the way, I noticed a tree whose roots have been exposed by the water washing away the soil over time. I just looked at the wonderful web of roots jutting from underneath the tree, each one taking its own path. I also wondered just how far in the ground those roots reach. I thought they have to reach down pretty far in order to keep that tree from being blown away by our Texas-sized storms.

In this same sense, a man or woman who lacks integrity cannot have a very strong root system. The storms of life come at them and WHAM!, they come crashing down. But look at the contrast of one who does have integrity. Their root system makes them immovable, able to withstand the storms life throws at them.

Develop a strong root system! Develop integrity!

Get your armor on!

as long as my breath is still in me and the breath from God remains in my nostrils, my lips will not speak unjustly, and my tongue will not utter deceit. I will never affirm that you are right. I will maintain my integrity until I die. (Job 27:3-5 NIV)

Job was speaking to a friend who was trying to help Job, but really was not. The friend wanted him to denounce God for all the horrible events in Job's life. And look at Job's response. He will maintain his integrity until he dies! Wow, what a statement! I can only hope and pray that I can have that type of resolve, not matter the circumstances. I pray you will, too.

Get your armor on!

INTEGRITY

The righteousness of the blameless keeps his way straight, but the wicked falls by his own wickedness. (Proverbs 11:5 NIV)

You lie, steal, and cheat; others will lie, steal, and cheat from you. You manipulate people to get your way; others will manipulate you to get their way. You gain by deceit; others will deceive you. Truly, the wicked falls by his own wickedness. BUT, the way of the righteousness is straight. You treat others with respect, you will be treated with respect. You deal honestly with others, others will deal honestly with you. Keep your way straight. Have integrity!

Get your armor on!

Here I am. Bring charges against me before the LORD and His anointed: Whose ox or donkey have I taken? Whom have I wronged or mistreated? From whose hand have I taken a bribe to overlook something? I will return it to you." "You haven't wronged us, you haven't mistreated us, and you haven't taken anything from anyone's hand," they responded. (1 Samuel 12:3-4 NIV)

Samuel is probably the greatest example of integrity in the Bible, aside from Jesus, of course. These verses came from his farewell speech. Samuel had led the children of Israel for years. He held himself accountable to the people he led. He opened himself up to the scrutiny of everyone with whom he had ever had dealings, challenging the crowd that if he had done any wrong, he would correct it. And what is even more impressive is how the crowd responded. No one was able to bring any wrongdoing before him. Samuel was definitely a man of integrity. Follow his example!

Get your armor on!

WISDOM

The wise will be put to shame; they will be dismayed and snared. They have rejected the word of the LORD, so what wisdom do they really have? (Jeremiah 8:9 NIV)

Wisdom defined is the comprehension of what is true or right coupled with optimum judgment as to action. In plain English, wisdom is knowing what to do and then doing it. You can look for wisdom in college degrees, self-help books, Dr. Phil or Oprah, and still not find it. All you need to do is read God's Word. What wisdom do you really have if you do not have God's Word? I'll let you answer that one yourself.

Get your armor on!

The fear of the LORD is the beginning of knowledge; fools despise wisdom and discipline. (Proverbs 1:7 NIV)

Remember when the Bible uses the phrase "fear of the Lord", it is not referring to scared type of fear, but a referent type of respect and awe of His great power. Respect of God is the beginning of knowledge and wisdom. Here, we are told fools despise wisdom and discipline. A fool is one who has poor judgment or little intelligence. If you do not want to be cast in that light, then I would recommend you learn to fear the Lord.

Get your armor on!

A fool's way is right in his own eyes, but whoever listens to counsel is wise. (Proverbs 12:15 NIV)

Insanity has been defined as doing the same thing over and over and expecting different results. The same can be said of a fool. He keeps thinking his way is best. Not wanting to listen to anyone else, he keeps marching to the beat of his own drum, even if that beat leads him to a dead end. If you want to develop wisdom, you will listen to counsel. But be careful that you select wise mentors who can train you in the way of the Lord.

Get your armor on!

WISDOM

The one who walks with the wise will become wise, but a companion of fools will suffer harm. (Proverbs 13:20 NIV)

Ever heard the term, "you are what you eat"? Here, we learn we are who we hang out with. All too often you hear of someone with good intentions, but weak spiritually. They start hanging out with the wrong crowd and before they know it, the snare of the evil one has caught them. You want to be wise and develop wisdom? Hang out with those who are wise. You will become like those you associate with the most.

Get your armor on!

Now if any of you lacks wisdom, he should ask God, who gives to all generously and without criticizing, and it will be given to him. But let him ask in faith without doubting. For the doubter is like the surging sea, driven and tossed by the wind. That person should not expect to receive anything from the Lord. (James 1:5-7 NIV)

You want wisdom? Simply ask God for it. Solomon was asked what he wanted. Of all the things he could have asked the Lord to give him, he asked for wisdom. And he was the wisest man to ever live. But when we ask for it, we must believe that God will give it to us. No doubting! Otherwise, as James explains, we are no different than the waves of the sea, drifting back and forth with the wind. Got wisdom? Ask God!

Get your armor on!

COMMIT TO THE LORD

For you were called to this, because Christ also suffered for you, leaving you an example, so that you should follow in His steps. (1 Peter 2:21 NIV)

Why did Jesus die? One obvious answer is so that He could provide salvation for all who believe in Him. Another not so obvious answer is to set an example for us. That does not mean He expects us to be crucified. We should be so willing to honor Him and bring Him glory that we would go to any length to spread the gospel, even if it meant losing our life. It is better to die than to deny the truth! Christ set the example of true servanthood. Now it is our decision to commit to Him and do the same.

Get your armor on!

Fight the good fight for the faith; take hold of eternal life that you were called to and have made a good confession about in the presence of many witnesses. (1 Timothy 6:12 NIV)

Even though this was written by Paul for Timothy thousands of years ago, it could easily have been written today for you and me! Get ready for battle! Fight the good fight for the faith you have been given. You have made a good confession of your faith and trust in Christ in front of many witnesses. Now is the time to commit to the Lord and show the world how great a God you serve! Do not put off until tomorrow what you should do today!

Get your armor on!

COMMIT TO THE LORD

Dear friends, although I was eager to write you about the salvation we share, I found it necessary to write and exhort you to contend for the faith that was delivered to the saints once for all. (Jude 1:3 NIV)

Jude was eager to write about the salvation all Christians share in Christ. However, he was compelled to write about something different. I want to draw your attention to the phrase, "contend for the faith." What does that phrase mean to you? It means we are to hold on to our profession of faith, hold on to our testimony, hold on to our usefulness and working for God. In other words, we are to constantly work for the faith, staying in the will of God and being useful to Him. Commit to the Lord and contend for the faith!

Get your armor on!

Commit your activities to the LORD, and your plans will be achieved. (Proverbs 16:3 NIV)

Do not you just love it when the Word of God is so black and white! Plain and simple: you want to succeed in life? Commit all your activities to the Lord! In all ways possible, honor God and He will honor you!

Get your armor on!

COMMIT TO THE LORD

Take delight in the LORD, and He will give you your heart's desires. Commit your way to the LORD; trust in Him, and He will act. (Psalm 37:4-5 NIV)

These verses are not a license to ask for whatever your heart desires and expect God to give it to you. No, the verse reads that you must first take delight in the Lord. Then He will give you your heart's desire. Because at that point, your heart will be in harmony with His heart. Commit to the Lord; trust Him, and He **WILL** act! Not He might act, or if He is not doing something else, He may act, or provided God is listening, He will think about acting. Verse 5 says God **WILL** act if we stay committed to Him.

Get your armor on!

GOOD CHARACTER

Do not be deceived: "Bad company corrupts good morals." (1 Corinthians 15:33 NIV)

Guilty by association. You have heard of people getting in trouble, even when they did not do anything wrong. Problem was they were with someone who did. You hang out with the wrong crowd and soon your reputation becomes like theirs. Do not think too highly of yourself to believe you will be the stronger personality and will influence them. In most cases, that does not work. Look back at the warning in this verse. Do not be deceived. Pay attention to who your "homies" are! Develop good character.

Get your armor on!

The one who searches for what is good finds favor, but if someone looks for trouble, it will come to him. (Proverbs 11:27 NIV)

You know very well the different paths two brothers can take. Not that one was perfect by any stretch of the imagination. You can be assured both make their share of poor decisions. However, for the most part, one tries to do what was right. For the other, it seems like everywhere he turns, trouble is there waiting on him. Someone looking for trouble does not really have to look for it. Trouble will find him! To have good character, search for what is good. You will find what you are looking for!

Get your armor on!

GOOD CHARACTER

He dug a pit and hollowed it out but fell into the hole he had made. His trouble comes back on his own head, and his violence falls on the top of his head. (Psalm 7:15-16 NIV)

The psalmist is referring to a wicked one. He digs his hole of wickedness and then falls into it. The trouble he has caused falls on top of him. You might read, too, that the wicked one is trying to cover / hide his wickedness by digging a hole and putting all the evil doings in it. Problem is, as is with most sins, the hole keeps getting bigger and bigger before you eventually fall in your own trap. Best not to cover up your sins, but confess them; ask for forgiveness; repent from them. A person of good character does not retreat and hide, but recognizes his sinfulness and gets right with God as soon as he can.

Get your armor on!

All you need to say is simply 'Yes' or 'No'; anything beyond this comes from the evil one. (Matthew 5:37 NIV)

My word is my bond. This phrase does not mean much anymore. Jesus spoke these words to the Pharisees who were all caught up in technicalities that allowed them to side-step certain obligations. Jesus accused them of mocking the truth. He expects His followers to be men and women of character, to remain true to their commitments and not look for a loophole or technicality to bypass them.

Jesus was true to His word. He was a man of character. And He expects you to be the same!

Get your armor on!

GOOD CHARACTER

Who can find a capable wife? Jessica is far more precious than jewels. The heart of her husband trusts in her, and he will not lack anything good. Jessica rewards him with good, not evil, all the days of her life. Jessica selects wool and flax and works with willing hands. Jessica is like the merchant ships, bringing her food from far away. Jessica rises while it is still night and provides food for her household and portions for her female servants. Jessica evaluates a field and buys it; she plants a vineyard with her earnings. Jessica draws on her strength and reveals that her arms are strong. Jessica sees that her profits are good, and her lamp never goes out at night, Jessica extends her hands to the spinning staff, and her hands hold the spindle. Her hands reach out to the poor, and she extends her hands to the needy. Jessica is not afraid for her household when it snows, for all in her household are doubly clothed. Jessica makes her own bed coverings; her clothing is fine linen and purple. Her husband is known at the city gates, where he sits among the elders of the land. Jessica makes and sells linen garments; she delivers belts to the merchants. Strength and honor are her clothing, and she can laugh at the time to come. Jessica opens her mouth with wisdom and loving instruction is on her tongue. Jessica watches over the activities of her household and is never idle. Her sons rise up and call her blessed. Her husband also praises her: "Many women are capable, but you surpass them all!" (Proverbs 31:10-29 NIV)

This is my prayer for you! That one day these verses can be said of you, just like, in my opinion, they speak about your mother! Be a woman of character!

Get your armor on!

GOOD CHARACTER

LORD, who can dwell in Your tent? Who can live on Your holy mountain? Scott, who lives honestly, practices righteousness, and acknowledges the truth in his heart– Scott does not slander with his tongue, Scott does not harm his friend or discredit his neighbor, Scott despises the one rejected by the LORD but honors those who fear the LORD, Scott keeps his word whatever the cost, Scott does not lend his money at interest or take a bribe against the innocent—Scott does these things [and] will never be moved. (Psalm 15:1-5 NIV)

This is my prayer for you. While I admit I am not perfect, I hope that I have been some form of example for you to follow. Be a man of character!

Get your armor on!

GOSSIP

Without wood a fire goes out; without a gossip a quarrel dies down. (Proverbs 26:20 NIV)

Remember playing the game as a child. Cannot recall the name, but you start with one person whispering a message to another and then go around the room, each person whispering the message told to him. The last person states aloud the message that was told to him. The two messages are not anywhere close to being the same. This is the very thing that happens with gossip. You hear something and tell someone else. That someone else tells someone else and so on. You end up with something totally different from the beginning message. You also end up with a lot of hurt feelings and misunderstandings. Best to adhere to Solomon's advice and remove gossip.

Get your armor on!

A gossip betrays a confidence, but a trustworthy person keeps a secret. (Proverbs 11:13 NIV)

You ever tell someone a secret and have them swear they won't tell anyone. Well, they do not tell everyone, just their roommate or one of their best friends. Before long, the secret is out. Bet you will not ever tell that person a "secret" again! Why? Because they betrayed your confidence in them. Do not be a gossip. Be a trustworthy friend!

Get your armor on!

GOSSIP

A contrary man spreads conflict, and a gossip separates close friends. (Proverbs 16:28 NIV)

Yesterday we read one of the benefits of avoiding gossip – building a trustworthy friend. Here, we read one of the dangers gossip can cause. It will eventually ruin a friendship. Some people thrive on gossip and look for ways to hurt others in hopes that they may receive more attention. All it does is tear a friendship apart and cast a shadow of doubt on a person's motive. You cannot be trusted if you gossip. You may get away with it for a while, but eventually, others will figure you out and cast you aside. Be a trusted friend. Do not gossip.

Get your armor on!

We hear that some among you are idle and disruptive. They are not busy; they are busybodies. Such people we command and urge in the Lord Jesus Christ to settle down and earn the food they eat. (2 Thessalonians 3:11-12 NIV)

I just love this verse. We all know people like this. They are so busy trying to find scoop about everyone else. Paul refers to these individuals as busybodies! Look at what he tells them: settle down and earn the food they eat. In other words, mind your own business and take care of yourself. Do not be a busybody. Do not gossip!

Get your armor on!

GOSSIP

The words of a gossip are like choice morsels; they go down to the inmost parts. (Proverbs 18:8 NIV)

Think of your favorite dessert. Now imagine you have a plate or bowl if it sitting right in front of you. You have not eaten all day and your stomach has been growling for hours. What do you do? Duh! You gobble it down like no tomorrow!! As each bit slides across your taste buds, you cannot think of anything better. But after you have gorged yourself, you do not feel so good. This is exactly what gossip does. It baits you, like your favorite dessert. Then you get all you can get. It goes down in your inmost parts and you do not feel so good after a while.

Be aware of gossip's enticing traits. Pray for discernment to identify gossip before you get entangled.

Get your armor on!

JEALOUSY

A heart at peace gives life to the body, but envy rots the bones. (Proverbs 14:30 NIV)

According to Wikipedia, jealousy is an emotion that typically refers to the negative thoughts and feelings of insecurity, fear, and anxiety over an anticipated loss of something that the person values. Jealousy is a negative emotion. What drives a person to be jealous is not healthy. The writer of Proverbs says it "rots the bones." I would rather give life to the body than to cause the body to rot. Get rid of jealousy and give life!

Get your armor on!

Saul was very angry; this refrain displeased him greatly. "They have credited David with tens of thousands," he thought, "but me with only thousands. What more can he get but the kingdom?" And from that time on Saul kept a close eye on David. (1 Samuel 18:8-9 NIV)

I bring up this verse because I wanted to share with you how jealousy destroys relationships. David was already appointed heir to the throne and Saul knew it. Saul's jealousy had already driven him to attempt to kill David on several occasions. Remember that Jonathan, Saul's son, was David's best friend. Remember, too, that David was married to Saul's daughter, Michel. Bet that was an interesting Christmas dinner!! Jealousy rarely impacts just 2 people. It has roots throughout many relationships, none of which can lead to anything positive. So beware of the tangled web of jealousy.

Get your armor on!

JEALOUSY

Resentment kills a fool, and envy slays the simple. (Job 5:2 NIV)

We have talked about how jealousy is a negative emotion that leads to nothing positive. This verse is more evidence of that fact. Resentment kills a fool. So who is the fool? The person to whom jealousy is intended or the person with the jealousy? My take is the latter. Only fools are jealous. And jealousy will tear the heart out of a person. Jealousy also slays the simple because, the majority of the time, the one to whom jealousy is intended has no idea of the jealousy towards them. They go through the relationship thinking all is well, when behind the scenes, your jealousy is cutting them to pieces. Beware of the dangers of jealousy!

Get your armor on!

And I saw that all toil and all achievement spring from one person's envy of another. This too is meaningless, a chasing after the wind. (Ecclesiastes 4:4 NIV)

Solomon could have and did have anything he ever wished for; nothing was withheld from him. And the conclusion from his pursuits? All was meaningless, like chasing the wind. Jealous never gets you anywhere. The toil and "achievement" gained from jealousy is worthless. Learn Paul's secret of being content in any and every situation (Phil 4:11-12). Avoid jealousy. It gets you nowhere.

Get your armor on!

JEALOUSY

When the Jews saw the crowds, they were filled with jealousy. They began to contradict what Paul was saying and heaped abuse on him. (Acts 13:45 NIV)

You cannot control other people's reaction to what you do. All you can do is control you. Paul was not doing anything wrong here. Yet the Jews in the crowd were filled with jealousy and began to cause trouble for Paul. You may encounter people just as Paul did, who want nothing more than to discredit you or cause your harm, all because of their jealousy towards you. Recognize jealousy and persevere against it.

Get your armor on!

LOVE OF MONEY

For the love of money is a root of all kinds of evil. Some people, eager for money, have wandered from the faith and pierced themselves with many griefs. (1 Timothy 6:10 NIV)

Let's make one thing very clear. Paul did not tell Timothy that money was the root of all kinds of evil. He said the LOVE of money is. It is not a sin to be wealthy. There are many strong Christian families who are wealthy and use their wealth to promote the Kingdom of God. But when the desire or pursuit of money becomes your idol, then we have a problem. Many have wandered from the faith, depending too much on their bank account or stock portfolio rather than the provisions of our Lord. And doing so has caused them many grieves. Pursue God and you will have all the riches you can handle!

Get your armor on!

Keep your lives free from the love of money and be content with what you have, because God has said, "Never will I leave you; never will I forsake you." (Hebrews 13:5 NIV)

Typically, when one pursues the almighty dollar, they start depending more upon their ability than the provision of the Lord. I created the wealth; I developed the product; I invested wisely; it was my idea. It is a bit one-sided thinking, would you not say? Who created the resources for you to use to develop your product? Who gave you the intelligence to invest wisely? Who gave you the creative ability to come up with the idea? You get the picture. Plus, the Lord already promised He would provide for us our every need. Just trust His provision and be content with it.

Get your armor on!

Now listen, you rich people, weep and wail because of the misery that is coming on you. Your wealth has rotted, and moths have eaten your clothes. Your gold and silver are corroded. Their corrosion will testify against you and eat your flesh like fire. You have hoarded wealth in the last days. Look! The wages you failed to pay the workers who mowed your fields are crying out against you. The cries of the harvesters have reached the ears of the Lord Almighty. You have lived on earth in luxury and self-indulgence. You have fattened yourselves in the day of slaughter. (James 5:1-5 NIV)

Why would you not think I would pull a verse from James!!! Again, do not get me wrong. James is not against people being wealthy. He is pointing out what usually happens when we pursue wealth. Look at the words he uses: "rotted", "corroded", "hoarded", "self-indulged", "fattened". These are not flattering words, but condemning words. Condemning because these rich people have replaced their dependence upon God with their dependence upon themselves and their wealth. Beware the pursuit of wealth. Pursue God instead.

Get your armor on!

Like a partridge that hatches eggs it did not lay are those who gain riches by unjust means. (Jeremiah 17:11 NIV)

Again, I will use the word "typically". Not all wealthy people fall into this category. Typically, when one has amassed a great deal of wealth, the desire for more just grows in intensity. They can already buy anything money can offer, but they want more. Never satisfied, they will go to most any means to acquire more, even if they have to lie, steal, or cheat to get it. Just like this verse reads, you hatch eggs that you did not lay. It is the struggle that makes you appreciate the benefits. Without the struggle, where are the benefits? There are none. Remember that!

Get your armor on!

LOVE OF MONEY

Those who trust in their riches will fall, but the righteous will thrive like a green leaf. (Proverbs 11:28 NIV)

I just love the analogy in this verse. Take a green leaf compared to a dead leaf. The dead leaf has all the characteristics of a green leaf in terms of shape and size. However, to the touch, the dead leaf is brittle and easily crumbled. To the color, the dead leaf is drab and, well, dead. The green leaf, on the other hand, is thriving, providing shade and coolness in the heat of the day. Its color is vibrant! Put your trust in your riches and you become like a dead leaf. Put your trust in the Lord, you thrive like a green leaf!

Get your armor on!

PRIDE

Pride goes before destruction, a haughty spirit before a fall. (Proverbs 16:18 NIV)

Probably the most commonly known verse regarding pride. Let's dive into this little word. Defined, pride means a high or inordinate opinion of one's own importance, whether as cherished in one's mind or as displayed in one's conduct. Pretty succinct definition. Your pride is shown either in your opinion of yourself or carried out in your actions for others to see. Oh, but watch out when pride creeps in. Because right around the corner comes destruction and a great fall. Do not be too prideful to think it will not happen to you.

Get your armor on!

"This is what the LORD says: 'In the same way I will ruin the pride of Judah and the great pride of Jerusalem. These wicked people, who refuse to listen to my words, who follow the stubbornness of their hearts and go after other gods to serve and worship them, will be like this belt—completely useless! (Jeremiah 13:9-10 NIV)

What caused the Lord to lash out so against the Children of Israel? It was their pride. Just like in the definition from yesterday, pride can be made visible for others to see. Judah and Jerusalem showed just that with their refusal to listen to God's word and their stubbornness to serve and worship other gods. Because of their pride, they would be completely useless. May God never use those words to describe me – completely useless! I pray they do not describe you either!

Get your armor on!

PRIDE

Before his downfall, a man's heart is proud, but humility comes before honor. (Proverbs 18:12 NIV)

Just like the first verse in this series, pride usually precedes a fall. You get all puffed up, depending on yourself rather than on God; your own intellect; your own abilities; your own finances and resources. You think you have this life all figured out. Then the bottom falls out and down you go! Look what comes before honor – humility – the opposite of pride. If you want a place of honor in God's household, then you must put away pride.

Get your armor on!

The vision of Obadiah. This is what the Sovereign LORD says about Edom— We have heard a message from the LORD: An envoy was sent to the nations to say, "Rise, let us go against her for battle"— "See, I will make you small among the nations; you will be utterly despised. The pride of your heart has deceived you, you who live in the clefts of the rocks and make your home on the heights, you who say to yourself, 'Who can bring me down to the ground?' Though you soar like the eagle and make your nest among the stars, from there I will bring you down," declares the LORD. (Obadiah 1:1-4 NIV)

How about that. I think this is the first verse from the book of Obadiah. I bet most people will have to look up that book in the table of contents in their Bible!!

Oh, the ways of pride. It deceives you. It makes you think you are invincible. You think you soar above all the "common folk" because of your position, possessions, or power. No matter how high you may think you can fly, God can fly higher! And from your self-appointed lofty position, God will bring you down. Beware of pride. Learn from Obadiah's vision.

Get your armor on!

PRIDE

If anyone thinks they are something when they are not, they deceive themselves. Each one should test their own actions. Then they can take pride in themselves alone, without comparing themselves to someone else, (Galatians 6:3-4 NIV)

Do not you just love the way Paul puts people in their places? If you think you are something when you are not, you just deceive yourself! Our problem with pride is when we start comparing ourselves to others. "Keeping up with the Jones" as the old saying goes. Paul tells us here to quit comparing ourselves to others. We are to test our own actions and whether they measure up to God's standards. When we do that, we do not need to compare ourselves to anyone else, for He alone is the sole measuring stick.

Get your armor on!

WORRY

Cast all your anxiety on him because he cares for you. (1 Peter 5:7 NIV)

Worry is hard not to express, especially if you are a parent!! But when we break everything down, worry means lack of faith. We are telling God that we do not believe He is big enough to handle our situation. We fail to remember He is the God of the Universe. He did speak all things into being. All we need to do is cast all our anxiety (worry) on Him for He longs to intercede for us to shoulder those burdens for us. Much easier said than done, I know that. But when you feel the tightness of worry around you, just remember God is waiting to take on that burden for you.

Get your armor on!

The animals going in were male and female of every living thing, as God had commanded Noah. Then the Lord shut him in. (Genesis 7:16 NIV)

If anyone in the world ever had a reason to worry, it was Noah. It had never rained on earth before. He had two of every known animal on board with him. What and how was he to feed them all? What and how was he to feed him and his family? How long would he be on the ark? Would the ark hold up? Would the food run out? Where would the ark eventually settle? How were they to carry on once the water subsided? So many more questions than answers. The key here is "...God had commanded Noah." Noah knew God commanded him. All Noah needed to do was obey! Sure, doubt will creep in; but you need to remind yourself that what God has promised, He is able to perform (Romans 4:21).

Get your armor on!

Why, you do not even know what will happen tomorrow. What is your life? You are a mist that appears for a little while and then vanishes. (James 4:14 NIV)

This verse just hits me between the eyes sometimes. And really puts things into perspective. We get all caught up worrying about tomorrow when tomorrow is not guaranteed to anyone. Do not take this wrong and think this verse is a license to not plan for tomorrow. But we should not be so concerned about tomorrow and forget about living today! Our life is just a mist. We only have a short window of opportunity to make a difference for Christ. Do not let tomorrow stand in the way of today!

Get your armor on!

Cast your cares on the Lord and he will sustain you; he will never let the righteous be shaken. (Psalm 55:22 NIV)

We have come full circle this week with worry. We started with the fact that God cares for us. We end on the fact God cares for us. Take Him for His Word! He will sustain you. He will never let the righteous be shaken. That does not mean life will always be rosy. Far from it. But through the peaks and valleys, God is there. We do not need to worry! Just trust in Him.

Get your armor on!

WORRY

"Therefore I tell you, do not worry about your life, what you will eat or drink; or about your body, what you will wear. Is not life more than food, and the body more than clothes? Look at the birds of the air; they do not sow or reap or store away in barns, and yet your heavenly Father feeds them. Are you not much more valuable than they? Can any one of you by worrying add a single hour to your life? And why do you worry about clothes? See how the flowers of the field grow. They do not labor or spin. Yet I tell you that not even Solomon in all his splendor was dressed like one of these. If that is how God clothes the grass of the field, which is here today and tomorrow is thrown into the fire, will he not much more clothe you—you of little faith? So do not worry, saying, 'What shall we eat?' or 'What shall we drink?' or 'What shall we wear?' For the pagans run after all these things, and your heavenly Father knows that you need them. But seek first his kingdom and his righteousness, and all these things will be given to you as well. Therefore do not worry about tomorrow, for tomorrow will worry about itself. Each day has enough trouble of its own. (Matthew 6:25-34 NIV)

I know, this is a long passage. In short, Jesus is telling us not to worry through life and gives us two illustrations why we should not: the birds and the flowers. You do not see birds storing up food in massive nests, do you? They are fed daily as they need. Yet, are not we more valuable than the birds? Anyone driving through Texas in the spring can see the fields of bluebonnets painting the landscape in all shades of blue. The Lord provides the necessary water and sunshine to make them grow. If God "clothes" the roadsides in bluebonnets, how much more will He care for you? Again, this is not a license to become lazy, waiting for God to provide everything. You get the idea. Do not be like the pagans, who run after these things. Our Heavenly Father knows our needs, even before we know them. We only need to look to Him for sustenance.

Get your armor on!

FEAR

The Lord is a warrior; the Lord is his name. Pharaoh's chariots and his army he has hurled into the sea. The best of Pharaoh's officers are drowned in the Red Sea. The deep waters have covered them; they sank to the depths like a stone. Your right hand, Lord, was majestic in power. Your right hand, Lord, shattered the enemy. (Exodus 15:3-6 NIV)

The children of Israel were so wishy-washy. One day praising the Lord and the next day cursing Him for bringing them to the desert to die. We really are no different. This was right after the crossing of the Red Sea, so of course they were praising His name. But look at how they describe the Lord: "a warrior", "majestic in power", "shattered the enemy". If we truly believed those descriptions, we would not have anything to fear. The Lord that did all those things in the desert is the same Lord we serve today. So do not be afraid. Just trust He will do the same to your fears as He did to Pharaoh's army.

Get your armor on!

Surely God is my salvation; I will trust and not be afraid. The Lord, the Lord himself, is my strength and my defense; he has become my salvation. (Isaiah 12:2 NIV)

Fear can be defined as a feeling of apprehension or alarm caused by impending danger. And just like worry, we can boil the definition down to lack of faith. Truly God is our salvation. He will rescue us in His strength. It is much easier said than done, but we need to trust He knows what He is doing and not fear anything. He is our defense. Rest in His salvation.

Get your armor on!

FEAR

So do not fear, for I am with you; do not be dismayed, for I am your God. I will strengthen you and help you; I will uphold you with my righteous right hand. (Isaiah 41:10 NIV)

There that phrase is again, "righteous right hand." What is the meaning of the "right hand of God"? Well, who ascended to the right hand of God? Who holds that precious high position? Jesus Christ Himself!! Remember, He is with us. He is our God. He will strengthen us and help us. He will uphold with His righteous right hand-the Lord Jesus Christ!

Get your armor on!

But Jesus immediately said to them: "Take courage! It is I. Do not be afraid." (Matthew 14:27 NIV)

This verse is taken from the story of Jesus walking on water. The disciples were in the middle of the sea, winds blowing, waves crashing against the boat. They saw a figure on the water and were frightened, thinking they were seeing a ghost. I do not blame them! I probably would have done the same. But look at what Jesus did. He immediately responded to them, calming their fear. He did not ignore them; He did not keep coming towards them causing fear to increase. Jesus does the same for us today. We need not fear anything. The future; graduation; career opportunities; marriage; kids; family. Take courage. He is with us. Do not be afraid.

Get your armor on!

FEAR

The Lord is my light and my salvation—whom shall I fear? The Lord is the stronghold of my life—of whom shall I be afraid? (Psalm 27:1 NIV)

When I am afraid, I put my trust in you. In God, whose word I praise—in God I trust and am not afraid. What can mere mortals do to me? (Psalm 56:3-4 NIV)

Two great verses on fear. I could not decide between the two, so you get both! Another two-for-one special.

If we truly put our trust in the Lord, then who or what should we fear? Really, no one and nothing. The Lord is the stronghold of our lives. A stronghold is a fortified place or a fortress, a place of survival or refuge. We can take cover under His arms. And, when the world gets the best of us (and it will!), and we begin to believe the lies Satan tells us: we are not talented enough; pretty enough; we'll never have enough money - we just need to put our trust in God. And when we do, what can mere mortals do to us? Think about it. Mere mortals. They do not hold a candle to our God. The finite compared to the Infinite. The limited compared to the Unlimited. The constrained compared to the Unconstrained. No comparison!

Get your armor on!

HOMOSEXUALITY

Because of this, God gave them over to shameful lusts. Even their women exchanged natural sexual relations for unnatural ones. In the same way the men also abandoned natural relations with women and were inflamed with lust for one another. Men committed shameful acts with other men, and received in themselves the due penalty for their error. (Romans 1:26-27 NIV)

I am probably going to make a lot of enemies this week!

Let me make one thing very clear. I do not hate homosexuals! As the saying goes, "love the sinner, hate the sin." We are so bombarded with the message that homosexuality is acceptable and should be tolerated. I wanted to point out the fallacies of this type of thinking.

The Bible is very clear on sexual relationships, inside the context of marriage, is between man and woman. Look at how the Apostle Paul describes these relationships in these verses: **"unnatural", "inflamed lust",** and **"shameful acts."** No glowing words of endorsement for this type of behavior. Besides, if this behavior was acceptable to God, then why would Paul have concluded they received "due penalty for their error"?

Get your armor on!

HOMOSEXUALITY

Do not have sexual relations with a man as one does with a woman; that is detestable. (Leviticus 18:22 NIV)

I just love it when the Word of God is very clear. These words were spoken to Moses by God Himself. If any homosexual tries to justify his/her behavior, he/she is directly disobeying God's explicit Word. There is no room for debate here. Let's look at what detestable means. Synonyms include vile, despicable, repugnant, revolting, abhorrent, and loathsome. I do not think I would want to be involved in any behavior with those adjectives.

Get your armor on!

They called to Lot, "Where are the men who came to you tonight? Bring them out to us so that we can have sex with them." Lot went outside to meet them and shut the door behind him and said, "No, my friends. Do not do this wicked thing. (Genesis 19:5-7 NIV)

These verses describe just how wicked a place Sodom was. Men had come to visit Lot. Others in the city saw them arrive and enter Lot's house. All these others could think about was "fresh meat." Two things to point out here. Even though these men were detestable (using God's word from yesterday's verse), Lot called them "friends." You can still have compassion on those wrapped up in sin. Second, Lot called what they wanted to do a "wicked thing." If this type of behavior is simply ok and should be tolerated, as Hollywood and main stream media want us to think, then why would Lot have described it as a wicked thing?

Get your armor on!

HOMOSEXUALITY

We also know that the law is made not for the righteous but for lawbreakers and rebels, the ungodly and sinful, the unholy and irreligious, for those who kill their fathers or mothers, for murderers, for the sexually immoral, for those practicing homosexuality, for slave traders and liars and perjurers—and for whatever else is contrary to the sound doctrine that conforms to the gospel concerning the glory of the blessed God, which he entrusted to me. (1 Timothy 1:9-11 NIV)

I do not want to get too philosophical with you today. Basically, the law (primarily the Old Testament) was given to point out our wrong doing and to show that no man can be justified in Christ just by keeping the law, for no one is perfect. Paul lists those for which the law was made. In essence, it was made for us all. However, I want to point out to you the list includes homosexuals and then includes a catch-all phrase of – "whatever else is contrary to sound doctrine" of the gospel of Christ. Point blank – homosexuality is flat out wrong. God did not make you that way. You were not born that way. If you are involved in homosexual activity, it is a choice you made and is contrary to the sound doctrine of God.

Get your armor on!

HOMOSEXUALITY

Or do you not know that wrongdoers will not inherit the kingdom of God? Do not be deceived: Neither the sexually immoral nor idolaters nor adulterers nor men who have sex with men nor thieves nor the greedy nor drunkards nor slanderers nor swindlers will inherit the kingdom of God. (1 Corinthians 6:9-10 NIV)

Now we cannot use this verse and therefore condemn all homosexuals to hell. That is not what this verse is referring to. Like any addiction, you can be cured. Whom these verses are referring to are those actively involved and continuing in this type of behavior without any remorse or conscience. You flaunt your evil behavior before man, woman, and child and try to convince anyone who will listen that it is within your right to do, go ahead. But remember this: You will NOT inherit the kingdom of God. You will be forever removed from Him. Not a place I want to be!

Get your armor on!

Those who walk righteously and speak what is right, who reject gain from extortion and keep their hands from accepting bribes, who stop their ears against plots of murder and shut their eyes against contemplating evil— they are the ones who will dwell on the heights, whose refuge will be the mountain fortress. Their bread will be supplied, and water will not fail them. Your eyes will see the king in his beauty and view a land that stretches afar. (Isaiah 33:15-17 NIV)

Remember at times, when you hear something you do not want to hear or should not hear, you tightly close your eyes, plug your ears with your fingers and say, "La La La La, I cannot hear you." This is the exact behavior we should have when approached by sin. We should **"shut [our] eyes against contemplating evil."** For when we do, look at the promises: **[we] will dwell on the heights, bread will be supplied, and water will not fail.** Better yet, our eyes will see the King in His beauty. Close your eyes to sin, open them to the beauty of the King!!!

Get your armor on!

I made a covenant with my eyes not to look lustfully at a young woman. (Job 31:1 NIV)

Even though Job is making a covenant here, we can also infer that a woman should not look lustfully at a young man. This is a pretty bold covenant. And a difficult one to keep! I do not believe Job's covenant included a glance. He did not say not to look. He said not to look lustfully. There is a difference. You can notice an attractive male or female. But it is another thing to stare and begin developing sinful thoughts about them. That is where the look crosses the line. Follow in Job's footsteps. Make that same covenant with your eyes. Guard them!

Get your armor on!

GUARD YOUR EYES

Do not lust in your heart after her beauty or let her captivate you with her eyes. (Proverbs 6:25 NIV)

You walk across campus and see someone in a distance. You do not really like that person or you know that person will stop you and talk your ear off. You do not want to listen or you do not have time to listen. If you do not make eye contact with them, maybe they will not "see" you.

Although Solomon's main intention was to guard his sons from adultery, I think we can take this a bit further. Yes, the "her" refers to a woman, but what about a new car? New clothes? New shoes? House, jewelry, golf clubs, boat, RV, you name it. Do not lust after these things. Do not let them capture you with their lure. Avoid "eye contact" with these things.

Get your armor on!

A discerning person keeps wisdom in view, but a fool's eyes wander to the ends of the earth. (Proverbs 17:24 NIV)

You want to affix your eyes on something? Keep wisdom in full view. That means you allow the wisdom of the Holy Spirit to guide and guard your eyes. And not necessarily the eyes in your head, but also the eyes of your heart. So much of life comes back to attitudes of the heart. Do not be like the fool whose eyes and heart wander aimlessly to the ends of the earth. Have purpose. Be intentional. Keep wisdom in full view.

Get your armor on!

GUARD YOUR EYES

Let your eyes look straight ahead; fix your gaze directly before you. (Proverbs 4:25 NIV)

Remember when you first started driving? How intently you looked straight ahead, not daring to look away from the road for fear of an accident. Our lives should be lived with our eyes affixed on the goal to win the prize for which God has called us to. To glance side to side might cause us to have an accident!

Get your armor on!

ALCOHOL AND DRINKING

Be careful, however, that the exercise of your rights does not become a stumbling block to the weak. (1 Corinthians 8:9 NIV)

Now before you completely tune me out, hear me out. The result may surprise you.

Nowhere in the Bible are we commanded not to drink alcohol. Many argue, "Even Christ drank wine, so why should I not?" While a Christian may be free to drink moderately as long as they do not become drunk (that is strictly forbidden as we will explore later), is that the highest activity we could do? Paul stated here that he would not allow this liberty to be a license to sin, nor would he do anything that would cause a brother to stumble. Like choosing on a multiple-choice test, the best answer when two answers appear to be right.

Alcohol is such a heated topic of debate these days. We know all too well the disastrous consequences of drinking. Look at my own family. One may never know the consequences of their drinking, how it may influence someone else who may be struggling in this area. You may feel comfortable doing so, but is that really the most Christ-like behavior we could be involved in?

Get your armor on!

ALCOHOL AND DRINKING

Wine is a mocker and beer a brawler; whoever is led astray by them is not wise. (Proverbs 20:1 NIV)

So if drinking is not forbidden, what should our position, as Christians, be regarding alcohol and drinking? We know that alcoholism is responsible for many broken homes; we know the many deaths on our highways are caused by drinking and driving; we know premature deaths are caused by health problems stemming from alcoholism. Millions of dollars are spent annually combating the ills of alcoholism. And it all starts with just one drink. I do not believe anyone ever starts drinking with the intent of becoming an alcoholic.

Look how Solomon describes alcohol in this verse: a mocker and a brawler. Anyone "led astray" by them is not wise. Does that mean we should not drink? Not necessarily. Alcohol can lead you where you ought not to be. Then, as Solomon suggests, you are not wise.

Get your armor on!

ALCOHOL AND DRINKING

"Speak to the Israelites and say to them: 'If a man or woman wants to make a special vow, a vow of dedication to the Lord as a Nazirite, they must abstain from wine and other fermented drink and must not drink vinegar made from wine or other fermented drink. They must not drink grape juice or eat grapes or raisins. (Number 6:2-3 NIV)

In the Old Testament, there was a group of people known as Nazarites that took a vow to separate themselves unto the Lord and therefore they would not drink any wine or alcoholic beverages.

Is it sinful to drink? Sin is a matter of the heart and does not exist in any one thing. It is the drunkenness and intoxication that comes about when one drinks too much that causes one to sin. The Bible teaches discipline and moderation not just with alcohol; even over eating is a sin (gluttony).

What we do know is that the Nazirites separated themselves unto God. In order to do so, they put away any alcohol. Be honest before God as to the issue in your own heart in this regard.

Get your armor on!

ALCOHOL AND DRINKING

For John the Baptist has come eating no bread and drinking no wine, and you say, 'He has a demon!' The Son of Man has come eating and drinking, and you say, 'Look at him, a glutton and a drunk, a friend of tax collectors and sinners!' (Luke 7:33-34 NIV)

You, my brothers and sisters, were called to be free. But do not use your freedom to indulge the flesh; rather, serve one another humbly in love. (Galatians 5:13 NIV)

John the Baptist was a preacher abstained from drinking. Jesus was The Preacher who drank alcohol. So what is our stance to be? We cannot say to abstain when one preacher drank. We cannot say it is ok to drink when one preacher abstained. Throughout Scripture, many references to wine were positive: a blessing from the Lord, something to be enjoyed. But like any good gift from God, it can be abused.

Now look at what Paul has to say. We are free from the law. Free from the bondage of sin and free from subjection to expensive and burdensome rituals and customs. We are now under grace (God's Reward At Christ's Expense). But that grace does not give us license to sin just so grace can be poured out. Hence, Paul's caution not to use freedom to indulge in the flesh. Just because we may be free to partake in alcohol does not mean that is the best thing we can do. Rather, the better thing to do is serve one another humbly in love.

Get your armor on!

ALCOHOL AND DRINKING

Do not get drunk on wine, which leads to debauchery. Instead, be filled with the Spirit, speaking to one another with psalms, hymns, and songs from the Spirit. Sing and make music from your heart to the Lord, always giving thanks to God the Father for everything, in the name of our Lord Jesus Christ. (Ephesians 5:18-20 NIV)

We must all give an account of ourselves before our Lord. What would please Him the most? Would it not be pleasing to Him if we loved others enough to give up those things we could have, for a greater cause? Would it not be a more powerful witness to others in our age to stand out as one who did not drink alcohol because we had no need to do so? When we are filled with the Spirit of God, His Spirit gives us the joy and release that many are seeking by drinking.

I find it so ironic that a slang word for alcohol is "spirits." So my question to you is: with which spirit do you want to be filled?

Get your armor on!

DEVELOP A CLEAR CONSCIENCE

So I strive always to keep my conscience clear before God and man. (Acts 24:16 NIV)

So what do I mean to develop a clear conscience? Free of guilt or responsibility. Innocence. At the end of the day, you can honestly look back and state with confidence that you did everything within your power to ensure you treated everyone you encountered with dignity and honor. That the words you spoke were helpful and beneficial for the building up of others. That you did your best to show Christ to all people. That you did not give anyone reason to question your motives as being self-serving.

Like Paul, strive to keep your conscience clear!

Get your armor on!

The mind governed by the flesh is death, but the mind governed by the Spirit is life and peace. (Romans 8:6 NIV)

I like the use of the word "governed" in this verse. It means ruled, controlled, or administered. If our mind, or conscience, is ruled by the flesh, or by worldly thinking, it leads to death. But if our mind is ruled by the Spirit, it breeds life and peace. Two very dramatic differences. When we have a clear conscience, we radiate with life and peace to those around us. That will not stop people from trying to give us a bad name or criticizing us behind our backs. But when these accusations come, those that hear them will automatically know they are false because of the way we live.

Let the Spirit govern you. Develop a clear conscience.

Get your armor on!

DEVELOP A CLEAR CONSCIENCE

A good name is more desirable than great riches; to be esteemed is better than silver or gold. (Proverbs 22:1 NIV)

Not too long ago, a man's word was his bond. A handshake was all it took to seal the deal. To go back on your word was frowned upon. Not anymore. Deals are made, contracts are signed, but they mean nothing if you have some slick lawyer who can find loopholes.

We need to get back to the basics and put emphasis on our word being our bond. We need to desire to have a good reputation in the community so that when someone hears the name Jessica Brooks / Scott Brooks, they instantly think, "I know her/him. I have heard of her/him. She/He is a really good person."

Desire a good name. Develop a clear conscience.

Get your armor on!

let us draw near to God with a sincere heart and with the full assurance that faith brings, having our hearts sprinkled to cleanse us from a guilty conscience and having our bodies washed with pure water. (Hebrews 10:22 NIV)

You can put up false fronts to people. Some you will be able to fool; others will see right through you. But you cannot fool our Lord. He knows your heart. We must come before Him with a sincere heart and ask Him to clear our guilty conscience and have our bodies washed with the pure water of the Spirit. Then, with the full assurance that faith brings, go out and live with a clear conscience with Christ on our side, living through us.

Get your armor on!

DEVELOP A CLEAR CONSCIENCE

Jessica / Scott, my daughter / son, I am giving you this command in keeping with the prophecies once made about you, so that by recalling them you may fight the battle well, holding on to faith and a good conscience, which some have rejected and so have suffered shipwreck with regard to the faith. (1 Timothy 1:18-19 NIV)

Ok, so this is not exactly how Scripture reads. But you know how I like to personalize Scripture!!

The verses were written from Paul to Timothy. Look at the encouragement from Paul. "Fight the battle well, holding on to faith and a good conscience." Look at the warning, "some have rejected and so have suffered shipwreck with regard to the faith." What caused the shipwreck? Not holding on to the faith or not having a good conscience? Perhaps both. Since we are focusing on a good conscience this week, let's go there. The fact that some did not have a clear conscience caused them to have a shipwrecked faith. What comes to mind with a shipwreck? Destruction; maybe death; a ship that is no longer sea worthy. Not words I want said about my faith.

Make sure your sails are full of wind! Make sure your hull is fortified! Make sure you are sea worthy! Develop a clear conscience.

Get your armor on!

NO EXCUSES

Elisha sent a messenger to say to him, "Go, wash yourself seven times in the Jordan, and your flesh will be restored and you will be cleansed." But Naaman went away angry and said, "I thought that he would surely come out to me and stand and call on the name of the Lord his God, wave his hand over the spot and cure me of my leprosy. Are not Abana and Pharpar, the rivers of Damascus, better than all the waters of Israel? Couldn't I wash in them and be cleansed?" So he turned and went off in a rage. Naaman's servants went to him and said, "My father, if the prophet had told you to do some great thing, would you not have done it? How much more, then, when he tells you, 'Wash and be cleansed'!" So he went down and dipped himself in the Jordan seven times, as the man of God had told him, and his flesh was restored and became clean like that of a young boy. Then Naaman and all his attendants went back to the man of God. He stood before him and said, "Now I know that there is no God in all the world except in Israel. So please accept a gift from your servant." (2 Kings 5:10-15 NIV)

Naaman was commander of the army of the king of Aram and was a valiant soldier. However, he acquired leprosy and sought after the prophet Elisha to be healed. When Elisha told him what to do to be healed, what was Naaman's response? He went away angry because he did not receive the cure he thought he would get. I love Naaman's servant's response: "...if the prophet had told you to do some great thing, would you not have done it?"

Sometimes we make excuses for not obeying God because He did not tell us what we wanted Him to tell us in the way we wanted Him to tell us. If we would just do what He said, when He said it, how He said it, life would be much sweeter!

What about you? What excuses are you giving to God?

Get your armor on!

NO EXCUSES

Then the Lord God said to the woman, "What is this you have done?" The woman said, "The serpent deceived me, and I ate." (Genesis 3:13 NIV)

The concept of finger pointing goes all the way back to the Garden of Eden. We are always excusing our sin and putting the blame on someone else. Seems like no one these days can accept personal responsibility. You spill hot coffee on your lap and you sue the company who made the coffee; you get caught drinking and driving and you sue the bar for serving you alcohol; you get lung cancer and you sue the tobacco industry. When are we going to stop pointing the finger at someone else and start taking personal responsibility for our choices, good or bad?!?!?!

Do not make excuses.

Get your armor on!

"But ask the animals, and they will teach you, or the birds in the sky, and they will tell you; or speak to the earth, and it will teach you, or let the fish in the sea inform you. Which of all these does not know that the hand of the Lord has done this? (Job 12:7-9 NIV)

How can we question the Creator? How can we assign credit for scientific order to mere coincidence? Just look around you. Watch the sun rise. Watch the sun set. Watch the leaves change their colors. Watch the flowers bloom. Watch the birds build their nests. These events are evidence of the Creator's existence. We are without excuse to the knowledge of a greater being; a higher power. The real question is whether we will acknowledge His existence or ignore it.

Get your armor on!

NO EXCUSES

"But they all alike began to make excuses. The first said, 'I have just bought a field, and I must go and see it. Please excuse me.' "Another said, 'I have just bought five yoke of oxen, and I'm on my way to try them out. Please excuse me.' "Still another said, 'I just got married, so I cannot come.' (Luke 14:18-20 NIV)

This is from the parable of the wedding feast. Everyone had an excuse why they could not attend the banquet. Jesus is calling us to participate in His kingdom work. He does not need us, but He desperately wants to use us so that we might receive joy in working alongside Him. When He calls, do not give Him excuses. Respond with, "Wherever You lead, I'll go!"

Get your armor on!

"I tell you," he replied, "if they keep quiet, the stones will cry out." (Luke 19:40 NIV)

I just flat out love this verse! Luke 19 is a record of Jesus' triumphant entry into Jerusalem. The people of the city were shouting His praises as He passed through the streets. Unfortunately, a week later, they would be calling out, "Crucify Him!" The Pharisees were rebuking the people and asked Jesus to make them stop. And Jesus uttered these words. As marvelous as it would be to see and hear the rocks cry out praises to God, let's not offer this as an excuse for keeping quiet. Shout it from the mountain tops! Do not let the rocks do our work for us!

Get your armor on!

TEMPTATION

Jesus, full of the Holy Spirit, left the Jordan and was led by the Spirit into the wilderness, where for forty days he was tempted by the devil. He ate nothing during those days, and at the end of them he was hungry. The devil said to him, "If you are the Son of God, tell this stone to become bread." Jesus answered, "It is written: 'Man shall not live on bread alone.'" The devil led him up to a high place and showed him in an instant all the kingdoms of the world. And he said to him, "I will give you all their authority and splendor; it has been given to me, and I can give it to anyone I want to. If you worship me, it will all be yours." Jesus answered, "It is written: 'Worship the Lord your God and serve him only.'" The devil led him to Jerusalem and had him stand on the highest point of the temple. "If you are the Son of God," he said, "throw yourself down from here. For it is written:"' He will command his angels concerning you to guard you carefully; they will lift you up in their hands, so that you will not strike your foot against a stone.'" Jesus answered, "It is said: 'Do not put the Lord your God to the test.'" When the devil had finished all this tempting, he left him until an opportune time. (Luke 4:1-13 NIV)

Luke's version of the temptation of Christ. There is so much in these verses, but I will only concentrate on two aspects.

#1 How did Jesus respond with every temptation? "It is written:..." He quoted scripture. If the Son of Man used scripture to ward off the devil's temptations, how much more important is it for us to do the same!

#2 The devil left him until an opportune time. You may record a victory against the devil. He may leave you for a moment. But trust me, he will return. He is relentless; always seeking whom he may devour. And at the most opportune time, he will strike. Always be on your guard.

Get your armor on!

TEMPTATION

For we do not have a high priest who is unable to empathize with our weaknesses, but we have one who has been tempted in every way, just as we are—yet he did not sin. (Hebrews 4:15 NIV)

After reading yesterday's verse, you may have thought to yourself, "Times are different today. There are so many more temptations these days. Jesus just does not understand what I am going through." Today's verse completely contradicts that rationale. Jesus was tempted in every way we are. Now, granted, maybe not in the same way with the same things, but understand, He was tempted with every type of desire whether it be power, position, or possession. So He does understand what we are going through and is standing by ready to offer help in our time of need. All we need to do is reach out to Him in those times.

Get your armor on!

Because he himself suffered when he was tempted, he is able to help those who are being tempted. (Hebrews 2:18 NIV)

Because Jesus was tempted just as we are, He can help us as we experience temptation. You may have experienced a victory over temptation. If so, then do not keep that to yourself. Share it with others so that it may help someone else going through the same thing. Or share your struggles with an accountability partner. It sometimes helps to know you are not alone. And remember, God is there waiting to help. We just need to reach up!

Get your armor on!

TEMPTATION

Let no one deceive you with empty words, for because of such things God's wrath comes on those who are disobedient. Therefore do not be partners with them. (Ephesians 5:6-7 NIV)

Empty words. I love this description. That is exactly what the devil's words are to us as he attempts to draw us off course. He will promise you anything just to entice you to turn your back on God. But look at Paul's warning in this verse. God's wrath comes to those who are disobedient. If you follow after empty words, be assured you will be punished. Follow Paul's recommendation – do not be deceived by or be partners with empty words.

Get your armor on!

No temptation has overtaken you except what is common to mankind. And God is faithful; he will not let you be tempted beyond what you can bear. But when you are tempted, the will also provide a way out so that you can endure it. (1 Corinthians 10:13 NIV)

If I have not said it before, now would be a good time to do so – IT IS NOT A SIN TO BE TEMPTED! In fact, we ought to praise God when we are tempted because that tells us Satan feels we are a threat to him. If we are complacent and apathetic towards the Gospel, why bother. That is right where Satan wants us.

Know this: when we are tempted, we can overcome! God is faithful. He will not allow you to be tempted beyond what you can bear. You may not think so in the midst of your struggle, but stand on God's Word. He will provide a way out so that we can stand up under it. Notice it does not say He will remove the temptation. It is up to us to use the escape hatch!

Get your armor on!

SATAN THE ADVERSARY

Then war broke out in heaven. Michael and his angels fought against the dragon, and the dragon and his angels fought back. But he was not strong enough, and they lost their place in heaven. The great dragon was hurled down—that ancient serpent called the devil, or Satan, who leads the whole world astray. He was hurled to the earth, and his angels with him. (Revelation 12:7-9 NIV)

Some believe there is no God; there is no Satan; there is no Heaven; there is no Hell. Those that believe this are sadly misled and will realize one day just how wrong they are. Here we see the origin of Satan. A spiritual war broke out in heaven. And Satan was not alone. He convinced other angels in his attempt to overthrow the kingdom of Heaven. He purpose is to lead the whole world astray. Note that he was not strong enough and lost his place in Heaven.

Know this: Satan is for real. He will stop at nothing to stop you from proclaiming the Gospel of Christ. But, no matter how hard Satan tries to steer you off course, he just does not muster enough strength to offset the power of God. We just need to tap into that power at the right times.

Get your armor on!

SATAN THE ADVERSARY

How you have fallen from heaven, morning star, son of the dawn! You have been cast down to the earth, you who once laid low the nations! You said in your heart, "I will ascend to the heavens; I will raise my throne above the stars of God; I will sit enthroned on the mount of assembly, on the utmost heights of Mount Zaphon. I will ascend above the tops of the clouds;I will make myself like the Most High." But you are brought down to the realm of the dead, to the depths of the pit. (Isaiah 14:12-15 NIV)

Yesterday we saw the origin of the fall of Satan. Now we see insight into why he fell. PRIDE. He wanted to become like the Most High. With great pride comes a great fall. And that is exactly what happened to Satan. He was brought down to the realm of the dead, to the depths of the pit. When we think we know more about our lives than God does, this very thing will happen to us. Take a lesson from the fall of Satan or you will end up with him.

Get your armor on!

Now the serpent was more crafty than any of the wild animals the Lord God had made. He said to the woman, "Did God really say, 'You must not eat from any tree in the garden'?" (Genesis 3:1 NIV)

Crafty is a pretty descriptive word for the devil. Synonyms include sneaky, shrewd, and devious. All of these words provide insight into the character of the devil. A couple other observations. One, the serpent was the craftiest of all animals **made**. The devil is a created being. Remember, the created cannot be greater than the Creator! Second, look at how crafty the devil is when tempting someone. He questions the very word of God. Even more reason why we should know His Word, the Sword of the Spirit, and use it to fend off temptation.

Get your armor on!

You belong to your father, the devil, and you want to carry out your father's desires. He was a murderer from the beginning, not holding to the truth, for there is no truth in him. When he lies, he speaks his native language, for he is a liar and the father of lies. (John 8:44 NIV)

Jesus speaking to the Jews who refused to believe He was the Son of God. Look at how he refers to the devil – a murderer, no truth in him, a liar, and father of lies. Know that nothing good ever comes from the devil. There is no truth or any good in him. He is completely evil. His native language is lies. He cannot tell the truth.

My prayer for you is that you will be able to detect the voice of God above the voice of the evil one. That the voice of the evil one will be quieted so you can hear the still small voice of God. Be on guard and keep the armor fully intact!

Get your armor on!

And the devil, who deceived them, was thrown into the lake of burning sulfur, where the beast and the false prophet had been thrown. They will be tormented day and night for ever and ever. (Revelation 20:10 NIV)

Oh, the victory is ours! It was determined thousands of years ago! The devil knows his fate. And he is determined to take as many with him as he possibly can.

Satan is for real. His plan is to call into question God's Word, Jesus's death and resurrection, even your salvation. Do not believe his lies. Do not fall prey to his deceit. Claim the victory that has already been won!

Get your armor on!

GOD HAS YOUR BACK

Dear friends, do not be surprised at the fiery ordeal that has come on you to test you, as though something strange were happening to you. But rejoice inasmuch as you participate in the sufferings of Christ, so that you may be overjoyed when his glory is revealed. (1 Peter 4:12-13 NIV)

So then, those who suffer according to God's will should commit themselves to their faithful Creator and continue to do good. (1 Peter 4:19 NIV)

Peter offers words of encouragement to those first century Christians who were experiencing significant turmoil and suffering. This is tough encouragement because we often view things in the present tense, meaning we do not normally look beyond our current situation. But Peter says to rejoice in that we are offered the opportunity to participate in the sufferings of Christ. Why? So that we might have the full joy when His glory is finally revealed. Do you think Christ rejoiced while being beaten, spat upon, stabbed, mocked, ridiculed, crucified? So what do you think got Him through His present suffering? Looking to the future when His glory would be revealed! Commit yourself to your faithful Creator and continue to do good. He has your back!

Get your armor on!

GOD HAS YOUR BACK

You will not have to fight this battle. Take up your positions; stand firm and see the deliverance the Lord will give you, Judah and Jerusalem. Do not be afraid; do not be discouraged. Go out to face them tomorrow, and the Lord will be with you. (2 Chronicles 20:17 NIV)

Words from the prophet Jahaziel spoken to King Jehoshaphat. The King was to face his enemies, the Moabites and Ammonites. But what did the King have to be afraid of? Nothing. And neither do you! When you step out to face your enemies, remember you have someone on your side who is greater; someone who will fight your battle for you. Go out and face them with confidence! And remember, the Lord will be with you! He's got your back!

Get your armor on!

But you will not leave in haste or go in flight; for the Lord will go before you, the God of Israel will be your rear guard. (Isaiah 52:12 NIV)

I want to focus on the final 2 words in this verse. The rear guard. What is the purpose of the rear guard? It is a military term used for the group responsible for the protection of larger numbers of military personnel during a retreat. The rear guard delays or interferes with advancing enemy forces in order to gain time for the remainder to regroup and reorganize. During struggling times when you feel the world caving in on your – you were just assigned another project and benchmarks are past due, your project does not fit right, you just received a new assignment in structures – retreat, retreat, retreat. Wave the white flag. Just remember, The Lord will go before you. The God of Israel will be your rear guard. He delays or interferes with the enemy to allow you rest to regroup and reorganize.

Get your armor on!

GOD HAS YOUR BACK

Then your light will break forth like the dawn, and your healing will quickly appear; then your righteousness will go before you, and the glory of the Lord will be your rear guard. Then you will call, and the Lord will answer; you will cry for help, and he will say: Here am I. (Isaiah 58:8-9 NIV)

You've had a bad day; bad week; maybe even a bad month. Nothing you do or say seems to be right. You need a do-over. These are the times we for sure need to drop to our knees in prayer, asking the Lord to intervene. When we do that and earnestly seek Him, Isaiah tells us this will be the result. There is that term again – the rear guard. He will go before you. He will cover your backside. You call to Him and He will answer. You cry for help and He will say: Here I am! Remember, God has your back.

Get your armor on!

Whoever dwells in the shelter of the Most High will rest in the shadow of the Almighty. I will say of the Lord, "He is my refuge and my fortress, my God, in whom I trust." Surely he will save you from the fowler's snare and from the deadly pestilence. He will cover you with his feathers, and under his wings you will find refuge; his faithfulness will be your shield and rampart. (Psalm 91:1-4 NIV)

Man, this verse is stocked full of good stuff. Look at the beginning of the verse. "Whoever dwells." The benefits listed in these verses only apply to those who dwell in the shelter of the Most High. We ought not take for granted that God will come to our rescue if we are not truly seeking after Him. But if we are, then look out! He will be our refuge; He will be our fortress; He will save you; He will cover you with His wings; He will be your shield and rampart (barricade). He will have your back!

Get your armor on!

JESUS' CLAIMS TO BE GOD

Again his Jewish opponents picked up stones to stone him, but Jesus said to them, "I have shown you many good works from the Father. For which of these do you stone me?" "We are not stoning you for any good work," they replied, "but for blasphemy, because you, a mere man, claim to be God." (John 10:31-33 NIV)

I am not sure we Christians fully understand Jesus' claims to be God. No other world religion has a savior who claimed equal footing with God. Muhammad did not. Joseph Smith did not. The Dahlia Lama did not. Yet Christ did. That alone separates Christianity from all other belief systems. We have a Savior who is Christ the Lord, who is God incarnate. The early religious leaders knew it, too. That is why they wanted to kill Him. They could not fathom a "mere man" could be God. Hard for us to comprehend as well. Scripture tells us it is true and I believe it. You should too!

Get your armor on!

Thomas said to him, "My Lord and my God!" Then Jesus told him, "Because you have seen me, you have believed; blessed are those who have not seen and yet have believed." (John 20:28-29 NIV)

Notice here Jesus did not correct Thomas for claiming Him to be Lord and God. If it were not true, do not you think Jesus would have corrected him? Rather, Jesus commended Thomas for making that claim. It is on this claim that our belief system rests. Without it, our faith is in vain. If Christ was not God, then everything He stood for, everything He taught is worthless. Praise Jesus Christ, My Lord and my God!

Get your armor on!

JESUS' CLAIMS TO BE GOD

"Very truly I tell you," Jesus answered, "before Abraham was born, I am!" At this, they picked up stones to stone him, but Jesus hid himself, slipping away from the temple grounds. (John 8:58-59 NIV)

Jesus references the phrase God said to Moses at the Burning Bush in Exodus 3:14. Moses wanted to know what to tell Pharaoh when asked who sent him. God answered, "I AM" sends you. The religious rulers of the day made the connection very quick. Look at their reaction – they picked up stones to stone Him. Jesus, in part, refers to the Trinity here as well, inferring He was with God before Abraham.

Remember Who it is that sends you, too. "I AM" is the one. No other Savior can claim this name but Jesus.

Get your armor on!

"But what about you?" he asked. "Who do you say I am?" Simon Peter answered, "You are the Messiah, the Son of the living God." (Matthew 16:15-16 NIV)

Many argue that Jesus never declaratively stated He was God. While that is false (see yesterday's verse), He did not have to; others did for Him, just as Peter did here. And nowhere does Jesus ever correct someone for making this claim. In fact, quite the contrary. In the verses that follow, Jesus went on to bless Peter for his revelation and to state that is upon this very claim (that Jesus is the Messiah, the Son of the living God) Jesus would build His church.

Today, we get a chance to make the very claim Peter made. Do not pass up the opportunity when it comes your way.

Get your armor on!

JESUS' CLAIMS TO BE GOD

In his defense Jesus said to them, "My Father is always at his work to this very day, and I too am working." For this reason they tried all the more to kill him; not only was he breaking the Sabbath, but he was even calling God his own Father, making himself equal with God. (John 5:17-18 NIV)

Jesus may not have clearly stated He was God, but so inferred it. His audience certainly picked up on it for it inflamed their desire to kill him even more. If Jesus was merely misunderstood, would He not have argued that point? "Whoa, guys, wait a minute. Did I say I was equal with God? Do not be ridiculous." Instead, in the verses that follow, Jesus further explained the relationship between the Father and the Son, never once denying His deity. If Jesus did not deny His deity, neither should we!

Get your armor on!

POWER OF CHRIST

When he had said this, Jesus called in a loud voice, "Lazarus, come out!" The dead man came out, his hands and feet wrapped with strips of linen, and a cloth around his face. Jesus said to them, "Take off the grave clothes and let him go." (John 11:43-44 NIV)

Christ has power over death. I have heard other commentators say that Jesus had to specifically call Lazarus to come forth. Had he not, all of the dead would have come forth! Now that is power. And that same power is given to us. Not that we can cheat death, but that death is not our end; it is only our beginning. Rest in the power of Christ.

Get your armor on!

The demons begged Jesus, "Send us among the pigs; allow us to go into them." He gave them permission, and the impure spirits came out and went into the pigs. The herd, about two thousand in number, rushed down the steep bank into the lake and were drowned. (Mark 5:12-13 NIV)

Christ has power over demons. Jesus had just restored a demon-possessed man. The demons were commanded by Jesus to come out of the man and they obeyed. I do not want to invoke scenes from The Exorcists, but Christ can do the same today. However, demons may not be the same. What about the demon of "I am not as smart as she/he is", or the demon, "I wish I made more money", or the demon, "It is so hard for me to memorize scripture, so why bother", or the demon, "I need *(fill in the blank)*". Draw on the power of Christ and overcome your demons!

Get your armor on!

POWER OF CHRIST

Jesus left the synagogue and went to the home of Simon. Now Simon's mother-in-law was suffering from a high fever, and they asked Jesus to help her. So he bent over her and rebuked the fever, and it left her. She got up at once and began to wait on them. At sunset, the people brought to Jesus all who had various kinds of sickness, and laying his hands on each one, he healed them. (Luke 4:38-40 NIV)

Christ has power over diseases. This is a tough one to grasp. There are so many examples of strong Christians who have succumbed to diseases after lengthy battles. Equal examples are those non-Christians who have overcome their diseases and continue their wicked behavior and lifestyle. Why does God save some and not others? I cannot answer that. God has His reasons for healing some and not others. What I can tell you is, if God so chooses, He can heal you from any sickness you may have. We must put our trust and faith in Him to know what is best for us in areas we are unable to see.

Get your armor on!

He got up, rebuked the wind and said to the waves, "Quiet! Be still!" Then the wind died down and it was completely calm. (Mark 4:39 NIV)

Christ has power over nature. And why not, He created it!! Remember this scene, Jesus and the disciples were crossing over the lake to the other side. Jesus was sleeping when a fierce storm arose. The disciples were fearful of their lives and awoke Jesus. After Jesus calmed the winds, he rebuked the disciples for their lack of faith. We, too, have storms that come up in life from time to time, like graduating college and starting a job on your own without Mom and Dad there to help. We get scared. But why? Our faith should be in Christ to calm the figurative storms of life just like He did the literal storms for the disciples.

Get your armor on!

POWER OF CHRIST

Some time after this, Jesus crossed to the far shore of the Sea of Galilee (that is, the Sea of Tiberias), and a great crowd of people followed him because they saw the signs he had performed by healing the sick. Then Jesus went up on a mountainside and sat down with his disciples. The Jewish Passover Festival was near. When Jesus looked up and saw a great crowd coming toward him, he said to Philip, "Where shall we buy bread for these people to eat?" He asked this only to test him, for he already had in mind what he was going to do. (John 6:1-6 NIV)

Christ has power over problems. Here is John's account of the feeding of the five thousand. What I did not include is Philip's response to Jesus' question. He said it would take over 1 ½ year's salary to pay for food for all the people. I love the last part of verse 6. Jesus already had in mind what he was going to do. He wanted to see if Philip had enough faith in Him or not. Jesus may do the same for us at times. He may prop us up just to see our faith in action. He may already know what He is going to do, but wants to see us act/react first. Just make sure you act/react in faith, no wavering! Easier said than done, I know. Just remember Christ has power over any and all of our problems.

Get your armor on!

POWER OF THE WORD

For the word of God is alive and active. Sharper than any double-edged sword, it penetrates even to dividing soul and spirit, joints and marrow; it judges the thoughts and attitudes of the heart. (Hebrews 4:12 NIV)

This is probably the most often quoted verse when referring to God's written Word. It is alive and active. How often have you read a verse numerous times when all the sudden, clarity comes and you understand both context and content? God's Word is sharp on both edges, able to cut both ways, convicting of wrongdoing, encouraging of right doing. And how often have we seen that God does not care about outward appearances, but the thoughts and attitudes of the heart, the inner core of your being.

When you put your armor on, remember the last piece – the SWORD OF THE SPIRIT, WHICH IS THE WORD OF GOD.

Get your sword up!

But the seed falling on good soil refers to someone who hears the word and understands it. This is the one who produces a crop, yielding a hundred, sixty or thirty times what was sown. (Matthew 13:23 NIV)

This is from the parable of the seeds. Jesus is explaining different types of people, referred to as seeds. Look at what happens to those who hear the word and understands it. They produce fruit. And what a bounty they produce! Some thirty, others up to one hundred times what was sown. This is the essence of the power of the Word. It produces fruit. But it has to fall on good soil – someone who is willing to listen, give it a try, and search to understand what it says.

Find some good soil and get your armor on!

POWER OF THE WORD

And the words of the Lord are flawless, like silver purified in a crucible, like gold refined seven times. (Psalm 12:6 NIV)

Puritan Writer **Thomas Brooks** said, "The Word of the Lord is a light to guide you, a counselor to counsel you, a comforter to comfort you, a staff to support you, a sword to defend you, and a physician to cure you. The Word is a mine to enrich you, a robe to clothe you, and a crown to crown you."

I do not think we realize just how powerful God's written word is. It is all the above and then some. More valuable and precious than any metal or gem. Applicable and relevant today as it was when it was written.

Treasure it; read it; memorize it; meditate on it.

Get your armor on!

The law of the Lord is perfect, refreshing the soul. The statutes of the Lord are trustworthy, making wise the simple. The precepts of the Lord are right, giving joy to the heart. The commands of the Lord are radiant, giving light to the eyes. (Psalm 19:7-8 NIV)

God's Word has been translated in whole or in part, in over 2,400 different languages and over 7 billion copies have been distributed. Just think, if each Bible were 3 inches thick, and you laid them back to back, you could circle the earth 13 ½ times with the number of Bibles distributed. And that number continues to grow each day.

Look at how the Word of God is described in these verses: perfect, trustworthy, right, and radiant. Now look at the effects of the Word: refreshes the soul, making wise the simple, giving joy to the heart, and giving light to the eyes. Name another written word that can do that!

Get your armor on!

POWER OF THE WORD

For everything that was written in the past was written to teach us, so that through the endurance taught in the Scriptures and the encouragement they provide we might have hope. (Romans 15:4 NIV)

Herein lays the whole intent of God's written word. That we might have hope. Hope is what gets us up in the mornings; what motivates us through our struggles; what carries us through dark days. God left His word to teach us and to encourage us. If we have that eternal perspective, we know that we might have temporary setbacks, but they are just that – temporary. Our hope is not just for the eternal. Our hope can be experienced today, knowing God is present. And if we ever lose that hope, go back to His word!

So word up and get your armor on!

ANGELS

Are not all angels ministering spirits sent to serve those who will inherit salvation? (Hebrews 1:14 NIV)

I thought this would be a good follow-on to last week.

So just who are angels? Where did they come from? What is their purpose? Can we see them? Lots of questions we will try to explore throughout this week.

All angels are created beings. They were in existence when God created the world (Job 38:4-7). The word angel means messenger. They can be human as in Matthew 28:5 or non-human as in Matthew 1:20. They are not equal with God and are not to be worshipped (Hebrews 1:4-6).

The writer of Hebrews hit the nail on the head with their purpose. Angels were created by God to serve His purpose. They serve God by helping Christians serve God. We will see just how they do that in the verses that follow this week. Stay tuned.

Get your armor on!

My God sent his angel, and he shut the mouths of the lions. They have not hurt me, because I was found innocent in his sight. (Daniel 6:22 NIV)

Here we see the protection aspect of angels. We all have heard the story of Daniel in the lion's den. Cast into the lion's den for breaking man's law while keeping God's law, Daniel defied all logic and survived. How? God sent his angel to protect Daniel. And He does that same with us today. Serving God has never been easy. At times, we appear to be punished for doing so. But remember Daniel's story. When we need it, God will send His angel of protection to see us through.

Get your armor on!

ANGELS

Now an angel of the Lord said to Philip, "Go south to the road—the desert road—that goes down from Jerusalem to Gaza." (Acts 8:26 NIV)

Here we see how angels direct us. I am sure Phillip questioned the direction of the angel of the Lord. Why go south to the desert road? But it did not take long for him to figure it out. For not too far into his trip, Philip ran across the Ethiopian Eunuch. The Eunuch was reading the scriptures of Isaiah and was confused. Philip did more than just explain the scriptures to him; he led him in the saving knowledge of Jesus Christ and baptized him on the spot. We might question the direction the angel of the Lord leads us, but our best response is to obey promptly. You never know who might be around the corner.

Get your armor on!

For he will command his angels concerning you to guard you in all your ways; they will lift you up in their hands, so that you will not strike your foot against a stone. (Psalm 91:11-12 NIV)

The angel of the Lord encamps around those who fear him, and he delivers them. (Psalm 34:7 NIV)

The verses clearly convey the guardian aspect of angels. Not that we have a specific "guardian angel" assigned to us, but I do believe God places angels around us to care for us and protect us at times. I remember driving home very late one night. I was tired and could feel myself nodding off at times. I remember specifically one time raising my head, realizing the car was headed for the median. It was then that I felt an angel caused my head to rise so I could avoid an accident. I am sure if you think hard enough, you will remember times in your life where an angel was watching over you as well.

Thank our Lord for sending us His angels.

Get your armor on!

ANGELS

Then the devil left him, and angels came and attended him. (Matthew 4:11 NIV)

An angel from heaven appeared to him and strengthened him. (Luke 22:43 NIV)

Two great passages that explain the encouraging aspect of angels.

Matthew's reference was right after the temptation of Christ. Luke's passage was the night of Jesus' arrest.

In both cases, Jesus was facing or had just faced a challenging time. In Matthew's reference, the word "attended" means to be present. Sometimes, we just need someone there with us to help us during a critical period in our life. They do not necessarily have to say anything; just be close. In Luke's reference, the angels appeared and offered encouragement. I can almost vision it this way: The angels appeared and told Him, "You got this! You can do this! This is why You came. Think of the glory which will be revealed in You."

Be aware of which type of angel you can be to someone today!

Get your armor on!

WITNESSING

But in your hearts revere Christ as Lord. Always be prepared to give an answer to everyone who asks you to give the reason for the hope that you have. But do this with gentleness and respect (1 Peter 3:15 NIV)

Witnessing really is not that hard, although we make it out to be sometimes. Simply put, it is just telling others the reason for the hope that you have. We should always be prepared to give an answer because you never know when the opportunity will arise.

Take note of the last sentence – "do this with gentleness and respect." We do not need to beat anyone over the head with our Bibles. We do not need to be demeaning of other's beliefs. With gentleness and kindness, share what Jesus has done for you. Then step out of the way and let the Holy Spirit do His thing!

Get your armor on!

As for us, we cannot help speaking about what we have seen and heard (Acts 4:20 NIV)

Peter and John answering to the Sanhedrin. I just love this verse. The Sandedrin were trying to stop Peter and John from spreading the Good News of Jesus Christ. Peter and John were warned to stop speaking the name of Jesus. And here is their response. Try as you may, we are not going to stop speaking about what we have seen and heard.

This is my prayer for you as well. That you will not be intimidated by anyone, but will continue to speak about what great things you have seen and heard!

Get your armor on!

WITNESSING

And because of my chains, most of the brothers and sisters have become confident in the Lord and dare all the more to proclaim the gospel without fear. (Philippians 1:14 NIV)

You may have witnessed to someone and got blasted for doing so. Ridiculed, made fun of, called "holier than thou." You may never know that in so doing, someone else was moved to do the same thing. They derived their boldness or confidence from your example. Paul was thrown into prison for proclaiming the Gospel of Jesus Christ. In so doing, many brothers and sisters in Christ became more confident in the Lord and began to proclaim the Gospel without fear of repercussion. Be that Paul to someone else. Proclaim the Good News without fear and perhaps encourage someone else to do the same.

Get your armor on!

so is my word that goes out from my mouth: It will not return to me empty, but will accomplish what I desire and achieve the purpose for which I sent it. (Isaiah 55:11 NIV)

One of the most common excuses given for not witnessing, "But what am I going to say?" What if they ask me a question I cannot answer?" Let me tell you, these are very poor excuses. I remember witnessing to a friend's brother. We had been talking for a while. Then I begin to quote John 3:16. First verse I ever memorized. Probably for you as well. I got tongue-tied and cannot remember the verse. The person I was witnessing to finished the verse for me! Now tell me God will not do the same for you. He will give you the words to say; if not you, he will give them to the person to whom you are witnessing.

His word does not return empty! It will accomplish what He desires.

Get your armor on!

WITNESSING

And I, when I am lifted up from the earth, will draw all people to myself. (John 12:32 NIV)

Jesus was referring to his impending death and resurrection, pointing to the fact that it is through Jesus Christ, alone, that all men are saved. We can do nothing to save ourselves. This is a key concept to understand. When we witness to someone, it is not our responsibility to "save" them. Our responsibility is to share the Gospel. Let the Holy Spirit do the saving.

You lift up the name of Jesus. Leave the saving to Him.

Get your armor on!

WORK

Those who work their land will have abundant food, but those who chase fantasies have no sense. (Proverbs 12:11 NIV)

According to the American Heritage Dictionary, work is defined as "physical or mental effort or activity directed toward the production or accomplishment of something; a trade, profession, or other means of livelihood."

Work can be used as an extension of our witness. People will see how we conduct ourselves in the workplace: the language we use; the ethics we prescribe to; the effort we put forth. After all, it is He who gave us the ability and desire to do what we do. Why not honor Him in how we work! Have some sense about you – honor God through your work!

Get your armor on!

Lazy hands make for poverty, but diligent hands bring wealth. (Proverbs 10:4 NIV)

Now do not take this verse out of context. Wealth depends on whose definition you use – the world's or God's. I believe the writer of this proverb is telling us that a lazy person does not produce much while one who is diligent about the task at hand has the ability and opportunity to produce a great deal. No one ever set their goals to be lazy and live in poverty. Be diligent about your work and thus produce the opportunity for great wealth – mainly for God's kingdom and perhaps in this life as well.

Get your armor on!

WORK

Anyone who has been stealing must steal no longer, but must work, doing something useful with their own hands, that they may have something to share with those in need. (Ephesians 4:28 NIV)

Why do we work? Well, to provide a livelihood for you and your family, but also to be able to share with those in need. Paul was speaking to the early church where members would share a great deal with one another. He is warning those who are "stealing", basically sharing in the taking but not so much in the giving. We all should take note of Paul's reprimand and ensure we are doing something useful with our hands. Then we will be blessed with the opportunity to share with those truly in need.

Get your armor on!

For a person may labor with wisdom, knowledge and skill, and then they must leave all they own to another who has not toiled for it. This too is meaningless and a great misfortune. (Ecclesiastes 2:21 NIV)

I have known people whose parents were very wealthy. They drifted through college life carefree, not really taking studies seriously. No drive. No ambition. Why? Because Daddy was going to give them whatever they wanted. This is a poor reflection on both the parent and the child. For what is the parent teaching the child? You do not have to work for anything. It will all be given to you. As Solomon says here, that is a great misfortune.

I am not saying parents should not give their kids things. But they need to teach them the value of working hard for what you have. I can tell from your summer jobs, you mother and I have taught you that. I trust you will pass that lesson on to your kids.

Get your armor on!

WORK

For even when we were with you, we gave you this rule: "The one who is unwilling to work shall not eat." (2 Thessalonians 3:10 NIV)

Pretty harsh consequence of not working. As we saw in a previous verse from Ephesians, the early church shared a great deal with each other. When one was in need, all pitched in to help. As it was in that verse, so it is in this verse - Paul is rebuking those who were being lazy and living off the generosity of others. You get much more joy from working hard for something rather than to be given something. So take this verse to heart. Work for what you have. Be proud of what you have accomplished, knowing Who it is that really gives you what you have.

Get your armor on!

'TIS AND TAT

Do not cut your bodies for the dead or put tattoo marks on yourselves. I am the Lord. (Leviticus 19:28 NIV)

This passage in Leviticus is specifically dealing with the pagan religious rituals. God's desire is that we set ourselves apart from other cultures. The focus here is prohibiting worldly worship and witchcraft. So am I saying tattoos are part of witchcraft? No. We must be careful to use this verse in its proper context. We must consider the overall theme of the context which is setting ourselves apart. Do you set yourself apart by getting a butterfly tattoo on your ankle or a cross tattooed on your arm? All innocent enough right? If you try too hard to justify something, then it tells me you know the answer. When in doubt, do not!

Get your armor on!

...everything that does not come from faith is sin. (Romans 14:23b NIV)

"To tattoo or not to tattoo?" I think the more serious questions to ask yourself are:
What are my motives for wanting a tattoo?
Am I seeking to glorify God or draw attention to myself?
Will my tattoo be a source of contention for my family/close friends?
Will my tattoo cause a "weaker" brother/sister to stumble?
Will I still want this tattoo years from now?

Instead of asking, "Is it okay for Christians to get tattoos," perhaps a better question might be, "Is it okay for ***me*** to get a tattoo?"

God has given us a means to judge our motives and weigh our decisions. It is called faith. Use it.

Get your armor on!

'TIS AND TAT

I have the right to do anything," you say—but not everything is beneficial. "I have the right to do anything"—but not everything is constructive. (1 Corinthians 10:23 NIV)

Go back to the 3rd week of your freshman year. We covered Spiritual Freedom. Sure, we have freedom to do and not to do many things - things that are not specifically forbidden or commanded in Scripture. Tattoos may be "permissible," but are they beneficial and constructive?

Certainly, a tattoo of a cross is better than a tattoo of a skull and cross bones. It may even be a conversation starter with some people. Before you tat, you must ask yourself two questions:

- What/who does this benefit?
- How is this constructively bringing glory to the Father?

If you cannot answer those two questions in the positive, then best you remain un-tatted.

Get your armor on!

To the weak I became weak, to win the weak. I have become all things to all people so that by all possible means I might save some. I do all this for the sake of the gospel, that I may share in its blessings. (1 Corinthians 9:22-23 NIV)

If you want to justify being tatted, this is probably the verse to use. If having a tattoo truly opens doors for sharing the Gospel that would otherwise be closed, then I guess this would meet Paul's qualifications of becoming all things to all people. However, I find it difficult to imagine that we cannot find some other opening that would allow us to share the Gospel.

Get your armor on!

'TIS AND TAT

I will accept you as fragrant incense when I bring you out from the nations and gather you from the countries where you have been scattered, and I will be proved holy through you in the sight of the nations. (Ezekiel 20:41 NIV)

I have said this probably a thousand times. No one should ever have to ask if you are a Christian. They should be able to tell through your actions, reactions, words, and behavior. I want to key in on the last part of this verse. "I will be proved holy through you in the sight of the nations." To me, this resonates with the same reasoning. God will be proved holy to others through the holy living of His children. If you can live holy and present the holiness of God to others with tattoos, then tat away. If not, then you know the answer.

Get your armor on!

THE GREATEST COMMANDMENT

Jesus replied: "Love the Lord your God with all your heart and with all your soul and with all your mind. This is the first and greatest commandment." (Matthew 22:37-38 NIV)

The Pharisees tried to trick Jesus by questioning Him on the greatest commandment. Here is His answer. Why would He say this is the greatest? Because without a right relationship with God, our relationships with others will not be right either. That is why the first four commandments contained in the 10 Commandments are about our relationship with God. The remaining six are about our relationship with each other. Get His relationship right, then all others will fall into place.

Remember the greatest commandment and get your armor on!

If you are pleased with me, teach me your ways so I may know you and continue to find favor with you. (Exodus 33:13 NIV)

We were created in the image of God to reflect His glory and name. But we cannot reflect what we do not know. So a key piece to the greatest commandment is to know Him and His ways. I pray you desire to know Him more and more with each new day. Then you will find favor with Him and reflect Him to others.

Get your armor on!

THE GREATEST COMMANDMENT

Show me your ways, Lord, teach me your paths. Guide me in your truth and teach me, for you are God my Savior, and my hope is in you all day long. (Psalm 25:4-5 NIV)

This verse goes hand in hand with yesterday. Show me your ways; teach me your paths. To be able to obey the greatest commandment, we must develop that eternal perspective and move from the temporal to the everlasting. This can only be done through a close walk with Christ. Hope in Him all the day long and you will not be disappointed.

Get your armor on!

Teach me your way, Lord, that I may rely on your faithfulness; give me an undivided heart, that I may fear your name. (Psalm 86:11 NIV)

I want to focus on the one phrase, "give me an undivided heart." We cannot sit on the fence with God. We must choose one side or the other. Fence sitting is like saying you are only a little pregnant. You are either pregnant or you are not. Same with God. You are either for Him or against Him. If we focus our undivided attention on the ways of the Lord, we will be in a position to obey the greatest commandment.

Pray the Lord will help you remove all the barriers and other attention grabbers so that you can focus on Him and Him alone. Then, go and obey the greatest commandment.

Get your armor on!

THE GREATEST COMMANDMENT

I will give them singleness of heart and action, so that they will always fear me for their own good and the good of their children after them. (Jeremiah 32:39 NIV)

When we decide to follow this greatest commandment, great things will follow. This verse is one example of that. Remember fear was a term used for utmost reverence. Not a scared fear, but a respectful fear; to be in awe of fear. So what is to follow when we obey this greatest commandment? The good of the next generation - our children's children and those after them. I, for one, do not want to be the generation that messed it up for those that follow. I pray you do not either.

Get your armor on!

DEFINING MOMENTS

But Rehoboam rejected the advice the elders gave him and consulted the young men who had grown up with him and were serving him. (2 Chronicles 10:8 NIV)

Rehoboam had just ascended to the throne of his father, Solomon. He had an opportunity to win the favor of the people. All he had to do was listen to the sage advice of his father's counselors.

Rehoboam was at a defining moment. He could listen to the wise counsel of the elders. Or he could listen to his "yes men", those men who grew up with him and most likely would give him the answer he wanted to hear.

Either because of pride or wanting to separate himself from his father, Rehoboam followed the advice of his friends. The result: the united nation under David and Solomon was split. More sadly, 2 Chronicles 12:14 states the result of Rehoboam: "And he did evil, because he prepared not his heart to seek the LORD."

Are you at a similar defining moment? Who will you listen to?

Get your armor on!

DEFINING MOMENTS

Then he reached out his hand and took the knife to slay his son. But the angel of the Lord called out to him from heaven, "Abraham! Abraham!" "Here I am," he replied. "Do not lay a hand on the boy," he said. "Do not do anything to him. Now I know that you fear God, because you have not withheld from me your son, your only son." (Genesis 22:10-12 NIV)

FYI, Abraham's willingness to sacrifice his son, Isaac, is a foreshadowing of the sacrifice God gave through His Son, Jesus.

You know the story well. Can you imagine the thoughts going through both Abraham's and Isaac's mind? Imagine how Abraham must have dreaded each step up the mountain. Imagine how confused Isaac must have been while being tied to the alter. How heavy Abraham's hand must have been as he raised it to slay his son, his only son.

Abraham, and Isaac for that matter, was at a defining moment. Would he be completely obedient to God, even if it called for the life of his only son? Would he forsake all for the greater cause of God? In the end, Abraham was the father of the nation of Israel and is considered one of the patriarchs of the Christian faith.

Your defining moment may not be as dramatic. But what will you decide?

Get your armor on!

When they had finished eating, Jesus said to Simon Peter, "Simon son of John, do you love me more than these?" "Yes, Lord," he said, "you know that I love you." Jesus said, "Feed my lambs." Again Jesus said, "Simon son of John, do you love me?" He answered, "Yes, Lord, you know that I love you." Jesus said, "Take care of my sheep." The third time he said to him, "Simon son of John, do you love me?" Peter was hurt because Jesus asked him the third time, "Do you love me?" He said, "Lord, you know all things; you know that I love you." Jesus said, "Feed my sheep." (John 21:15-17 NIV)

Peter had failed the Lord in His hour of need, denying three times that he ever knew Jesus. Yet Jesus loved Peter. A great attribute about our God is that He pursues the fallen, the downtrodden, the sinner. Perhaps you think you have sinned against God so badly that He would never forgive you. Perhaps you are where Peter was. Would He ever accept me back? Would He ever forgive me? Could He ever use a failure like me? The answers are Yes, Yes, and YES!

Peter was at a defining moment. Would he / could he move on and become the disciple Jesus called him to be or would he sink back into obscurity? We know Peter's story. He became the greatest evangelist to the Jewish nation. What about your story?

Get your armor on!

DEFINING MOMENTS

But Ruth replied, "Do not urge me to leave you or to turn back from you. Where you go I will go, and where you stay I will stay. Your people will be my people and your God my God. (Ruth 1:16 NIV)

Ruth and Naomi had just experienced great tragedy. Ruth's husband, Naomi's son, had just died. There was no one left to care for them. In those days, widows were left to fend for themselves and treated like outcasts. Naomi pleaded with Ruth to return to her family, thinking she would marry again, for she was relatively young.

Ruth was at a defining moment. She could leave her mother-in-law and go back to her home country where she would likely marry again and be taken care of. Or she could stay with Naomi in a foreign land, worship a new God, and the two of them could figure things out together. Ruth's story ends well. She met and married Boaz. She is included in the lineage of David which ultimately leads to Christ.

What lineage will you leave?

Get your armor on!

DEFINING MOMENTS

But the men who had gone up with him said, "We cannot attack those people; they are stronger than we are." And they spread among the Israelites a bad report about the land they had explored. They said, "The land we explored devours those living in it. All the people we saw there are of great size. We saw the Nephilim there (the descendants of Anak come from the Nephilim). We seemed like grasshoppers in our own eyes, and we looked the same to them." (Numbers 13:31-33 NIV)

Oh the children of Israel! We really are no different. After all they have been through – walked through the Red Sea on dry land; fed with manna from heaven; drank water from a rock; led by a cloud by day and a pillar of fire by night. What more could God have done to show His presence to the nation??? Yet, they continued to doubt the ability of God Almighty!

Here they stood on the banks of the Promised Land. Will they enter and take possession? Or will they continue to wander aimlessly in the desert? A defining moment for sure! And we know too well the result. Forty years of wandering. All those that then said no to the Promised Land were not allowed to experience its wonder. And you know, Israel has never fully possessed all the land the Lord was willing to give them. Why? Because of their lack of faith and trust.

Remember this: The Will of God will never lead you where the Grace of God cannot keep you. In their defining moment, the children of Israel did not or would not accept this. In your defining moment, what will you do?

Get your armor on!

GROW SPIRITUALLY

Like newborn babies, crave pure spiritual milk, so that by it you may grow up in your salvation (1 Peter 2:2 NIV)

Our growth as spiritual warriors is never over. We should never reach the position where God cannot teach us anything new. Just as you were when you were a baby, crave that spiritual milk. And believe me, you craved it!!! Sometimes faster than I could give it to you! That is how we should be as we mature and "grow up in [our] salvation."

So crave that milk mustache and get your armor on!

Now the Berean Jews were of more noble character than those in Thessalonica, for they received the message with great eagerness and examined the Scriptures every day to see if what Paul said was true. As a result, many of them believed, as did also a number of prominent Greek women and many Greek men. (Acts 17:11 NIV)

Why were the Berean Jews of more noble character than those in Thessalonica? Because they received the message with great eagerness and examined the scriptures daily. In order to grow spiritually, we need constant nourishment. Ever go a day without eating? Probably not. I bet you cannot go 10 hours without hunger pains setting in. But yet so many of us go days without even picking up our Bibles; without even sitting for just a moment to thank God for His many blessings. How can we then expect to grow spiritually without ever taking part in spiritual food?

Be like the Berean Jews. Ensure you have your daily intake of spiritual food!

Get your armor on!

GROW SPIRITUALLY

But grow in the grace and knowledge of our Lord and Savior Jesus Christ. (2 Peter 3:18 NIV)

It has been said that crocodiles never stop growing, albeit the pace of their growth slows as they age. I think this is what Peter had in mind with this verse. A more apt translation would be, "But continue to grow in..." We should never be content in our current spiritual state, but keep on growing, striving to do better, to know more, straining for the prize of the high calling of our Lord and Savior (a preview of verses to come, stay tuned). Pray the Lord brings something new to you each and every day. Wake each day expecting something new!

Get your armor on!

But solid food is for the mature, who by constant use have trained themselves to distinguish good from evil. (Hebrews 5:14 NIV)

You did not start eating solid food until you were nearly one year old. Your body had not grown enough yet to be able to digest solid food. But as you matured, you were able to eat and digest solid foods. When you first started swimming / playing tennis, you were not breaking records / winning matches. You had to train yourself to swim / play tennis. You had to learn to pace yourself / learn how to place your shots. By constant training and development, you were able to set personal records with almost every swim / you were able to win matches.

Our spiritual walk is no different. As we grow, we are able to digest more things about God and His relationship with us. By constant training, we can distinguish good from evil, even the best of two right answers.

Never give up. Never stop learning. Never stop training yourself.

Get your armor on!

GROW SPIRITUALLY

Not that I have already obtained all this, or have already arrived at my goal, but I press on to take hold of that for which Christ Jesus took hold of me. Brothers and sisters, I do not consider myself yet to have taken hold of it. But one thing I do: Forgetting what is behind and straining toward what is ahead, I press on toward the goal to win the prize for which God has called me heavenward in Christ Jesus. (Philippians 3:12-14 NIV)

What Paul had not yet attained was complete Christlikeness. But what he did was continue, daily, to press on to achieve that goal. I love the word picture Paul describes. Like an Olympic runner straining to the finish line – leaning forward, arms thrown back, neck stuck out, lunging towards the finish line. May we never get too old to press on in our spiritual growth to be like Christ.

Get your armor on!

DROP YOUR ANCHOR

We have this hope as an anchor for the soul, firm and secure. (Hebrews 6:19a NIV)

What is an anchor? What is its purpose? Normally used in reference to a floating vessel, it is used to prevent that vessel from drifting. But we can apply an anchor to anything, ourselves included. The hope the writer is referring to is the certainty of God's promises. This certainty serves as an anchor to our souls, making us firm and secure.

Make sure you do not go adrift. Drop your anchor in God's promises.

Get your armor on!

he said to them, "Take to heart all the words I have solemnly declared to you this day, so that you may command your children to obey carefully all the words of this law. They are not just idle words for you— they are your life. (Deuteronomy 32:46-47a NIV)

Moses' final words to the children of Israel right before Joshua took over the responsibility for leading the people into the Promised Land. Note how Moses refers to God's Word. They are not just mere words, they are **your life**! We are to take them to heart, meaning we are to take it seriously. We are to obey them carefully, meaning to pay attention to detail. His commands are not something we do occasionally, or when we feel like it, or it fits the moment. We are to live it out daily. Treat His commands like spiritual food. You would not go a day without eating would you? Do not go a day without feeding on His Word.

Drop your anchor on God's Word and get your armor on!

DROP YOUR ANCHOR

You will keep in perfect peace those whose minds are steadfast, because they trust in you. Trust in the Lord forever, for the Lord, the Lord himself, is the Rock eternal. (Isaiah 26:3-4 NIV)

When an anchor is dropped, it usually drags along the sea floor until it catches on something. Then, anchored to that object, the vessel remains in place. So what do we want our anchor to catch on to? The Rock eternal Himself – God Almighty! Only He can keep you in perfect peace. Only He can keep you steadfast in His faithfulness. Do not be tossed to and fro with the winds of the world. Drop your anchor on the Rock.

Get your armor on!

Therefore, since we are receiving a kingdom that cannot be shaken, let us be thankful, and so worship God acceptably with reverence and awe, (Hebrews 12:28 NIV)

What happens to our anchor when it attaches to something loose on the sea floor? Whatever object that is not firmly affixed to the floor will eventually move. When the object moves, so does the vessel. When that happens, the fact that you dropped your anchor is meaningless, because the anchor can only do what it is intended to do when it attaches firmly to something stable.

If you affix your anchor to anything other than the Kingdom of God, expect it to move. Good looks turn to wrinkles and gray hair. Those 6-pack abs turn into the Pillsbury doughboy. That stock portfolio is lost in the next business downturn. That house rots and the new paint fades. That new car ages with every mile. But the Kingdom of God cannot be shaken. It cannot be moved. It is firmly secured in place. Dropping your anchor on anything else will only lead to disappointment.

Get your armor on!

DROP YOUR ANCHOR

That day when evening came, he said to his disciples, "Let us go over to the other side." Leaving the crowd behind, they took him along, just as he was, in the boat. There were also other boats with him. A furious squall came up, and the waves broke over the boat, so that it was nearly swamped. Jesus was in the stern, sleeping on a cushion. The disciples woke him and said to him, "Teacher, do not you care if we drown?" He got up, rebuked the wind and said to the waves, "Quiet! Be still!" Then the wind died down and it was completely calm. He said to his disciples, "Why are you so afraid? Do you still have no faith?" (Mark 4:35-40 NIV)

You would think that, after spending so much time with Jesus, the disciples would not be afraid of anything. Yet, they still kept Jesus inside a box, with human limitations. They had yet to develop that eternal perspective and understanding of just Who Jesus was. I think we get that way too. We may drop our anchor, but then think that there is no way the anchor will hold through the swift currents and waves the world brings upon us. You see how concerned Jesus was during the storm – He was sleeping on a pillow!!! Our storms are nothing to Him. He has no fear of them for He has overcome them all.

So get your pillow and drop your anchor. Then rest in His peace.

Get your armor on!

KEEP THE FIRE BURNING

Do not quench the Spirit. (1 Thessalonians 5:19 NIV)

Just what exactly this this verse mean? What does "quench" mean? I looked it up and found a variety of meanings: to put out, to extinguish, to cool, or to prevent from continuing. I happen to like this last meaning. So let's review the verse again with this phrase substituted:

"Jessica/Scott, Do not prevent the Spirit from continuing."

Now we have a verse that makes sense to me. Whatever we hold on to that prevents us from spending time with God is quenching the Spirit. Whenever we fail to read His Word or spend time with Him in prayer, we quench the Spirit. Whenever we fall asleep reading His Word or praying to Him, we quench the Spirit. Whenever we conform to the world around us, we quench the Spirit.

Let the Spirit continue to mold you into the godly woman/man you are intended to be. Keep the fire burning.

Get your armor on!

For this reason I remind you to fan into flame the gift of God, which is in you through the laying on of my hands. (2 Timothy 1:6 NIV)

To "fan the flame" means to make something more intense. Before the days of gas grills and fire places, we had to light the fire by hand, then blow on the fire or "fan the flame" to make it spread to the rest of the coals or wood. A friend in college showed me the trick of using a hair dryer to make the fire spread faster. Paul is encouraging Timothy to make the gift of God more intense within him so that Timothy could share the Good News with others. The flame will not burn on its own; it must be nurtured, or in keeping with this verse, fanned into flame! So get the hair dryer out and fan into flame the gift God has given you!

Get your armor on!

KEEP THE FIRE BURNING

But if I say, "I will not mention his word or speak anymore in his name," his word is in my heart like a fire, a fire shut up in my bones. I am weary of holding it in; indeed, I cannot. (Jeremiah 20:9 NIV)

Oh, Jeremiah, no wonder they called him the weeping prophet. Here he is voicing his frustration in delivering God's message. Why continue? No one is listening anyway. I might as well stop speaking his word or speak anymore in his name. But you see, the message of God is indeed like a fire surging within you, just like it was within Jeremiah. Trying as hard as he could, he was incapable of holding it in. Indeed, he could not. He had to share. My prayer for you is that you, too, would have such a fire burning within you, that there is no way you can hold it in. Explode like a volcano the good news of Jesus Christ.

Get your armor on, and watch for falling ash!

my heart grew hot within me. While I meditated, the fire burned; then I spoke with my tongue: (Psalm 39:3 NIV)

David is meditating on his own adversity, while looking on at the prosperity of others. All the while, he kept his thoughts to himself until he could no longer hold them in. His anger and resentment grew hot within. While he thought about the goings on, the fire burned within him until he could no longer suppress his feelings.

I may be taking a bit of a stretch here, but this is what I want you to get from this verse and it fits with yesterday's verse. We receive the Good News of Jesus Christ. We see the events shaping and sharpening our lives, molding us to reflect His image. As we dwell on His love, as we meditate on His divine word, our hearts grow hot within us; a fire begins to burn so that we cannot keep it in. Then we burst out with words. May your words burst with clarity, sincerity, and compassion to all those around you.

Get your armor on!

KEEP THE FIRE BURNING

They asked each other, "Were not our hearts burning within us while he talked with us on the road and opened the Scriptures to us?" (Luke 24:32 NIV)

Ever been in a position where you know beyond a shadow of a doubt that you are exactly where God wants you to be? It's as if you are sitting in front of a roaring fire, wrapped up like a cocoon in your favorite blanket. You feel warm inside. Comfort. At peace. Never before have I been more confident of being in that place than the day I asked your mother to marry me.

This is what these disciples were referring to when they asked each other, "Were not our hearts burning within us..." Can you imagine walking along the road to Emmaus, listening to Jesus explain Scripture and prophecy? His words spoken with such evidence, power, and conviction. The disciples must have found His words to be as a burning fire within them.

This is my prayer for you. That you find that warm, snuggly spot right were Jesus wants you. That His words burn within you, keeping you at peace with Him, finding rest. And that you keep the fire burning!

Get your armor on!

CONTINUOUS OBEDIENCE

if my people, who are called by my name, will humble themselves and pray and seek my face and turn from their wicked ways, then I will hear from heaven, and I will forgive their sin and will heal their land. (2 Chronicles 7:14 NIV)

This is God's answer to Solomon's prayer regarding provisions for when the Children of Israel sinned. I want to point out there are 4 things we are to do in this case.

- Humble yourself. That means to recognize just who you are and Whose you are. You do not deserve anything by rite or inheritance. It is only by God's grace that we have life.
- Pray. Not as you drive; not as you fall asleep; not intermittently as you answer text messages or phone calls. Separate yourself from all distraction and have dedicated one-on-one time with God alone.
- Seek my face. Truly fix your eyes heavenward to God. Desire His will; desire to live the life worthy of the calling you have received.
- Turn from their wicked ways. In other words, repent; make a 180° turn; go in the opposite direction.

Only after the children of Israel did these 4 things would God hear from Heaven. Only after the children of Israel did these 4 things would God forgive their sin. Only after the children of Israel did these 4 things...you get the message. Start doing these 4 things and all your worries will take care of themselves.

Get your armor on!

CONTINUOUS OBEDIENCE

Son though he was, he learned obedience from what he suffered. (Hebrews 5:8 NIV)

This verse is referring to Christ and contains a key concept regarding obedience. Obedience is not easy and sometimes leads to suffering. Even Christ Himself learned obedience through suffering. We read in Matthew 26 where Jesus prayed to God on three different occasions to remove His future suffering from Him. Yet Jesus was obedient, even unto death. Why should we expect anything different?

Obedience is not easy. It may sometimes lead to suffering. It may even lead to death. But the rewards are literally out of this world! Which is a good teaser for tomorrow. Stay tuned.

Get your armor on!

However, as it is written: "What no eye has seen, what no ear has heard, and what no human mind has conceived"— the things God has prepared for those who love him— (1 Corinthians 2:9 NIV)

Paul quotes from Isaiah 64. This is a conditional promise; the promise is only offered to those who love Him. If you love Him, you will keep His commandments (John 14:21).

Can you imagine? If we only are faithful to love Him and keep His commandments, what blessings we will see. Honestly, we cannot imagine it because this verse tells us that no eye has seen, no ear has heard, no human mind has conceived what blessings are to come from the Father! Wow! More than enough incentive to be continuously obedient.

Get your armor on!

CONTINUOUS OBEDIENCE

We know that we have come to know him if we keep his commands. Whoever says, "I know him," but does not do what he commands is a liar, and the truth is not in that person. (1 John 2:3-4 NIV)

The "him" in this verse refers to God. What does it mean to "know Him"? It means to become aware of, to acknowledge, to recognize. And how do we know we "know Him"? By keeping His commands. The word "keep" conveys the idea of continuous action. We are to continue to obey His commands so that we, and others, will know that we "know Him."

Verse 4 contains the kicker. If we say we "know Him", but do not continue to obey His commends, John calls us a flat out liar! And further, "the truth is not in [us]."

Now, read through the verse again,

> Jessica / Scott knows that she / he has come to know Him if she / he keeps His commands. If Jessica / Scott says, "I know Him," but does not continue to do what He commands, Jessica / Scott is a liar, and the truth is not in her / him.

Adds a whole new meaning does not it.

Now get your armor on!

CONTINUOUS OBEDIENCE

So we fix our eyes not on what is seen, but on what is unseen, since what is seen is temporary, but what is unseen is eternal. (2 Corinthians 4:18 NIV)

I want to focus our attention today on the word fix. When we fix our eyes on something, we look with a purpose. In context, this verse tells us to keep fixing our eyes. In other words, make it your habitual practice to fix your eyes. And where are we to fix our eyes? On what is unseen – heavenward, into the eyes of Jesus. A key point to make here is that we do not have to wait until death to meet Jesus face-to-face. We can experience the joy of seeing Christ right now. Make it your habitual practice to do so.

Get your armor on!

BUILDING A HOME

Wives, submit yourselves to your own husbands as you do to the Lord. For the husband is the head of the wife as Christ is the head of the church, his body, of which he is the Savior. (Ephesians 5:22-23 NIV)

This verse has caused a great deal of debate. Men use it to support treating their wives as slaves. Women argue against it, stating women are on equal ground with men. I think all those arguments for and against are completely out of context. What does "submit" mean? It means to give in to the authority of another. And Paul goes further to provide a perfect example of submitting: Christ and the Church. The Church gives in to the authority of Christ. That does not mean wives do not have a voice. They most certainly do. Your mother has many times offered her advice on a subject throughout our marriage. We discuss a matter and I make the final decision. She then gives in to my decision, even if it differs from hers. I will be held responsible for my decision making. Your mother will be held responsible for yielding to my decision.

You have the perfect pattern to follow. Just do what your mom has done!

Get your armor on!

Husbands, love your wives, just as Christ loved the church and gave himself up for her (Ephesians 5:25 NIV)

The greatest thing you can do for your family is love your wife. Your kids will take note. Not sure if you remember or not, but as we would head off to church each week, I would say to you and your sister, "I love your Mommy and does she not look good today!" This verse is one of the reasons why I would do that. I wanted you to know that I loved your mother.

One day, you will be the head of your household. One day, your kids will look up to you to emulate. I pray they know you love their mother – not just in words, but actions, too.

Get your armor on!

BUILDING A HOME

But if serving the Lord seems undesirable to you, then choose for yourselves this day whom you will serve, whether the gods your ancestors served beyond the Euphrates, or the gods of the Amorites, in whose land you are living. But as for me and my household, we will serve the Lord." (Joshua 24:15 NIV)

One of the keys to any structure is a good foundation (a hint of tomorrow's verse). A key to any marriage is also a good foundation. You must make a conscience decision on who you will serve from the very beginning of your relationship. God will not force Himself on you; you must decide whether to follow. You must be intentional with your decision and never waiver.

Your mom and I made that decision. In fact, this verse was part of our wedding vows. We decided from the very beginning we would serve the Lord. It has not always been easy, but it has been most rewarding! I pray you and your future mate will decide the same.

Get your armor on!

BUILDING A HOME

"Therefore everyone who hears these words of mine and puts them into practice is like a wise man who built his house on the rock. The rain came down, the streams rose, and the winds blew and beat against that house; yet it did not fall, because it had its foundation on the rock. But everyone who hears these words of mine and does not put them into practice is like a foolish man who built his house on sand. The rain came down, the streams rose, and the winds blew and beat against that house, and it fell with a great crash." (Matthew 7:24-27 NIV)

What did we say yesterday about a good foundation? Why is it important? Because the rest of the house is dependent upon it. If the foundation is weak, so too will be the structure. Just like building upon sand. The structure will not be able to sustain the turbulent times of this world and it will fall with a great crash! Marriages and homes not built on a firm foundation are doomed to fail.

But if you build upon the Rock (see Psalm 18:2), then when the turbulent times of this world come, you will be able to withstand it. And trust me, turbulent times will come. Which church to attend? How to discipline your children? How much freedom do you give your children as they grow and mature? To relocate or not? To make a career change or not? Where to spend the holidays? (silly question - with your mother and me of course). How to manage your finances? Tons more questions that will strain a relationship.

Make the decision to build upon the Rock of your Salvation. Then when the rains come, you will be able to stand and not fall!

Get your armor on!

BUILDING A HOME

By wisdom a house is built, and through understanding it is established; (Proverbs 24:3 NIV)

This verse, too, was part of your mother's and my wedding vows. Two vital characteristics for a successful marriage and home: wisdom and understanding. Wisdom is a rather broad term. It really refers to what you do with knowledge. Using it smartly for the betterment of the whole. Not using it as an arrow in your quiver to be pulled out when you are losing an argument. Understanding is being considerate, thoughtful, and accepting. "My way or the highway" does not work in a marriage. Your mom and I have not always seen eye-to-eye on every topic, but I do think we have tried to gain an understanding of each other's opinion and reasoning.

Make sure you have these key attributes when building a home!

Get your armor on!

Unless the Lord builds the house, the builders labor in vain. (Psalm 127:1 NIV)

Do not you just love it when Scripture says it all and you need no commentary!

Get your armor on!

YOU ARE CHOSEN

But you are a chosen people, a royal priesthood, a holy nation, God's special possession, that you may declare the praises of him who called you out of darkness into his wonderful light. (1 Peter 2:9 NIV)

Peter wrote these words to those who were believers in Jesus Christ. If you are a child of God, these verses pertain to you as well. As believers, we are chosen to be a royal priesthood; chosen to be part of God's very special possession – His Church. But the verse does not stop there. We have a purpose. We have been chosen to be a part of something BIG. We have been chose to declare the praises of Him to others; to make Him known to others. Being a part of His royal priesthood; His holy nation; His church, is not a one-and-done type of event. It is a lifelong journey. So get up off the couch! You have work to do!

Get your armor on!

And you will be called priests of the Lord, you will be named ministers of our God. You will feed on the wealth of nations, and in their riches you will boast. (Isaiah 61:6 NIV)

Jesus read from Isaiah 61 at the beginning of his ministry (Luke 4:18-19). Back then, as today, we have those whose careers are to preach the gospel. We have pastors and teachers who make a living doing just that. But what about the rest of us? Jesus intended for all His followers to be "priests of the Lord...ministers of our God". This may not be our job per se, but it is certainly an expectation of a true believer. We may actually have a different vocation – teaching elementary school, designing buildings, being a homemaker, or working at Peterbilt. But we are all chosen to make Him known.

Get your armor on!

YOU ARE CHOSEN

For you are a people holy to the Lord your God. The Lord your God has chosen you out of all the peoples on the face of the earth to be his people, his treasured possession. (Deuteronomy 7:6 NIV)

When we become children of God, we are certainly special. We become God's treasured possession. However, we should not let that go to our head. We are chosen not by our merits or potential. We are chosen solely based on Christ's work on the cross. It is because of His great love for us that we are even allowed to live. Death is a worthy and justified sentence for our sin. Because we have been spared, we should live our lives in a way that shows our appreciation for being His treasured possession.

Get your armor on!

who is a deposit guaranteeing our inheritance until the redemption of those who are God's possession— to the praise of his glory. (Ephesians 1:14 NIV)

Three of the four verses this week have called believers in Christ "God's possession". Have you ever given that much thought? You are His possession! He bought you with the blood of His Son. Think back to something you purchased with your own money. I remember your first flat screen TV / ping pong table. You were very proud of your purchase, and rightly so. You worked hard for it. It was your first big purchase and I am sure you look upon it differently than other things in your room / apartment. We are no different in God's eyes. Praise be to His glory!

Get your armor on!

YOU ARE CHOSEN

"This is the covenant I will make with the people of Israel after that time," declares the Lord. "I will put my law in their minds and write it on their hearts. I will be their God, and they will be my people. (Jeremiah 31:33 NIV)

The Lord is referring to a new covenant He will make with the people of Israel. And not to the literal nation of Israel, but to the spiritual nation of Israel, meaning all believers. This covenant will be special in that it will be no longer communicated by means of a priest or rabbi, but by the works of the Holy Spirit – "put the law in their minds and write it on their hearts." The Gospel will become an inner force shaping one's character from the inside out.

The "their" and "they" in the last sentence is you and me! So let's read it this way:

"I will be Jessica's / Scott's God and Jessica / Scott will be my people."

Jeremiah was written sometime between 630 B.C and 580 B.C. That means more than 2,600 years before you were ever born, God was thinking of you! What a mighty God we serve!

Get your armor on!

FINISH THE RACE

Do you not know that in a race all the runners run, but only one gets the prize? Run in such a way as to get the prize. Everyone who competes in the games goes into strict training. They do it to get a crown that will not last, but we do it to get a crown that will last forever. Therefore I do not run like someone running aimlessly; I do not fight like a boxer beating the air. (1 Corinthians 9:24-26 NIV)

I am sure you have heard of athletes and actors who have immense talent but have squandered their opportunity for success. Why? Because they were satisfied at being mediocre. They were satisfied just being in the race. They did not run to get the prize. Do not run aimlessly or beat the air. Have purpose. Remember to chase after the prize that will last forever! Run in such a way as to get that prize!

Get your armor on!

Watch your life and doctrine closely. Persevere in them, because if you do, you will save both yourself and your hearers. (1 Timothy 4:16 NIV)

I bet if I asked you go swim a 500 / play a tennis tournament, right now, you would not perform very well. Why? Because you have not practiced. You have not kept up your training / workouts. As the swim / match continued, you would grow weary, performance would begin to drop off, strokes become slower, and power would be reduced. Paul knew this would happen, so he encouraged Timothy even more. The main word here is "persevere": persist, endure, to continue, to sustain. For if we continue to persevere in our faith and walk with Christ, knowing what and why you believe, we will secure our salvation in Christ and people will begin to take notice. Who knows? They may even begin their journey with Christ, all because you finished the race!

Get your armor on!

FINISH THE RACE

Therefore we do not lose heart. Though outwardly we are wasting away, yet inwardly we are being renewed day by day. For our light and momentary troubles are achieving for us an eternal glory that far outweighs them all. (2 Corinthians 4:16-17 NIV)

I am sure you had days during your freshman year where you wondered, "Did I make the right career / college choice?" And I am sure during your sophomore and junior years, you probably wanted to throw in the towel. "These crazy professors!! Do they realize I have a life and 4 other classes!!!" But you see, it was all a long distance journey. Along the way, you had hills to climb and obstacles to avoid / overcome. Other days the wind was at your back and all was smooth sailing. Now as you approach graduation, it was all worth it. And so goes our walk with Christ. Do not give out when the times get rough. They are but temporary troubles. Just remain faithful in His faithfulness and soon the wind will be at your back. Your relationship with the King is a long distance journey. Do not quit on Him too soon. Finish the Race!

Get your armor on!

Do not let anyone who delights in false humility and the worship of angels disqualify you. Such a person also goes into great detail about what they have seen; they are puffed up with idle notions by their unspiritual mind. (Colossian 2:18 NIV)

Along your journey in life, you will run across people or things that will try to distract you from your course. People may show good intentions outwardly, but inside they have a hidden agenda. You may convince yourself that you really need that coveted item. Beware! It is a ploy used by Satan to try and pull God's children away. Pray the Lord will give you a discerning mind to be on the lookout for these individuals or things. We do not want to be disqualified from the race by not focusing on the prize. We want to finish the race!

Get your armor on!

FINISH THE RACE

I have fought the good fight, I have finished the race, I have kept the faith. (2 Timothy 4:7 NIV)

Sis / Bubba, we have come to the end of your college experience. What a ride it has been! It is with bittersweet emotions as I type this today. I now know what Paul might have felt as he sent Timothy on his way after mentoring him for more than 14 years. I have watched you grow and mature as an adult, but also as a follower of Christ. You have made me very proud to call you my daughter / son.

Although you may have completed your college experience, you have so much more to see and do. You are just beginning. I pray that as you look back on your years at school, you can honestly say you fought the good fight; you have finished the race; you have kept the faith.

This may be the end of our "verses of the day", but I certainly hope this is not then end of your journey with Christ. May you read back through the verses and draw inspiration, encouragement, restoration, excitement, and purpose. God has so much more He wants to do through you. Let Him do it!

May your armor grow thick and impenetrable.

Keep your armor on!

CPSIA information can be obtained
at www.ICGtesting.com
Printed in the USA
BVHW071119260219
541199BV00001B/35/P

9 781973 646778